John Hoblyn Appleton, Archibald Henry Sayce

Dr Appleton

His Life and Literary Relics

John Hoblyn Appleton, Archibald Henry Sayce

Dr Appleton
His Life and Literary Relics

ISBN/EAN: 9783337053901

Printed in Europe, USA, Canada, Australia, Japan

Cover: Foto ©ninafisch / pixelio.de

More available books at **www.hansebooks.com**

D̲R̲ APPLETON:

HIS LIFE AND LITERARY RELICS.

BY

JOHN H. APPLETON, M.A.,

LATE VICAR OF ST. MARK'S, STAPLEFIELD, SUSSEX;

AND

A. H. SAYCE, M.A.,

FELLOW OF QUEEN'S COLLEGE, AND DEPUTY PROFESSOR
OF COMPARATIVE PHILOLOGY, OXFORD.

LONDON:
TRÜBNER AND CO., LUDGATE HILL.
1881.

LIFE OF DR. APPLETON

AND

INTRODUCTION.

CONTENTS.

	PAGES
LIFE OF DR. APPLETON	1–107
INTRODUCTION, CONTAINING FRAGMENTS OF AN UNFINISHED ESSAY ON DEVELOPMENT	109–128
WHAT IS THE EGO ?	
CHAPTER I. STRAUSS AS A THEOLOGIAN . . .	129–159
CHAPTER II. A PLEA FOR METAPHYSIC, I. .	160–195
CHAPTER III. A PLEA FOR METAPHYSIC, II. .	195–243
AMERICAN EFFORTS AFTER INTERNATIONAL COPYRIGHT .	245–280
ATHEISM . .	281–310
DOUBT	311–326
FRAGMENTS .	327–350

LIFE OF DR. APPLETON.

CHARLES EDWARD APPLETON was born at Reading, on March 16, 1841. His father, the Rev. Robert Appleton, had at that time been recently appointed to the Head Mastership of Reading School, a well-known foundation of Henry VII. which, during its long and useful existence, has trained many eminent persons for the service of Church and State. The Head Master was an excellent classical scholar, and also gradually succeeded in organizing, under considerable difficulties, what would now be called the "modern side" of education; so that Mathematics, History, the German and French languages and general Literature formed, to a remarkable degree for those times, an important feature in the work of the School.

To the very favourable circumstances of his home and school life must be attributed the early formation of those habits of industry and accuracy, as also the first beginnings of that wide and cultured sympathy, for which Dr. Appleton was afterwards so remarked. He himself was always most loyal and grateful to Reading School, where he received the whole of his education up to the time of his entering the University: he took great interest in its recent re-organization, and used any influence he might possess to secure for it, in a time of change, those features which he felt were of so much value in his own case.

As a young boy he was rather delicate, but strength seemed to come to him as he grew older, and he was able not only to study regularly, but also to take a fair share in the sports of the playground: indeed, he bore throughout his life distinct traces of an ugly blow he received in the cricket-field when about sixteen years old.

He was of an impulsive, sanguine temperament, and this, rather than physical strength, supplied much of the motive power both in his boyhood and throughout his busy, energetic life; enabling him to carry out, to at least some measure of completeness, many schemes which in other hands would probably have fallen to the ground. His single-hearted zeal won him allies both at school and in the world; he was born to be the leader of a forlorn hope, and he was, to a remarkable degree, successful in his enterprises. One who knew him well in later life makes a remark which applies to a much earlier period of his career:—"He was one of those rare natures who convince practical people against their slower judgment, and achieve impossibilities by the contagion of their own enthusiasm. *Possunt quia posse videntur.*"

Fortunately, moreover, his impulsiveness did not merely accumulate force to be wasted, as so often happens, in spasmodic, ill-sustained effort. Method, rather in his case an acquired habit than a natural gift, characterized him even as a boy to quite a curious degree. He set an object steadily before his eyes, calculated, so far as he could, the means that would reach the end, and then sternly disciplined himself with a view to the accomplishment of his cherished purpose. An old friend, who had ample means of studying his character both at School and at Oxford, says,—"His days were bound each to each by conscientious adherence to a well-considered, self-imposed plan of life. In an age which is spendthrift of time and too much open to casual impulses, he never drifted: he always seemed to be steering straight at a mark. . . . . He was the least pushing of men, and little careful of external success; but nothing turned him aside from what seemed to him the line of his chosen duty."[1]

And yet withal he was a most genial, lovable boy, full of fun and with a keen appreciation of all the lighter sides of life; of quick and ready sympathies, fond of society as he grew older, and generally popular. Indeed, it was an early and almost precocious realization of the risks to which he was exposed by his social gifts and natural temperament, that made him set himself firmly to acquire those habits of self-restraint and methodical study without which he felt any intellectual self-development was impossible.

It is a great pleasure to me to recall that, while holding a curacy in Reading after taking my degree, I was able to be of service to my brother in his preparation for his University career. I have a very distinct recollection, for instance, of reading the Latin satirists with him, and of the eager and intelligent interest he took in all the social and historical questions which arise in the course of such a study. This must have been in 1858 and in the first part of 1859.

At this time it was proposed that Charles should compete at some scholarship examination at Oxford; but nothing definite had been arranged, when, quite unexpectedly, an opportunity came at St. John's College. Reading School had the privilege of sending two scholars to St. John's; but no vacancy was likely to occur, and consequently it seemed well nigh impossible that my brother could ever be upon the foundation of that college to which the thoughts of a Reading boy would naturally turn. But during a visit of a few hours to Oxford in June, 1859, I fortunately heard from one of the Reading Fellows that Tunbridge School, a sister foundation to Reading in the privilege of sending scholars to St. John's, had just presented a candidate whom the college had

[1] From a letter from the Rev. Edward Harris, M.A., Head Master of Exeter School.

determined to reject. The result was that the Scholarship was thrown open to public competition, a valuable prize in those days, for it led in due course to a Fellowship. I well remember the astonishment of the future Fellow, when, on his return from a boating expedition that evening, he was told he must start next morning for Oxford. However, not much persuasion was required, and, although there were some worthy competitors, Charles was successful at the examination; the thing that struck the examiners being the wide range of his reading for so young a man. The preferment then won he retained till his death.

At Oxford he was a diligent, energetic student, reading widely and systematically; and, although he failed to obtain the highest honours in the University examinations, he was generally allowed to be one of the ablest men of his standing.[1] Perhaps in reading he did not keep the schools sufficiently in view to achieve the greatest success; but I suppose few at the present time will be found to maintain that a competitive examination is the most desirable stimulus for the best minds, or even an infallible means of discovering them.

I am sorry to have but few records of my brother's undergraduate life, which admit of being introduced in a memoir. The following extracts, however, will serve to give some glimpses of a routine of hard work lightened by genial sympathy with the thoughts and pursuits of others:—

As an undergraduate he was a very industrious student.

---

[1] "In the Moderations List he obtained a second class, but was so little below the standard of a First as to make me feel (I was an Examiner at the time) that a very slight difference in the chances of the Examination would have secured him that position."—From a letter rom Mr. Robinson Ellis.

Another Examiner also writes,—"I examined him in the Final Classical School. He showed great ability and very considerable knowledge. His philosophical papers I thought quite on a level with the best sent in that time."

with a decided bent towards speculative philosophy. . . . Even in his freshman's term, nearly twenty years ago, two or three of his friends used to meet on Sunday evenings in each others' rooms and read philosophical books, among which Mansel's Bampton Lectures, then in the height of their fame, found a prominent place. The choice was not very happy, perhaps, and it was only Appleton's philosophical ardour which kept the little band together; the others soon found the food too strong for them, but he relished it heartily, and would not allow his friends to relinquish their chosen task.[1]

A contemporary adds the reminiscence:—

If one was with him late in the evening, one would invariably see the faggot brought in and laid in the fender, that he might light his own fire and begin work before any servants came into college.

Another friend writes to me as follows:—

When I went up as an undergraduate to Oxford in October, 1863, my first visit was to Appleton's rooms. It was on a Saturday night, at about half-past seven, when I found my way to "No. 1, first quad., 1 pair, left hand door;" his "oak" was "sported," but as soon as he discovered it was none of his college friends, he opened the door and welcomed me warmly to Oxford. He was now reading steadily for "Greats," and made a point of arranging his work so as to get to bed very early; but he went out of his way to keep me talking, and even walked out with me to see my rooms and gave me some hints about furnishing. It was the first of the many proofs he gave me of the genuine, practical interest he took in his friends.

This term it was his custom to get up at four o'clock in the morning, light his fire, make some coffee and then work till nine. After a short interval for breakfast, he read on till midday, and then gave a long afternoon to exercise and recreation.

Though he was so busy, he allowed me to see a good deal of him even before the schools began. I found he had given up the idea of taking Orders and was now thinking of the Bar. One day we had a long talk about "Church principles," and he seemed satisfied that a good case could be made out for them. He was at this time inclined to the opinions of

---

[1] From the obituary notice in the *Athenæum*, Feb. 22, 1879.

Maurice and Stanley, and something gave me the impression that Stanley had had a good deal of influence upon him.

On November 21, 1863, I wrote in my diary: "Appleton has just been to see me and we have had a walk. He has missed his First, but in very good company; for there are two or three men in the second, whom everybody expected to find in the first class."

His disappointment in the final schools did not make him a less eager student than he was before. Having put aside, at least for the present, the thought of the Bar, he gave himself up earnestly to philosophy. I saw much of him during the next three years; and he used to talk often, and always with deep seriousness, of the questions which lie at the foundation of philosophy and theology. He was one of those men—not too many—who are in earnest about philosophy. His conversations gave me a clear idea of the nature and the bearings of the Hegelian system, and he put before me with great plainness and force the reasons which led him to think this philosophy the true one. . . . .

On Monday, October 22, 1866, I wrote in my diary: "Appleton lunched with me to-day and we walked out afterwards. He has been much troubled lately with weakness in one eye, and Dr. Symonds has advised him to avoid all reading for a time; so I have promised to read to him in the evening three times a week out of some book that may be useful to both of us. We shall begin with Mill's "Examination of Sir W. Hamilton's Philosophy." Dr. Symonds' treatment was successful, and by the end of term the weakness was nearly cured.

About this time your brother took an interest in a friend of mine, A——, of Balliol, who had just been received into the Roman Catholic Church, and showed all that earnest curiosity about a position so different from his own, which I had noticed so often before to be characteristic of him. We had some talk about an article, which appeared at the beginning of November in the *Daily News*, accusing the High Church party in Oxford of systematic proselytism by means of brotherhoods, party lectures and personal influence. This charge Appleton did not think a fair one, and could not agree with his Liberal friends about it.

After I had taken my degree, I saw Appleton oftener than before, in company with his graduate friends, and used to enjoy listening to his conversation with them. One evening

I remember Laing of Wadham dining with him and discussing the subject of Monasticism in England, on which we afterwards heard Appleton read a paper at a meeting of the Architectural Society.[1]

About this time (Lent Term, 1868), he used to join me in going to Green of Balliol's college-lecture on Modern Philosophy. His interest in this subject seemed always to be uppermost, and to find its centre in the great problems common to philosophy and theology. He was reading, about this time, the history of the Port Royal, and studying the subject of miracles. . . . .

When I returned to Oxford in January, 1870, after an absence of a year, Appleton was kind enough to ask me to be sub-editor of the *Academy*, which he had recently started. He was enthusiastic about the undertaking . . . . and gave up nearly all his time to it. We used to sit down to work at a quarter-past nine in the morning, and left off about half-past three, allowing a very short interval for lunch. Sometimes also, we worked in the evening, and then Cheyne came to help us. . . . .

Shortly after I went to Cambridge in January, 1877, your brother wrote to tell me of his intention to send a paper on the subject of "Doctrinal Development" to the *Contemporary Review*, or the *Nineteenth Century*; and I think I wrote to him twice in reply, sending (as he had requested me) what struck me as the best references to various works of Dr. Newman. . . . .

A few days before coming to the Oratory on Michaelmas Day, 1877, I dined with him at Hampstead and slept at his house. We had a long talk on the question of Development and the nature of Revelation, and next morning I parted from him and said "Goodbye" for the last time.

I am indebted to the Rev. T. A. F. Eaglesim, of the Birmingham Oratory, for the above interesting communication. It passes considerably beyond the time which we have reached in our narrative, but it seemed best to let it run on without interruption to the end.

My brother took his B.A. degree in October, 1863,[2] and,

---

[1] At the first Meeting of the Society in Trinity Term, 1868. An abstract of the Lecture was published.

[2] He subsequently took the Degree of D.C.L., in June, 1871.

after a short holiday, drew out for himself a course of reading in Philosophy, Law and History, which, with the occasional interruption of pupils, fully occupied his time until a long-cherished project[1] of a residence at one or more German universities could be realized. His scheme of study was no doubt framed in great measure with a view to the proposed sojourn in Germany, so that he might be able to gain the greatest advantage from the lectures he hoped to hear from the professors at Heidelberg, Halle and Berlin. He marked out his time and work with characteristic method:—

Each month must consist of four weeks of six days, and each day of a good six hours' reading .... the hours kept and the work done to be noted in this book; public lectures, and light biographical, poetical and novel reading not to count.

It is interesting to observe that he read Hegel's "Propädeutik" in the early part of 1864, and soon commenced a translation of it, upon which he spent a considerable time during the next three or four years, until the engrossing work of the *Academy* compelled him to lay it aside. On Dec. 23, 1865, I find the following note, written at Berlin, which shows the expansion of his plan under the influence of his German studies:—

My so-called "Translation of the Propädeutik" has increased into the following scheme:—

Table of Contents.

Introduction: (*a*) Characteristics of Propädeutik; (*b*) Explanation of technical terms, with parallel passages; (*c*) Analysis of the four parts of the work; (*d*) Account of the Parallel Works"—*i.e.*, i. "The Philosophy of Right"; ii. Phenomenology; iii. Logic; iv. Encyclopædia—in outline.

A. Essay on Philosophy of Right.
Notes and Translation.

---

[1] An old schoolfellow writes; "Long before he left school he had formed the plan, which he afterwards carried out, of adding study in Germany to the university course at Oxford."

B. Essay on Phenomenology.
   Notes and Translation.

C. Essay on Logic.
   Notes and Translation.

D. Essay on Encyclopædia.
   Notes and Translation.

Excursus —

i. Summary of Hegel's system up to the idea of a State.
ii. The Italian School.
iii. Criticism of Herbart and the Empirics :—Schopenhauer.
iv. History of Philosophy since Hegel.

The notes are to consist of a carefully digested parallel from the four great corresponding works.

In the summer of 1865, Dr. Appleton, in company with his friend, Mr. Owen, of Cheltondale, Cheltenham, studied for some time at Heidelberg, where he heard Zeller and Bluntschli, and in October of the same year commenced his residence at Berlin, of which University he became a matriculated member. Here is an account of the ceremony :—

You will rejoice to hear I am now a matriculated member of the University, for which honour I paid 18s., and received a whole heap of big, printed papers, in which I am described as "*vir juvenis ornatissimus*," which is, of course, a delicate allusion to my personal appearance. The authorities keep my passport till I leave Berlin, and give me a kind of *testamur* instead, which the police have insisted upon seeing, along with particulars as to my age, social position, object in living here, &c. The police surveillance is very silly, although not in the least annoying. . . . . Professor —— had his sister staying with him, and the police came with their inquiries, as to what *her* object was, &c.; to which the Professor being provoked replied, that her object was *to found a republic!*. . . . Well, as to matriculation, it was a long business, lasting an hour and a half, from the great number of candidates. Our names and particular descriptions were written in about six big books, and then the "Rector Magnificus," a most meek old man, the Professor of Botany, made a speech, and shook hands formally with us all, *jurisjurandi loco*, — i.e., we thereby engaged to obey the University regulations. He then singled me out, and said very kindly in German, "You are a foreigner; I must shake hands again with you; my best blessing on your work,"—which was jolly of him.

He finds comfortable quarters in the house of Professor Solly, and soon gets into harness, being much pleased to find Hegel so well represented at Berlin:—

I am getting nicely into work and have heard Michelet, the man I came to hear, for a fortnight with great effect. He delivers his lectures, which are very suggestive, with tremendous energy, throwing his arms about in the wildest way all the time. He is quite an enthusiast in philosophy, which suits me very well. Trendelenberg and Werder have not yet begun. I am most agreeably surprised to find that there are no less than four Hegelians lecturing in Philosophy and Art; three of them personal friends of Hegel, and editors of his works.

(Sunday, Nov. 12.) I had a charming talk with Michelet, this morning, for an hour and a half. He seemed very pleased to have got a disciple, and begged me to call again, and to bring any difficulties to him.

In reply to a request that he would explain briefly what the Hegelian philosophy is, he writes:—

It is difficult to state in short what Hegel is, or what German philosophy is. From a letter from a friend to-day I gathered that he thought it was something like what we call in England "Low Church!" This, it is needless to tell you, is not the case. . . . . So far as I can describe it in an intelligible manner, I should say it was simply the consummation of the attempt, which has been going on in the best minds, for the last two thousand years, to find an absolutely certain basis for complete knowledge. Four weeks ago we began with the first principle of the Hegelian Logic, " Pure Being is Pure Nothing," which appears, at first sight, an absurdity, but, on closer scrutiny, to be the last point of abstraction to which Thought can go, and consequently to form a beginning which is absolutely such, *i.e.*, which takes nothing for granted, not even, like the celebrated *Cogito, ergo sum*, the thinking mind itself. It would take an essay to explain this fully; and, as the first point of all, in which Thought and Being are fused in complete indifference, it is the most abstruse. But when we have got this principle, we don't stop, as the old philosophy did when it said, "Whatever is, is;" or, "The one is, the many is not;" but our principle involves its own development; it contains the necessity of motion in itself, and this necessity is its contradiction. Just as we see nothing in pure light, any more than in pure darkness; the only possible thing for us to see is their union in what we call, Colour. This is only an illustration; as also is Life, which is a complete fusion of the contradictories, growth and decay. This principle, then, is not developed by the application of an external method, which must always be arbitrary, but is its own method, or, as the Germans express it, "The form and the matter are absolutely identical." It developes itself through every stage of thought, then of nature, and then, lastly, of mind, which, instead of being a starting-point, is our last result. And thus the physical sciences, law, morality, politics, art, religion, philosophy proceed in regular and necessary order, until at last a point is reached, which the Germans call *Geist*, in which the whole universe is subdued to the Infinite Reason.

Professor Croft, Director of Public Instruction, Bengal, has been kind enough to send me the following extracts from letters written to him, in the autumn of 1865, by my brother from Berlin. They are humorous and characteristic:—

After a fortnight's intense thought, we of Michelet's class have arrived at the momentous proposition that "Being is Being:" and, with this formula upon my lips, I feel that I have my finger on the great pulse of the universe.

Being is good, but Not-being is better, because it adds to the notion of Being the notion of Not.

When we enunciate the truth—"Being is, and not-Being is not," you must not suppose that there is no such thing as not-Being. Verily, there is such a thing as not-Being, only it is Not.

Hegel has found a word which approximates to the meaning of οὐσία in the German *dingheit*, which a learned Italian, M. Vera, translates into French *choséité*; I suppose the English equivalent must be "thingamy-tight."

I have discovered a threefold theological argument, which is completely efficacious in confuting unbelievers. The first is called *ignoratio elenchi,* and is a very valuable instrument: it consists in passing over the point to which your opponent wishes to bring you, and in proving something else. But if your opponent is a sharp man and drives you from this standpoint, there remains a second serviceable weapon; it is called *petitio principii,* and consists in assuming the point to be proved—generally (though this is not essential) in a slightly altered form. If your opponent has had a logical training, he will detect your device and wrest the weapon from your hands. You will then take refuge in the last and impregnable stronghold, which is called *maxima refutatio,* and which consists in denying that there is any point at issue.

But this was not the whole of his life at Berlin. Partly, no doubt, through the influence of his kind host, he was welcomed into some very pleasant society, and greatly enjoyed his experiences of German home life. His letters are full of the good music he heard, the interesting people he met, and the places he visited. A few extracts shall be given:—

On Wednesday I sat an hour with the great jurist, Gneist, and smoked a cigar with him. He promised me tickets for the House of Parliament, of which he is a member; cut up our English notions of philosophy, in which I quite agreed with him; and finally told me that three Mondays in every month he should be at home in the evening and should be glad to see me. I enjoyed my visit to him extremely. . . . .

The political excitement is increasing, and Gneist had a demonstration from three or four hundred students the other day, of whom I was one, though rather as a spectator. As he entered, everybody stood up and shouted "Hoch!" which is the formula used instead of our Oxford "For he's a jolly good fellow, &c." It is at least simpler. He made a little speech in answer.

A couple of nights ago I attended a meeting of the Theological Society, where the Philosophy of Spinoza was fairly thoroughly discussed by about ten students out of a larger circle of forty or fifty. You would scarcely find forty English undergraduates, or people of any sort, capable of discussing such a question or listening to an essay intelligently upon it. There was no irreverence or lightness of any kind, and altogether I was much pleased with my evening. The Germans are certainly much more adapted to abstract thought than we are, but, as far as my experience goes, are mere children in practical matters.

I got home [from a four days' walk in the Hartz] in time for the so-called *Polter-abend*, that is, the evening before the wedding, of a relative of Professor Ranke. . . . . The play representing the different scenes in the lives of the happy couple, with good fairies in blue and silver, and bad fairies in red, was a very happy thought, and, upon the whole, was very well acted. . . . . The pair sat in the front row just under the stage, which was placed in the middle of the drawing-room. Several prologues were spoken, some by young ladies, who then descended and hugged the bride; and after all was over, they were both dragged by the players behind the curtain for the same process. Then the stage, scenery &c., were cleared, and the whole room thrown open, with a ballroom beyond. At the other end of the suite of four rooms was the professor's study, which was devoted to the reception of presents for the bride.

We sat up till twelve last night, and drank the old year (1865) out in punch with German pancakes, which are the orthodox thing for the occasion. Each of us poured a spoonful of molten lead into a basin of water, and then did our best to interpret the fantastic shapes of the lead as prophecies of our fortunes during the coming year. The Professor sang a comic song or two; after which we danced a quadrille as the clock was striking, and then opened the windows to hear the noise of the congratulations passing on through the streets. The city is quite quiet till the moment, and then you might imagine that a riot had suddenly broken out.

In March, 1866, Dr. Appleton joined me at Genoa, after a few days' stay at Halle, where he heard Erdmann. His own comment upon his residence in Germany, written apparently some years after, seems, at first sight, a little disparaging :—" The nett result of my visit to Berlin, and in the previous summer to Heidelberg, was not any great increase of philosophical or other knowledge such as I might not have acquired in England, by reading the books published by the professors whose lectures I attended;" but there can be little doubt that his future career was

largely shaped by his sojourn in Germany. It may have
been that such matters as those with which his name was
afterwards so closely associated, the organization of
academical studies, the endowment of research, and even
the foundation of a review like the *Academy*, had previously come into his thoughts ;[1] but certainly the contrast between a German and English university, a contrast
realized strongly by actual experience of the former, must
have served to emphasize his impressions and to direct
them to a definite result ; while the original plan of the
Academy was undoubtedly modelled on that of the
Literarisches Centralblatt. The *Athenæum* of Feb. 22,
1879, has an interesting passage on this point, in the
obituary notice from which we have already made an
extract :—

Soon after taking his degree, Appleton went for some time
to Germany, to perfect himself in a language which he already
knew fairly well, and to prosecute his favourite studies. He
spent some time at Heidelberg and afterwards at Berlin. The
contrast between German and English universities impressed
him, as it has done most of those who have studied both
impartially, and he came home confirmed in the opinion that,
while Oxford and Cambridge are admirable finishing schools
and consummate examining machines, they are far surpassed
by Germany in that important function of a university, which
consists in keeping alive a spirit of mature and disinterested
learning and of original research. In order to give expression
to this view, he translated and published[2] a pamphlet by Dr.
Döllinger on " Universities, Past and Present ;" and to the
propagation of a higher conception of the function of universities, in regard to learning as opposed to teaching, he subsequently devoted a great part of his life and energy. He projected
a learned journal, after the model of similar publications in
Germany, in which all books were to be noticed by persons
specially qualified by the course of their own studies to deal

[1] See page 89.
[2] In 1867,—" in order that it might appear before the several Bills
relating to the University of Oxford come again under the consideration
of Parliament."

with them, and prepared to give their names as a guarantee of their fitness. This was the origin of the *Academy*.

Genoa was our starting-point for a three months' tour in Italy, of which many pleasant memories remain, though few are of such a character as can well be transferred to these pages. Florence, Milan, Bologna, Padua, Venice, Naples, a visit to Pompeii, a scramble up Vesuvius, above all a month in Rome, where we certainly worked hard at churches, pictures and ruins of every date—all this is a well-worn theme; but, at the risk of telling again an oft-told tale, a few extracts from letters shall be made:—

The want of sympathy with art and with practices to which we are unaccustomed, and which we don't take the trouble to understand, is a most serious drawback to the enjoyment of a foreign tour, and, more than all, of such a place as Rome, which is a very hive of art, as well as a place proud of its past, tenacious of its peculiarities and the very centre and focus of Catholic Christendom. We really *must* put our dignity in our pocket in the face of the gigantic fact of Roman history, Roman art, Roman religion, Roman manners, and the great swarming city itself. How seldom do you find a German or a Frenchman impervious to all these influences; he will talk to you by the hour about a picture, or a foreign language, or the antiquities of a place like Rome, the architecture of its palaces, the last new phase of its politics, the significance of Catholicism in the world. Whereas—but I am quite ashamed to go on condemning our countrymen in this root and branch manner; and besides, we are not all equally bad. . . . . There are many English people of whom Rome herself is proud, and Gibson, Miss Horner and Nathaniel Hawthorne are a host in themselves, and may stand surety for us that the modern Anglo-Saxon is not quite hopeless.

The Pope himself [Pius IX.] is a dear, fatherly, gentle, spiritual-looking old man. His is scarcely an Italian face, but a kind of universal, indeterminate face—just the face for the father of a world-wide, manifold, struggling Christendom; and it does you good and makes you more of a Christian to look at its serenity.

He was much impressed by the service at St. Peter's

on Good Friday morning, a description of which ends thus :—

The people went up two and two, men and women, the former, if anything, slightly in the majority; all classes alike, soldiers, nobles and peasants, knelt, uttered a short prayer, and kissed the symbol of man's reconciliation. As a moving service, this to my mind is unequalled during the week; and so far from the adoration of the emblem seeming superstitious, it appeared the most obvious and natural thing in the world; a great improvement on the British "Dearly beloved brethren," some of us thought, at such a place, and at such a time.

One is struck by the exceeding plainness of the Roman churches. If the sacramental lamp were removed, one might fancy oneself in England. . . . . In the churches where Catholicism is presented publicly and authoritatively to the world, one looks in vain for the abominable and shapeless dolls, with their twopenny-halfpenny tinsel dresses, which distress one in France or Belgium. The mother of Christ is presented, by the authority of the Holy See, as the object and stimulator of devout aspiration, under the conception of Perugino or Raphael or Michael Angelo, as *un gran pezzo di donna*, "a splendid piece of womanhood," which will really elevate the mind by its very beauty above the level of ordinary life. I can't help thinking that a great picture by its very excellence keeps people from abusing it as an object of worship, and that when we hear of winking pictures or miraculous images we may be quite safe in assuming that they are rude blocks and miserable daubs, which depress the soul instead of raising it. . . . . Who ever heard of a Vandyke or a Titian working wonders? People say that going to Rome in the flesh is the best preservative against going over to Rome in the spirit: I think that this is quite the opposite of the truth. If you don't see the Bambino, and if you take the trouble to understand what is going on in the services, you will be led to feel that what divides Christendom is not religion, but prejudice, ignorance, misunderstanding, differences in words and in the outside rind of thought, want of sympathy and communication, a host of habits which grow up, dividing man from man, and which prevent us from seeing that we are all aiming the same way, thinking at bottom the same thoughts, hoping, aspiring after, feeling the same thing.[1]

On his return from the Continent Dr. Appleton resumed his residence at Oxford, and in October, 1867, was appointed lecturer in Philosophy at his own college. His note-books bear ample testimony to the conscientious labour bestowed upon the subjects which he taught, and I am glad to be able to add a statement by one of his pupils as to the value of his lectures, and the estimation in which the lecturer was held at this time at St. John's:—

To the general body of students he was above all things the representative of German ideas, German thought, learning, method; and was consequently regarded with mingled feelings of jealousy, mystery and admiration. . . . . He was the only efficient tutor we had upon "Greats'" subjects, and his lectures on the History of Philosophy, which I attended, were undoubtedly very valuable; more particularly as, at that time, there were very few men in the University who knew anything of the German language, and Zeller and a variety of works, which have been since translated, could only be read in the original.

The qualities for which Dr. Appleton was most remarkable as a lecturer were, I should say, subtlety, clearness, system and power of compression. He took a great delight in putting the minds of his pupils through the exercise of differentiating nice shades of thought; while nothing could exceed the neatness with which he would reduce a large mass of matter to a small compass. His style was always lucid and animated, and calculated to fix what he said in the memory of his hearers. . . . . For myself, I always think with pleasure and gratitude of the time when I was under him.

Amongst many, however, in his own college, it would perhaps be correct to say that he rather inspired respect than won any high degree of popularity. Taught by his course of reading for the final classical school to subject everything to a strict analysis, and armed with rather a powerful dialectic, he was, we can well imagine, a sore

[1] The above extracts are from letters to a "Long Vacation Journal" started by an Oxford reading party in North Devon in 1866.

trial to men of fixed opinions, even if he did not sometimes permit his love of mischief to triumph over prudence, and prompt him to shock the propriety of the common-room by advancing some highly revolutionary thesis. He was an energetic product of new Oxford, with a high ideal of what a university ought to be; and this ideal he pressed upon all, with whom he came in contact, in season and out of season. He desired to see his own college taking its place in the intellectual regeneration, and so his projects of reform were many and far-reaching: he was known, moreover, to be the personal friend of the leaders of the re-organizing movement, which has produced, and is producing, such important results at Oxford. All this was, no doubt, disquieting to those who, if not altogether satisfied with the old régime, were content to put off the day of change—were "opportunists" in reform, and feared to drift away from their old moorings. But from all he certainly won respect to a high degree: his aims, if to some they seemed impracticable, were, at least, perfectly disinterested: he sought no private ends, shrank from no sacrifice: he did not preach what he did not also practise; if he made ruthless war upon idleness and self-indulgence, he was himself an example of hard work and vigorous intellectual life; if he was, in his public capacity, as holding a trust for his college, stern and inexorable to vice, he was one of whom the following testimony could be given by one of his contemporaries:—

The signal purity of his habits of life, and his rare gentleness, might well have earned him Milton's Cambridge nickname—the Lady; for, more than any man whom I have known, he seemed to me to combine feminine graces with true manliness.

The following letter which I have received will be read with interest:—

From the Rev. F. E. Warren, Fellow of St. John's College, Oxford.

I gladly comply with your request that I would put down on paper some of my recollections of C. E. C. B. Appleton's career at St. John's College, Oxford.

When I matriculated and came into residence, in October, 1861, he had recently passed through Moderations, and was regarded by a freshman with the sort of awe which is inspired by a senior man. This feeling was, however, modified in my case by the fact that I had known him for some time previously, during the vacations spent by him under his father's roof at Reading, where I was a pupil; and, as a consequence of this previous acquaintance, an intimacy sprang up between us at college, greater than would be usual between undergraduates of such different university standing.

The points in his character which impress me most—writing of events which occurred nearly twenty years ago—are these:—

(1) His great industry and powers of application to work. He read for seldom less than eight, and often for ten hours a day. Not being of a very robust constitution, cricket, football, and other violent pastimes had little attraction for him; and the comparatively gentle exertion of an afternoon walk was usually sufficient for him by way of bodily exercise. His reading was not only steady and continuous, but far wider in its range than was usual among men of his standing, or than was required by the exigencies of university examinations. But self-culture and general research were the objects at which he aimed, rather than any temporary distinctions in the schools, or triumphs in the narrower grooves within which special subjects, as parts of the curriculum of the university, are confined.

(2) His great earnestness, both intellectual and moral. Self-cultivation to the highest point which, with the limited capacity with which our nature is endowed, it was possible to obtain, was the goal of his efforts; and in the determination to make the best use of his mental powers he never wavered. His moral earnestness was of a similar intensity. Apart from the supernatural sanctions of morality, an immoral life in any sense, and certainly in its worst sense, was incompatible with the highest cultivation of intellectual life, and as such was consistently avoided. Shunning any deviation from a high

moral ideal himself, he could not tolerate it, if he saw it, or thought he saw it, in others. And here, perhaps, was his weakest point—a want of sympathy with, or of toleration for, the moral or intellectual weaknesses of others. Stern, and justly stern in himself towards any development of idleness or viciousness, he was equally stern towards others; and no private consideration of friendship or of pity for the inexperience of youth, or of allowance for juvenile extravagance, would induce him to condone deviations from the path of rectitude. Yet even here, on occasions where, a few years later, his position as Fellow gave him a voice and vote in college meetings, he acted certainly not under the influence of resentment against an individual, but of indignation against the abuse of position and powers, and from a sincere desire to protect the best interests of his college. But, if ever his conduct may have, for a time, given rise to a feeling of hostility, those who felt it would probably now be the first to acknowledge that his actions were never the result of personal pique, but the necessity, real or supposed, of virtuous resentment.

(3) Another point in his character, which was especially worthy of notice, was his unselfishness and readiness to help others. In his busiest moments, if any one approached him with any doubt, or any question of difficulty, he was sure of a patient hearing, and probably of an exhaustive reply. It might be a question of grammar, or of translation, or of ethics, or of theology. The question was carefully listened to, and, when the questioner's back was turned, every available authority on the subject was ransacked, and a complete résumé of opinions would be frequently drawn up on paper, and criticized at length, and sent to you the next morning by the college messenger.

If there have been those who have reached a greater zenith of popularity among their contemporaries than Charles Appleton, there can be few who can look back on their past lives, and say they have done less evil, or whose example has been of more substantial advantage to those with whom they have been from time to time brought in contact.

In 1868 Dr. Appleton contributed an article on "The Dark Ages" to the June number of the *Contemporary Review;* and again, in June, 1869, a criticism on Mr.

Lecky's "History of European Morals." Also in the summer of 1868 he undertook a series of articles, chiefly on subjects which lie on the border-land between religion and philosophy, for Blunt's "Dictionary of Doctrinal and Historical Theology" and for the "Dictionary of Sects and Heresies" (Rivingtons); but the pressing nature of his duties with regard to the *Academy* made him unable to complete his engagement. He, however, finished fourteen papers, which appeared in the former work, and several of them were selected for very favourable criticism, while all bear the evidence of careful, conscientious study. The following is a list of the completed articles, of which the two first are permitted to appear in the present volume.

Atheism	Affections
Doubt	Cenobites
Dualism	Emanation
Eternity	Infinite
Buddhism	Hermit
Head	Heart
Dark Ages	Conceptualism.

On Feb. 24, 1871, Dr. Appleton gave evidence before the Select Committee on University Tests, and was further examined on March 7. His evidence was the subject of an interesting debate in the House of Lords on Monday, May 8, and attracted much general attention at the time. His own recapitulation, given on the second day of his examination, may be quoted in this place. It is hardly necessary to premise that he was in favour of unreserved abolition.

I first meant to say, respecting the application of tests at present, that the men affected by them or by their abolition were a small number; secondly, that the influences under which these men came were not influences exercised by persons who might be restrained from exercising such influences by law, but were influences partaking more of the nature of general causes, to which Acts of Parliament do not apply; and thirdly, with respect to the operation of tests, I meant to say that they do not at present act in preventing a destruction of belief, but they intervene at the most inopportune moment in preventing its natural re-construction.

These statements involved a criticism on the system of education for the final classical school at Oxford, which awakened considerable discussion, and to which I shall have occasion to refer again as we proceed.[1] Dr. Appleton then went on to speak of safeguards:—

I mentioned three, which I thought existed at the present time in Oxford quite independently of the tests, and which would continue to exist if tests were abolished. The first and most important of these, in my opinion, is the common feeling of honour existing among tutors of colleges, which would prevent a man, who was slightly older than his pupil, or even a great deal older than his pupil, from abusing his power over that pupil's mind. I think, so long as the tutors and fellows of colleges are gentlemen, we may rest assured that that restraint will operate. The second safeguard, which I conceived to exist already, was the increasing practice of dividing the branches of knowledge; so that a philosophical question, such as a question in moral philosophy, may be decided, and men are educated to decide it, without bringing in any religious considerations. The third safeguard was that there already existed in Oxford a number of religious influences quite independent of the university organization.[2]

He now desired to mention a fourth and new safeguard, which would be introduced by the very fact of the abolition of tests, in addition to the three which exist already: this would consist "in a large infusion, in the course of time, of Roman Catholics and Protestant Dissenters into the universities." His experience had led him to the conclusion that Nonconformists, as a rule, were more carefully trained, both religiously and theologically, than members of the Church of England of the same age,

---

[1] See pp. 93–5.
[2] He explains that he is alluding to the "immense influence exercised by Dr. Liddon," and, to a less extent, by some of the parochial clergy.

and he consequently argued that their presence at Oxford, their interest in theology, and their religious influence socially, would have the desirable effect of keeping "undogmatic Christianity" at bay, and preserving the definite outlines of the faith.

Another incident of 1871, connected with the siege and capitulation of Paris, shall be recorded in the words of an accomplished writer in the *Revue critique*, M. Paul Meyer:—

Si Appleton n'avait été qu'un littérateur de talent, nous bornerions à enregistrer sa mort dans notre chronique, les notices nécrologiques ne pouvant être dans la *Revue* qu'une exception toujours motivée par des circonstances particulières.

Mais la *Revue critique* a contracté envers Appleton une dette de reconnaissance. Au commencement de février 1871, alors que les portes de Paris venaient d'être ouvertes par la capitulation, celui qui écrit ces lignes reçut la visite d'une personne arrivant de Londres—c'était le P. Hyacinthe—qui lui remit, au nom d'Appleton et de l'*Academy*, une somme de 10,000 fr., pour être distribuée entre les érudits et littérateurs que nos malheurs auraient mis dans une situation embarrassée.[1] Cette somme était le produit d'une souscription faite entre les collaborateurs de l'*Academy*. Elle fut, selon les intentions du donateur, employée partie en dons, partie en prêts. Ce fut un acte de bienfaisance accompli avec discrétion. Ceux-là seuls le connurent qui y contribuèrent ou qui en bénéficièrent. La direction de la *Revue critique*, choisie comme intermédiaire, fut profondément touchée de l'honneur qui lui était fait, et si ces lignes tombent sous les yeux de ceux qui, en de douloureuses circonstances, à l'initiative d'Appleton, ont accordé aux savants français un témoignage de sympathie, elles leur porte-

[1] Extrait d'une lettre d'Appleton, 19 février 1871 :—"The object of sending it (the sum) was to help in the first place the collaborators of the *Revue critique*, especially those who collaborate for the *Academy*. After them for the collaborators of the *Revue archéologique*, &c. It appears to me that in these categories would be found many men who held several offices, and had lost by the war all or most of these; .... and that, by placing the sum at the disposal of yourself, or one of your colleagues in the redaction of the *Revue critique*, it could be used here and there with discretion, lent or given as seemed most acceptable, in all ways tendered in such a way that a gentleman could accept it."

ront l'expression de notre vive reconnaissance. Et quant à ceux de nos compatriotes qui furent relevés d'une gêne momentanée grâce à l'*Academy*, ils n'apprendront pas sans regret la fin prématurée d'un homme qui, dans ses actes comme dans ses écrits, fut toujours conduit par la passion du bien. (15 mars 1879.)

I am glad to be able to carry on the narrative of this important part of my brother's life by means of a contribution from Mr. James S. Cotton, late Fellow of Queen's College, Oxford, one of the essayists in the volume on "The Endowment of Research," who also has ample knowledge of the circumstances connected with the history of the *Academy* :—

Those who knew Dr. Appleton best would be disposed to dwell most upon the theoretical bent of his mind, as its dominant characteristic. He himself always regretted that his other duties never allowed him leisure to formulate in detail those metaphysical speculations of which he has left us but a single incomplete specimen. What he might have accomplished in this direction is now unknown. The world judges, and necessarily must judge, by work done, and not by hopes held out. The work to which Dr. Appleton gave his life was practical. To philosophy, his first love, he was never inconstant; but the call of duty compelled him to postpone his courtship to another day, which he was never destined to see. In default of others, he voluntarily undertook the obligation of leading a public life, and immersing himself in the details of business. While his friends stayed at Oxford, he went forth into the world, willing to spend and be spent for the sake of the common object they all alike had in view —the promotion of learning.

Dr. Appleton's practical talents were chiefly manifested in two arduous enterprises, by both of which his name will long be remembered. He founded the *Academy*, and he organized the movement in favour of the endowment of research. Concerning both of these it is necessary that something should be said in this place, but matters so recent and so intimately connected with the names of persons still alive can only be treated with a considerable measure of reticence.

For some time before the foundation of the *Academy*

Dr. Appleton had been considering how best he might devote himself to the cause of learning. His residence in Germany, and his experience of German universities, had deeply impressed him with the dignity of the life of the savant, and with the importance of diffusing the results of scientific study more widely among the cultivated classes of this country. It was at about this period that he eagerly took up a scheme for the publication in English of the master-works of the political thinkers of all ages and of all countries.[1] This scheme failed of accomplishment; but meanwhile the idea of the *Academy* was gradually gathering shape in his mind. In concert with a band of Oxford friends, almost every one of whom survived him, he planned and laboured and agitated, with all the enthusiasm of youth and of disinterested purpose, until at last the *Academy* was brought into existence. At first it was proposed that the journal should consist largely of original communications, with résumés of recent publications by competent hands rather than what is generally understood in England by "reviews." In short, the well-known *Literarisches Centralblatt* was to be taken as a model. At this stage, also, it was suggested that the journal (still without a name) should be divided into six departments, each under the direction of a separate editor skilled in his own branch of learning. At a somewhat later date, when the number of departments was to be reduced to three, Dr. Appleton modestly described his own position as being concerned with only "the mechanical part of the labour of editing." The first draft prospectus of the proposed new *Monthly Journal of Science* was privately circulated in April, 1869. The favour with which this prospectus was received at once forced attention to some details of business which had hitherto been lightly regarded. It was felt that the undertaking, from its growing magnitude, demanded that one man must stand forth as responsible editor, and also that the editor must take up his home in London. The universal consensus of his fellow-projectors pointed to Dr. Appleton as the person who could best satisfy the requisite conditions. He had not yet settled down as an Oxford teacher, nor in truth was he particularly anxious to do so. His Fellowship supplied him with that hold upon the university which was essential from the point of view of the original scheme. His exu-

---

[1] See pp. 84 5.

berant energy, his keen knowledge of men, his practical grasp of details, his devotion to an idea once firmly conceived, the wideness of his intellectual sympathies and the charm of his social manners—all these were qualifications for the editorship, each of them strong, but in their combination unequalled. It thus happened, as it were by natural selection, that Dr. Appleton, who had founded the *Academy*, became also its first editor. Shortly afterwards, he removed his permanent residence from Oxford to London;[1] and the projected journal was launched, not in the quiet of a university town, but amid the busy stir of the metropolis.

Oct. 9, 1869, was the date of the first appearance of the *Academy*, "A Monthly Record of Literature, Learning, Science and Art," with the motto "*Inter silvas academi quaerere verum.*" The number consisted of 30 quarto pages of text, with 20 additional for advertisements. The following is a list of the contributors, according to the order in which their names occur:—Matthew Arnold, H. de B. Hollings, G. A. Simcox, Gustave Masson, H. Lawrenny (Edith Simcox), Sidney Colvin, J. B. Lightfoot, T. K. Cheyne, T. H. Huxley, Sir J. Lubbock, A. Neubauer, H. N. Oxenham, C. W. Boase, G. Waring, H. F. Tozer, Th. Nöldeke, Mark Pattison, D. B. Monro, J. Conington, R. Ellis.

It was scarcely to be expected that the *Academy* would maintain the high-water mark of distinction implied by such a collection of names as this. But, despite all the vicissitudes to which it has been subject, it has always attempted to hold fast the principles upon which it was founded, and at least it has never abandoned the rule of admitting none but signed reviews.

From February, 1871, the *Academy* appeared fortnightly instead of monthly. Three years later, in January, 1874, it gained a publisher of its own, and began to appear every week. It has survived the crisis in its existence caused by the death of its founder and editor, and it still continues under the management of one who worked in

---

[1] After living for a short time in London, Dr. Appleton took up his quarters at Netley Cottage, Hampstead, the pretty artistic home where it was his pride and pleasure to bring together gradually the goodly collection of books, engravings, china, old furniture, &c., which formed, as it were, the setting of his busy life. Many of those who read these pages will, I am sure, have very pleasant memories of this hospitable retreat.—J. H. A.

willing subordination to Dr. Appleton for more than five years, and who was designated by him as his successor at the very last.

The present occasion is not suitable for tracing the history of the *Academy*. So far as Dr. Appleton is concerned, it is sufficient to say that for almost ten years his life was identified with it, as the life of a parent sometimes is with that of a child. As founder, as editor, and as part proprietor, he united in his own person all the multifarious duties that can arise in a literary concern. He was familiar with every detail of the publishing and advertising departments. He maintained communications not only with contributors and authors, but also with booksellers, with printers, with advertising agents, and with men of capital. It was not so much a paper that he edited as a business that he conducted. Wherever he went, whether paying visits of pleasure or travelling for health, the *Academy* was ever in his thoughts, and its name was ever foremost on his lips. Anxieties, from which an ordinary editor is free, daily pressed upon him, but only stimulated his courageous heart to fresh exertions. Nothing could dim his enthusiasm or daunt his perseverance. In season and (as some might think who knew not the simplicity of his nature) out of season, he advocated the claims of his paper upon the public with all the ardour of a projector, and with all the eloquence of a man of letters. Unfortunately, his physical strength proved unequal to the continual strain imposed upon it. His friends observed with pain that work and anxiety were gradually sapping a constitution that was at no time robust. To have argued with Dr. Appleton that he should spare himself while the *Academy* was in need of his services, would have been futile. But his labour had the only reward he desired. Before he left England for the last time he had the satisfaction of knowing that his paper was placed, by his own exertions and at his own pecuniary sacrifice, in a position where he could securely leave it for a time.

Absorbing as was the business of founding and watching over the *Academy*, Dr. Appleton's activity found vent in a second practical enterprise, which would have been enough in itself to occupy the time and establish the reputation of most men. He invented the phrase, once ridiculed but now generally accepted, of "the endowment of research," and he organized a public movement in its favour. University reform had always been a favourite subject with him, as with most Oxford men of his standing. He belonged to a generation which grew up under the immediate influence of the reforms inaugurated by the Commission of 1854. Open competition and abolition of tests were the two watchwords of that school; and to these principles Dr. Appleton always remained constant. But these principles were negative, and not constructive. They represented a protest against the unreformed colleges, rather than an ideal of what a university might be. Such an ideal Dr. Appleton constructed out of his German experiences, and set to work to preach it as a new gospel of academical reform. Recognizing, as he always did, the high character and even the commercial value of an Oxford education, he refused to admit that teaching, however excellent, and examinations, however searching, were the sole or indeed the main duty of a university. The average Oxford Liberal, on the other hand, was satisfied to acquiesce in the existing state of things, as being the best of which human nature was capable. "Permit the colleges a little more liberty in initiating legislation, and remove the few remaining clerical restrictions, and all will be well." To this Dr. Appleton replied: "You misconceive the proper functions of an endowed university. It does not exist to be a cramming and boarding school of the first magnitude, but as the home of students who devote themselves to a life of learning for its own sake. History proves that this was so; and the present circumstances of England imperatively require that original research should be encouraged, or we shall be shamed by the Germans."

The rallying cry of the new band of Oxford reformers was sounded by the Rector of Lincoln in his "Suggestions on Academical Organization," published in 1868. The attention of the reading public was thus called to the subject, and the followers of physical science fancied that they had discovered a breach through which they might enter into the treasure-houses of the old universities. Dr. Appleton was not content to let the matter rest with the inarticulate approval of the reading public, nor was he any the more disposed to allow learning to be swallowed up by physical science. He stirred up a practical movement, and founded an association; and he popularized the word "research," as including all branches of study. With one foot planted in London as editor of the *Academy*, and with the other not yet withdrawn from

St. John's College, he occupied a most convenient position from which to appreciate the various opinions of savants, of university reformers, and of men of business. For the second time, he planned, worked and agitated, until the "Association for the Organization of Academical Study" was established. This association included a long list of distinguished names, from London, from the provinces, from Oxford, and from Cambridge. Its first meeting was held in the Freemasons' Tavern, Great Queen Street, on November 16, 1872. The chairman of the meeting was the Rector of Lincoln, who delivered an address emphasizing what he had already written in his book. The general object of the association may be gathered from the following resolution, which was passed by a full body without a dissentient:—

"That the chief end to be kept in view in any redistribution of the revenues of Oxford and Cambridge is the adequate maintenance of mature study and scientific research, as well for their own sakes as with the view of bringing the higher education within the reach of all who are desirous of profiting by it."

The Association for the Organization of Academical Study held one more meeting on May 24, 1873, with Sir Benjamin Brodie in the chair. On this occasion a divergence of opinion between two sections of the members became manifest; and for reasons it would be idle now to discuss the association was allowed by its promoters to die a natural death. But although a most valuable instrument with which to influence the public mind thus broke in his hand, Dr. Appleton never abandoned his convictions or ceased to work by all the means that remained to him. In concert with the editor of *Nature*, a journal founded in the same year and the same month as the *Academy*, he set to work upon a private propaganda to influence all those with whom he came into contact, and bided his time for a favourable opportunity for a second public demonstration. This opportunity came when the Royal Commission appointed by Mr. Gladstone to inquire into the revenues of the two Universities presented its report. Popular interest was aroused by the apparent magnitude of the wealth disclosed; and Dr. Appleton's essay on "The Endowment of Research" in the *Fortnightly Review* of October, 1874 (afterwards published as one of a collection of essays bearing the same title), was assured of a hearing. Dr. Appleton was not one to let the iron, when once struck, get cool. He replied with vigour to the criticisms on his essay which appeared in the periodical press, especially in the *Spectator*, the *Pall Mall Gazette* and the *Athenæum*. A second essay on "The Endowment of Education," in the *Theological Review* for January, 1875 (read before the Oxford Political Economy Club in the preceding November), was intended to carry the war into the enemy's country by showing that unremunerative study possessed a claim for subsidy higher than that of education. This essay was noticed at length in the *Times*, which also opened its columns to a correspondence in which Dr. Appleton re-asserted his position with additional arguments. Of this long discussion, in which Dr. Appleton, single-handed, fought with a cloud of opponents, the most important part, in his own opinion, was that in which he met the common objection that his "researchers" would only be a new order of sinecurists. To conquer practical difficulties of this nature was a task peculiarly adapted to his energetic and hopeful mind. In the *Spectator* of October 24, 1874, he published a "Draft Scheme for the Endowment of Research," which he afterwards circulated in a separate form among eminent men of science for their advice and suggestions. As this draft scheme still remains the only attempt to organize the endowment of research, not by sporadic grants to individuals, but as a systematic part of the duty of a university, and as it met with a considerable measure of approval and but little criticism, it has been thought desirable to reprint it in full in this place. It reveals Dr. Appleton's mind at its best, when dealing with a practical problem, and is also a favourable example of his lighter style of composition.

"*Draft Scheme for the Endowment of Scientific Research.*

"1. Given, a number of young men who are receiving a liberal education, under the guidance of competent professors, and within the limits of a sufficiently elastic and varied curriculum. A considerable number of these will probably waste their time, or, from different causes, never attain anything like proficiency in their studies. We are not concerned with these. The remainder will fall into two classes, perfectly distinguishable by a teacher of ordinary experience, of those who shine because they have naturally agile and vigorous minds, who succeed in study because they would succeed in anything else; and of those who have a particular aptitude for study, and for a particular kind of study.

"2. In this latter group, consisting of men endowed with different varieties of a special faculty, we thus arrive, by a method of exclusion, at the raw material—the first draft, so to speak, of the scientific class of the next generation. Under our present arrangements, the members of both these classes alike are attracted into the practical professions—educational, legal, medical, civil, &c.—by which money may be made. As life goes on, the distinction between the two kinds of men becomes obliterated, and society suffers a double loss. First, it loses the additions to knowledge which the members of this latter class, or some of them, might have made; and it loses, secondly, by having a portion of its routine business performed by men whose temperament is studious and inventive, rather than practical. This happens because we have no career to offer to the savant at the outset.

"3. But if we had such a career to offer, what would happen is this:—The man who, at the age of twenty, say, felt within himself, or thought he felt within himself, the scientific impulse, would go to the professor under whom he had chiefly studied, and would say, "Now you have seen my work for a couple of years, and you know pretty well what I can do; do you think I shall make anything of a scientific career, or shall I go into a profession?" The recommendation of a professor who knows his pupils and possesses their confidence, being given and followed, would then form the first stage in the "sifting process," and out of the class of promising students, with apparently special capacities, who desire to try the career of research, we should get a still smaller group of men whom an experienced teacher recommends to try it.

"4. Can the professor tell without a formal examination? It is suggested that he can, for this reason: Because two or three years' experience of the quality of a man's work, under a variety of conditions, is better than three days' experience of the same work done under pressure. But for the satisfaction of the public, whose money is to be spent, by all means let us have an examination; only not a competitive examination. For we want to know whether the applicant is adequately acquainted with fact, and with the present state of inquiry, as well as adequately trained in scientific method, before we trust him to make investigations himself, for which we are to pay. We do not want to know whether and to what extent (if the expression be pardoned) he has been induced by the prospect of a glittering prize to allow himself to be fattened for the market. But the simple examination which reveals the candidate under pressure, and the professor's opinion of him independently of the examination, should be weighed together by the Board of Electors who have to grant the endowment for research.

"5. As to the composition of this Board, it may suffice for the present to say, that it should always contain external and independent elements capable of checking the recommendation of the local professor, and some men at least of acknowledged eminence as discoverers.

"6. Now, as to the nature of the grant to be made. In annual amount it should be equal to, but not greater than, the average income which the candidate would make if he went into practical life. Otherwise, if a premium be put on research which shall make it monetarily *more* desirable than other occupations, we shall be embarrassed by an "ugly rush." Let us say enough to live upon, to begin with—perhaps not enough to marry upon.

"7. But the essential point about the grant of endowment for research is, that it should be made for a very limited time, and for the performance of a specific piece of research, to be chosen, of course, by the candidate, subject to the approval of the Board. This will ensure its being a real, and not a fanciful or fruitless investigation, and its being within the lines along which a particular science is advancing. At the same time it should be something distinctly modest in its extent, which will not take more than a year, or a couple of years, to get done. And the recipient of the grant should fully understand that he has vested no right to have a similar grant for another research when this is over. He is simply paid handsomely for doing a particular job; nothing more.

"8. It is easy at this point to think of a number of means whereby he may be made to put forth his whole strength upon this first research. He may do it under the eye of the professor, or, what is more satisfactory, the research may form a part of a larger investigation in which some discoverer of eminence is engaged. In this way he is at once made a citizen of the Republic of Science, and a healthy emulation will spring up in him by intercourse with those who are engaged on other parts of the same investigation.

"9. Let us now suppose the term of the first grant nearly expired, and the first research done. It should then be presented for acceptance in the form of a paper to the Royal Society, or to one of the other learned societies of London. It is either accepted or rejected. If rejected, it is clear that the author has mistaken his vocation, and that both the professor and the Board have made a blunder. But it is a blunder, both in reference to the community and in reference to the person more immediately concerned, of the very smallest practical consequence. A few hundred pounds have been spent in trying an experiment; a further grant, if the candidate desires it, which is improbable, will be refused; and he is not too old to enter with success upon some other walk of life. If, on the other hand, the learned society accepts his research as a real contribution to knowledge, we shall let him choose another problem of larger dimensions, occupying a longer time, and with an increase in the annual payment, but in all other respects upon the same terms.

"10. This *precarious* and terminable, as opposed to *permanent* endowment, such as we have in a Fellowship, should go on, with slight increase in the annual amount of each successive grant, for ten or twelve years—*i.e.*, until the scientific habit of mind has been thoroughly formed in the recipient, and he has arrived at an age at which the choice of another profession is practically closed to him. He would, according to the hypothesis, have done by this time a good number of thoroughly real researches, and then we could safely give him an endowment for life, the amount of which should be equal to the income of a barrister or a medical man in fairly good practice, of a clerk who had been a dozen years in a public office, or of a junior partner in an average business—say £800 or £1,000 a year. And if he at any time of his life makes a *great* discovery, let him be rewarded as Sir Garnet Wolseley has been rewarded for his conduct of the Ashantee campaign—by an additional annuity on an equally liberal scale. In this way, the profession of Science could be made to compete on equal terms with the practical professions; and it should be remarked that during the period of probation, the endowment, although precarious and terminable, is really continuous, and not only continuous, but increasing in value, just as the income derived from a practical profession would have been.

"11. Lastly, the learned and scientific societies should be endowed to an extent which would enable them to carry on their business and to print their transactions; because it is a well-known fact that, in the case of some of them, it is found necessary, from sheer want of funds, to admit to membership a multitude of persons who have no pretension to the character of savants. It is probable that, in the majority of cases, the council of an unendowed society might be trusted, for competence, to perform the part, which in the present scheme is assigned to them, of accepting or rejecting the researches which we have supposed our young scientific men to make; but if the society be dependent upon its subscriptions, it is obvious that the introduction of incompetent persons upon the council is within the bounds of possibility; whereas, in the case of a learned body like the Royal Society such a contingency and its consequences are scarcely conceivable."

The year 1876 was a memorable one for the cause which Dr. Appleton had at heart. The Conservative Ministry brought forward their long-expected measure for the reform of the Universities by means of a Commission; and it was found that "research" figured prominently in their permissive scheme. In the first blush of surprise, it appeared as if Dr. Appleton's arguments, which had never been refuted by his anonymous opponents in the press, had carried conviction to the minds of responsible politicians. In his address as Lord Rector to the students of Edinburgh on Dec. 17, 1875, the Earl of Derby had foreshadowed the coming measure in words which justified all that Dr. Appleton had ever written:—

"Who knows how many discoveries might be worked out, how many conquests of man over Nature secured, if for, I do not say a numerous body, but even for some 50 or 100 picked men, such modest provision were made that they might be set apart, free from other cares, for the double duty of advancing and diffusing science. . . . . Whatever is done, or whoever does it, I think that more liberal assistance in the prosecution of original scientific research is one of the recognized wants of our time."

In moving the first reading of the Oxford Bill in the House of Lords on February 24, 1876, the Marquis of Salisbury made the following statements:—

"The only point in this connection to which I wish to call attention is that referring to research. We are of opinion that the mere duty of communicating knowledge to others does not fulfil all the functions of a university; and that the best universities in former times have been those in which the instructors, in addition to imparting learning, were engaged in adding new stores to the already acquired accumulation of knowledge. .... Another consideration which weighs upon me in urging the claims of research to a full recognition is that in recent times it has suffered some detriment from the fact that it has been pursued by men who have not possessed arms sufficiently robust to enable them to fight their way."

It is given to few men who lead a forlorn hope, as Dr. Appleton had done, to see their repeated assaults suddenly result in what looked like an unconditional surrender. The actual working of the University Commissioners, so far as it has become known, has unfortunately given little confidence that they are themselves imbued with the spirit of Lord Derby and Lord Salisbury. It may be that the obstructiveness characteristic of all ancient corporate bodies, the dead weight of vested interests, and, still worse, of vested anticipations, and possibly the fall in agricultural rents, have hampered their good intentions. Whatever the immediate results may be, it is something to be able to say that "research" will henceforth be officially recognized as one of the duties of a university, and will appear side by side with religion and education in the statutes of every college. Besides taking part in preparing the scheme for St. John's College, Dr. Appleton was examined before the Oxford Commissioners on October 24, 1877. As the Report has not yet been published, it would be improper to refer more particularly to his evidence. As usual, he dwelt most upon the practical objections urged against the scheme for the endowment of research with which his name is identified.

But to return to 1876. In May of that year also appeared a volume of "Essays on the Endowment of Research," by various writers (Henry S. King & Co., London), which Dr. Appleton edited, and in which he republished the two essays already referred to. The Rector of Lincoln wrote an introduction entitled "Review of the Situation;" and the other contributors were Professors Nettleship and Sayce, the Rev. T. K. Cheyne, Mr. H. C. Sorby, Mr. W. T. Thiselton Dyer, and Mr. J. S. Cotton. These names are but a sample of those who were proud to follow Dr. Appleton's lead, and are now honoured by the recollection that they were associated with him in a movement that has not been altogether barren of results, and is every day spreading its influence though its champion is gone.

On the last day of July, 1875, Dr. Appleton left England for America. The journey was undertaken chiefly for reasons connected with the *Academy*, and consequently a great part of his time was occupied with literary business, while his movements were largely determined by the same cause. He, however, had many friends in America, who gave him a hearty welcome, and ensured his introduction into the best circles. I have selected a few passages from his diary, some of which may perhaps be open to the criticism of saying what many have said before; but they will be interesting to many, and will at least serve to illustrate his wide sympathy and powers of observation.

Of the voyage over the Atlantic he writes:—

There were two episodes .... which I would willingly remember. On the day after we left, Aug. 1, the ship called at Queenstown about 2 o'clock and stayed till nearly 6. It is a wide and beautiful bay, with green low hills on either side, and Italian and Swedish ships riding at anchor. .... Here the women came out in a boat to sell grapes and lace; and we pulled up the articles in a basket and let the money over the side of the ship. I fancy I must have sold somewhat over £4 worth for a good woman, who rewarded me for my pains by the gift of a lace necktie. .... The other episode was the singing of hymns by the Americans, who composed the majority of our party, on the following Sunday. The tunes were new to me and exceedingly beautiful, of the Dissenting chapel type, but thoroughly refined; the hymns were many of them well-known English ones, such as "Rock of Ages." As we sat in the waning twilight, with the sun setting on our port, I could not help thinking of the good people on the *Mayflower*. .... The women sang well and sweetly, and there was a simple charm about the whole thing.

He notes carefully some features of the domestic architecture of New York:—

The predominant appearance of the streets, at first sight, is foreign—French or German. The shops, with cellars underneath and with gold letters on a black ground, savour of Germany; while the frequent sight of mountain ashes in the streets, and the green louvre shutters everywhere observable and standing in strong contrast with the red brick of the houses —a red produced by painting on the brick—confirm the impression. As one looks more closely at the structure of the houses, one sees that this is based on the old English "Queen Anne" house of the last century. There is the same general squareness and solidity of build; the same row of formal windows, set flush with the woodwork instead of four inches back, as we set them now, the frames delicately and severely moulded; the same square and ample doorway, with pilasters, and horizontal 'tooth' moulding along the top, with rosettes in the angle of intersection and panelling in the doors and in the frames. Occasionally these doors have a semicircular top, like ours of the period of the Regency. The same modelling is to be found in the old wooden houses of the Massachusetts villages, with greater slightness of appearance, arising from the use of wood instead of brick. In New York the more modern houses are built of brown sandstone or of white granite and marble; but they preserve the essential features of the style of English last century work. The Gothic revival and the gin-palace style have not yet invaded America.

After a visit to Philadelphia and the Centennial buildings, he went on to Newport, Rhode Island, where his friendship with Mr. Andrews and his family gave him a very pleasant visit. Here also he made the acquaintance of Col. Higginson, Professors Rogers, Cooke and Gibbs, Mr. Calvert, Mr. Lafarge, Mr. Lathrop, Mr. Agassiz and others. On Aug. 25 there is the following entry:—

Drove to the meeting of the Town and Country Club to hear a paper read on old notices of Newport by Colonel Higginson. He .... gave, from some old letters and documents, ... an account of the advent of French troops and officers under Count Rochambeau, when the English were encamped on Long Island. The French seem to have made furious love to the Newport beauties, amongst whom were mentioned Miss Hunter and Miss Champlain, whose names are still handed down in connection with the Hunter and Champlain houses, which I have visited. The most renowned of them all was the beautiful Quaker maiden, Polly Leighton or Lawton—the name is still borne in Newport—who wore a bewitching cap, concealing all her blonde hair but half an inch, and a white dress and plentiful white neckerchief, and who startled the Frenchmen with her "thees" and "thous," and with her disapproval of their coming and meddling in the war. One notice described Washington leading off a minuet at Newport with the beautiful Miss Hunter. . . . . I talked some time with Mark Twain (Mr. C. Clemens) who sat next me, and appeared to have a very fine head and face.

He was delighted with the old Newport houses, as also with some he saw in Nantucket and Middleborough: the descriptions are too long and minute for quotation, and are illustrated with rough pen sketches, showing the care with which he examined every point. Shortly after, he visits Berkeley's Rock:—

A mass of pudding-stone overgrown with lichens. . . . . The swampy ground around abounds in crickets and mosquitos, and I got badly bitten on the hands. . . . . Bishop Berkeley's house is about two miles up the country beyond the rock. The wooded ravine behind the rock, called Paradise, is a favourite resort of artists. . . . . A picture of it would give the idea of an extensive mountain scene, although the place is very small and one wall of the glen singularly thin; but there are no houses near, and the trees are all stunted, so that there is no standard of size.

He observes that the grasshoppers are very large:—

I saw one at Nantucket which was beautifully coloured on the inside of its wings—black, with a pale yellow border. The crickets keep up a perpetual chirp day and night, even in the region of the hotel, and their various notes seem to amalgamate into a shrill low whistle, swinging in regular time.

A "spread" is a new sensation to him:—

I went down at 1 o'clock to bathe. At this hour the "full dress" is not required, and it is the custom, after coming out of the water, to lie down and roll in the dry sand for half an hour or an hour. It gives a glow to the system, and goes by

the name of "sun-bath," "sand-bath," or vulgarly, "spread."
Some forty or fifty people were lying about to-day, rolling,
jumping, turning summersaults, conversing with their friends,
smoking, &c. I tried it, and found it fairly agreeable. . . . .
Many go into the water again after the sand-bath; to-day I
did not, but simply wiped the dry sand off the skin, after
lying for about twenty-five minutes.

After a few more experiences he becomes more enthusiastic, and writes:—

August 30, 1.30.—Bath and "spread," lasting an hour
and a half altogether, including walk. . . . . It does one a
great deal of good.

From Aug. 31 to Sunday, Sept. 5, he stayed at Shelter
Island, under the hospitable roof of Professor Horsford.
It was a period of repose he much enjoyed after three
weeks of almost incessant movement and business. "The
long mornings spent on the lawn under the shade of the
trees were very restful;" and he seemed "so thoroughly
and cordially welcome" that he felt able to prolong his
visit beyond the time originally contemplated. There is
naturally little to record of such a period; but the idyllic
"straw-ride," when "we all got into a country cart filled
with straw, and sang songs by starlight, while driving
through the country lanes," must not be entirely passed
over.

After a short stay at Naushon Island, and a visit to
the Fish Laboratory at Wood's Hole, where he was
received with "much courtesy by Professor Verrill,"[1] he
hurried on to the White Mountains, so as to be in time to
hear Henry Ward Beecher preach, on Sunday, Sept. 12.
He was not much impressed with the "worshippers" of
the great preacher, who crowded the hotel, and whose
talk was "underbred, loud, incessant;" but of the sermon
he speaks thus:—

The sermon was on the text, "Let your light so shine
before men," &c., and urged the importance of commending

[1] He afterwards had the advantage of a long chat, at Boston, with
Professor Baird.

Christianity, by making the life of the Christian visibly beautiful and attractive. There were several allusions to the late Beecher-Tilton scandal, to which I understand the preacher is fond of referring. As a literary composition the sermon was inferior to one of Spurgeon's; it repeated itself, and was occasionally guilty of the sort of grammatical slips which may pass in conversation, but ought to be avoided by a trained orator. Beecher walked about a little as he delivered the discourse from copious notes; and he not unfrequently condescended to raise a laugh by a good story, a pun, or a bit of Yankee dialect. But there was a good deal of sound experience, and a thoroughly moderate, human and possible view of the religious life.

He was disappointed with Quebec; "altogether the impression was one of dulness, bleakness, squalor and excessive provinciality." Perhaps the weather had something to do with it, which was cold and windy, and gradually developed into a tremendous hurricane or "gulf-storm." The appearance, on the other hand, of Montreal "was bright and cheerful:" here is a description of the market:—

I took a turn in the Bonsecours Market, overlooking the river, and among the fruit and other stalls in the street below. It was a very bright and busy scene, more like an Italian seaport—Genoa, for instance—than anything I remember. The view of the wharves and the bridge, which spans the St. Lawrence, and of the stalls below, from the balcony of the market, was very delightful. As one walked along till one came inside the meat market, the view of the stores was most picturesque, with the wide sunny outlook over the river seen through the window, partially shrouded by bits of thin louvre blind, ragged and hanging all askew. A Dutch painter might have made a charming *genre* picture out of any of them; and then this meat market was thoroughly pure and sweet, and the butchers well-looking and courteous men.

He rarely criticized unfavourably what he saw or heard in church, but he thus records his experience of a Sunday at Montreal:—

Went to high mass at Notre Dame, a church with a fine exterior, but ugly and tawdry within. The music was ambitious, but badly played and sung, and we had a very foolish sermon, in French, on the " Seven Dolours of Mary :" it struck me as thoroughly hollow and unreal. The preacher prefaced his discourse by reading a pastoral from the Archbishop, declaring that, for the pacification of the public mind, he advised no further opposition to the burial of Guibord, the excommunicated member of the Institut Canadien, in the Catholic part of the cemetery ; but that, by " the divine power" committed to him, he interdicted the site of this tomb in particular as an unholy spot.

At Toronto he met Goldwin Smith. A few notes are preserved of a long and interesting conversation :—

He took a pessimist view of the literary acquirements and demands of Toronto. He could only remember one literary man, or man with literary tastes, amongst his acquaintances, and he thought that " even now"—*i.e.*, after the main bulk of his library had been given to Cornell—he had the best collection of books, public or private, in Toronto. The people were for the most part " lumberers," and those who were not were the flunkeys of the mock Court of Ottawa. He thought the allegiance to a distant throne was the bane of Canada, and must sooner or later come to an end. The Canadians would get into some complication, pecuniary or otherwise, and would fly for help to the United States. At the same time, he regarded the distinct existence of Canada as a boon, because Democracy in the United States was anything but perfect, and Canada provided for a balance in the political opinion of the continent. The weakness of the Canadian people, which made it so difficult for it to combine together into an independent nation, was its heterogeneous character and the want of sympathy between the two races of its population. The union with the empire of Great Britain led Canada into acquisitions—as, *e.g.*, of the N.W. Provinces—which could only be a burden to it by itself, and was simply the carrying on of the imperial idea over an area in which it should find no place. Then, again, the Canadians had learned of Great Britain the miserable system of government by party, which had no *raison d'être*, as there was no important point of difference between the two parties.

We then spoke of International Copyright. He thought the best policy to advocate was free trade in books, and

considered that Mr. —— was under some misapprehension
in saying that the position of the American author and artist
was defined by the constitution in terms express and distinct
from those protecting any other producer. He was himself
in favour of protection under certain limitations—*i.e.*, he
thought that no more imposts should be laid on than were
required for revenue purposes, and that these should be made
to fall so as to benefit, and, in cases where it was weak, protect the industry of the country itself. This clearly had the
first claim. As to the American publishers, he thought that
they were too much in love with the profits of piracy to be
willing to have the duty taken off foreign books, or to have a
copyright treaty.

We then turned to the subject of the Endowment of
Research. He thought that the Fellowship reform was
bearing such good fruit, considering the short time Oxford
" had really been a university," that this was the proper way
of endowing it. The Fellows had half the year to themselves;
but what impeded research was the Sybaritism which of late
had been creeping over Oxford. I said this arose from the
depressing quality of the climate. He answered that, except
whilst at Magdalen, he had not found it depressing. I spoke
of the competitive system being prejudicial to original work,
in that it made the student mercenary and limited the curriculum. He thought that the mercenary motive of getting on
could not be eliminated from human action: certainly, in his
own case, it was the desire to please his friends, by getting a
good class, and registering in some tangible way his powers and
acquirements, which led him to take an interest in letters at
all. Otherwise, he should have preferred to keep a horse and
enjoy himself. As to the limitation of the curriculum, he
thought it was quite possible to introduce any amount of
variety into this, and of option, compatibly with the competitive system.

I then said that the Fellowship system was universally condemned by public opinion of all parties, and was regarded by
everybody as certain to go. This he regretted, and thought
it had not yet had time to give itself a fair trial.

I reminded him, too, that the great manufacturing towns
were putting in an imperative claim for portions of our old
endowments. This he thought ought to be resisted: it was
a mistake to try to carry away to the provinces the semblance
of university culture, without the reality. . . . . I told him

that the American scientific men were, almost to a man, much more unreservedly with me than the English. He answered, "That is because they have known nothing but the endless routine of education, and have not enjoyed the leisure which English Fellows have."

I asked him if Canada had any future before it: he said, "Yes, if she can become a nation."

A visit to Niagara has been made and described so often, that I give only one characteristic extract:—

The view on the top of the extreme left brink of the Horseshoe Fall is certainly very grand, and the bright green of the water as it tumbles over extremely beautiful.... You get here an idea of the vast body of water.... I was very much pleased with the view of the rapids on this side, fringed by the low woodland to the right, and extending to your left away to an indefinite distance. It recalled a picture of this precise spot which I had seen in my childhood, and which gave me the notion that all scenery in America was like this: just as I once dreamed that in India the air was black and all the objects golden—a fancy derived, no doubt, from the black and gold Indian or Japanese cabinet with which I had always been familiar.

At Cleveland, Ohio, he gives the palm to Princes Street, Edinburgh, and High Street, Oxford, over Euclid Avenue; but he is much struck with the brightness of the place, and is conscious of a general "impression of refinement," which he did not remember striking him to the same degree elsewhere. Then, after a short stay at Chicago, we next find him at St. Louis, where he is pleased to meet a brother Hegelian, Dr. Harris, the editor of the *Journal of Speculative Philosophy*:—

He (Dr. Harris) seemed right glad to see me, and honoured Professor Gilman's introduction with great cordiality. We talked about Hegel, whom he finds time to read and develop; and about Green, Wallace, Caird, and other English philosophic writers, about whom he seemed very pleased to hear personal details. He said the members of the Hegel Association were just then engaged in reading Wallace's book at their meetings. His own especial study for some years had been the *Phenomenology*, about which we talked a good deal, as we walked up and down the Mississippi bridge by lamp-light. Like all Hegelians, he would not give a direct answer to a question, but allowed his mind to play freely over Hegelian topics, and let me gather his reply from the general tenor of his remarks. One point he seemed to have a clear notion about—or rather two points—which I have never been able to determine so exactly; the meaning of the *Begriff* and the *Idee*.

The *Begriff* is a thing as determined by the sum of its conditions, in the metaphysical sense of absolutely all its conditions, or the Universe *quoad* one point of it.

The *Idee* is the complexus of all the *Begriffe—i.e*, of each of the things which in the *Begriff* figure as conditions, regarded themselves as cosmically conditioned in like manner.

Thus the *Begriff* of a is a as conditioned by b, c, d, &c., to n.

The *Idee* is the complexus of

a as conditioned by b, c, d, &c., to n.
b „ „ a, c, d, „ to n.
c „ „ a, b, d, „ to n.

and so on to n.

Another point about Hegel, which Dr. Harris accentuated, was this: when Hegel, in the course of his dialectic, arrives at a certain stage, *he always names it* before passing on.

In the evening I went to Harris's private house, after the walk on the bridge, and met Mr. D. J. Snider, a master in the High School, a very able man, who talked well and precisely about Hegel, and corrected me in my rusty inaccuracies more than once. We ate a kind of sour cream and biscuits, and drank copious draughts of the most excellent Lager Bier I ever tasted.

After a short stay at Cincinnati, where he made the acquaintance of Judge Stallo, and heard Governor Hayes address the mob on the hard money and school question in Ohio—" he spoke well and soberly, reasoning out the money question clearly "—he went on to Washington, " 936 miles, which we accomplished in about twenty hours," a large part of the journey being through " the lovely valley of the Potomac " :—

I had a comfortable armchair in the smoking-room of the parlour car .... which was conveniently at the end of the train; so that we could look not only through the windows on all sides, but through the open door, and see this charming scene perpetually receding before us. The colours of the trees were very varied - puce, orange, orange-red, straw-yellow, crimson, scarlet, brown and green. The country on each side of the river was as broken and full of variety as in the Passumpsic valley, and the sunshine was most brilliant. Harper's Ferry is a lovely spot, and the old building used in the skirmish of John Brown was still in ruins. I read Colonel Higginson's book, "History of the United States for Young Folks," as I passed through the scenes of the war, and got a sort of general outline.

At Washington he is full of business, chiefly connected with the *Academy*, for which he took out a copyright: "Spofford declares that it will protect me from being quoted without acknowledgment." He also had an interesting conversation with Sir E. Thornton, the British Ambassador.

Of the Library of Congress, where he had occasion to work for some hours, he says :—

It was as deserted as the Bodleian, and as comfortable to read in, everything being brought quite promptly, and there being no interruptions.

Two more extracts may be made—the second, if the information given was correct, revealing rather a strange state of things :—

Was driven into the country by Mr. Spofford in his buggy. The environs of Washington are very charming, and quite English in their aspect. We drove up to the Soldiers' Home, situated on a hill amidst beautiful trees, from which we got charming views of the town and river—notably one, of the white dome of the Capitol, through a gap in the trees, called Capitol Vista. . . . .

Lost my umbrella in the lavatory of the hotel: a lot of noisy groups crowded the whole area of the entrance-hall. The porter told me that not a few were bad characters, and that almost all carried revolvers and bowie knives!

On Oct. 8 he went to stay at Irvington with Mr. Cyrus Field, whose name has become historical in connection with the great work of laying the Atlantic cable. It was evidently a very interesting and enjoyable visit; but the diary at this point becomes rather fragmentary, and does not readily admit of quotation. A few extracts shall, nevertheless, be given :—

We drove this evening to the house of Washington Irving, and were admitted to see his study. The house is of stone, with gables, having flowing outline, and gives one the impression of a seventeenth-century building. I understand, however, that the old house was destroyed and the present one built within the memory of my informant. . . . .

Mr. Field talked this evening very agreeably about his English friends, amongst the most intimate of whom was John Bright. He also had a great regard for Dean Stanley, whom he knew well, and had "the highest opinion of his mind and his charitable goodness."

Went out after breakfast with Mr. Field in the carriage, and drove to Sleepy Hollow, a lovely spot, with gently undulating ground on either side, crowned with woods in all their autumn glory.

In the afternoon I went another drive with Miss Field to various points from which good views of the Hudson could be obtained. The great river reminds one of the Rhine, and is all the better for the absence of the chess-board pattern made by the vineyards upon the hills. Here they are clothed with trees, at present beautifully variegated with red and gold and russet and brown.

One more quotation must bring the American episode to an end. On Oct. 30 he dined with the Saturday Club at Boston, where he met, amongst other celebrities, Mr. Emerson, Mr. Lowell, Professor Wolcott Gibbs, Mr. J. M. Forbes, Professor Peirce, Dr. Oliver Wendell Holmes, Mr. Howells, Mr. Clemens (Mark Twain), Dr. Cabot, &c.

Dr. Holmes was highly talkative and agreeable. He converses very much like the Autocrat of the Breakfast Table, wittily and in a literary way, but perhaps with too great an infusion of physiological and medical metaphor. . . . . He is a little deaf, and has a mouth like the beak of a bird: indeed, he is, with his small body and quick movements, very like a bird in his general aspect. When poor Kingsley was in Boston he met Holmes, ... who came in, frisked about and talked incessantly, K. intervening with a few words only occasionally. At last Holmes whisked himself away, saying, "And now I must go." " He is an insp-sp-sp-ired j-j-j-h-ack-daw," said Kingsley.

After dinner, Mr. Emerson, who had greeted me most warmly on my entering the room, came up to Dr. Holmes' end of the table for a talk. He said he had hoped to have me as *his* guest—so also said Mr. Lowell—if another arrangement had not been made. He talked very freely and pleasantly, but his memory seems considerably impaired, especially in regard to names. . . . . Speaking of Shelley, he said that he thought the English were quite wrong in admiring him; but few of his lines were really good, and many of his subjects were horrible. "There is one of his tragedies—what is it called?" "Queen Mab?" said I. "No." "Cenci, perhaps?" "Yes, Cenci; that is horrible. But there is another man, who has written a poem which I like; I can't speak his name at this moment." "Keats?" "Yes, Keats; and there is a poem of his with gods and goddesses in it, which is good." Byron he admired, as a real poet who was to his mind. I said that to me he did not appeal as an imaginative writer; but as a writer in verse of agreeable and pointed narration and fine thoughts. He thought "Childe Harold" particularly good.

I asked him why he had put six poems of William Allingham in his "Parnassus," and only three of Browning? He said that he could not admire or read Browning; a principal merit of a poet was lucidity, and Browning was not lucid. I said that in a room in which Browning was life-size, Allingham would be invisible to the naked eye. "Yet 'Touchstone' is a good poem," he replied. "Browning's obscurity," I said, "arises from his being the child of his age. We are all in these days detached from our old moorings, and are reaching forward, both in thought and emotion, into the unknown, and putting to sea without a compass. Our thoughts, instead of being thought out to the end of them, are crossed by other thoughts, and these by others; so that they are all broken and incomplete. Browning represents this turmoil in his diction." To this, Emerson said little or nothing.

He spoke of his acquaintance with John Sterling, Carlyle's friend, and of the correspondence Sterling (whom he called Stauning and something else at times) had opened with him. He liked his poems.

I told Emerson that we regarded Swinburne as one of our greatest poets. "Swinburne is a leper," he said. "Mr. Swinburne has written against me, that Mr. Emerson has called him a leper. I do not remember that I ever said so; but as he puts the word into my mouth, I adopt it."

I mentioned to Mr. Emerson an opinion expressed to me by Mrs. Fanny Kemble, that there was a great deal more talent for poetry and art spread about among the young men and women of America than was to be found in England; only it came to nothing for lack of discipline. Emerson, instead of meeting the main point of the remark—viz., the question as to the presence or not of a greater quantity of æsthetic talent—said that poetry was not the same as verse-making, and that discipline would not avail without talent. This habit of his—I suppose it has grown upon him in his old age—of not taking the real point of an observation, but fixing upon some quite trivial detail, was exemplified at my first interview with him, two years ago, at the soirée in the Beethoven Rooms, in Harley Street, London, the night when Tom Hughes was installed as President of the Working Men's Club in Great Ormond Street, in the place of F. D. Maurice. Emerson was very silent that night, and I said, by way of trying to interest him, that a friend of mine, a young barrister, now deceased, had a class of sixteen working men, earning but poor wages, button-makers and the like, with whom he had read Sophocles in the Greek, and that they had shown more appreciation of Greek tragedy than the ordinary undergraduate at Oxford. Instead of entering into the main point of the remark, he merely said, "What was your friend's name?" "Robinson." And he then passed on into the crowd. This trait of mind, which tends to seize on the trivial element in a statement, I have also noted and wondered at in Professor Jowett.

His fit of forgetfulness came over him in speaking of Nichol. .... He asked me to come over and see him on Tuesday, November 2, at one o'clock, and that he would ask Mr. Alcott to meet me. "Alcott, he said, is really a man of genius. But be sure you come to Concord, Massachusetts; not Concord, New Hampshire. There was a very good man— he was a Professor in Scotland, at Glasgow—who came to the wrong Concord, and went sixty miles out of his way." "Was it Professor Nichol?"—who had given me a letter to him— "Ah, yes; Nichol was the man."

Some one told me that his forgetfulness was to some extent an affectation; .... but I fear it is only too real a loss of memory, and it embarrasses conversation a good deal.

We also talked of Ruskin. .... Emerson said he had told his friends at Oxford that he would only come there on a day when he could hear both Ruskin and Max Müller lecture. He was charmed with R.'s lecture, but when R. carried him off to his rooms at Corpus, and began a tirade against railways, telegraphs, and modern civilization generally, Emerson said to his daughter, "I cannot hear this: we must go." So he left Ruskin. He said he had been to see Carlyle, who said that Ruskin was the best man who came now habitually to see him.

Speaking of copyright, Emerson said, "Well, you see, we have no writers in this country." He then rose to catch his train.

Mr. Emerson speaks with great modesty and diffidence, whilst a smile covers his whole face—forehead, chin, eyes, nose, all taking part in the muscular modification. He has a way of raising one eyebrow a good deal, which gives him the aspect of having one eye somewhat above the level of the other; and in conversation he is fond of using the phrase, "You shall find," &c., which occurs very often in his essays.

A long chat with Mr. Lowell and "Mark Twain," chiefly about the *Academy* and International Copyright, brought a most enjoyable evening to a close.

Dr. Appleton started for England on Nov. 10, in the Cunard ship, *Scythia*, and arrived in Liverpool on Saturday, Nov. 20.

His American tour had been a great success in every way but one. His business arrangements were satisfactorily completed, he had made many friends, he was sincerely touched by the warmth of the welcome he had received, while of his keen appreciation of American life and scenery the above extracts are a sufficient proof. The one drawback, at which he probably would have laughed at the time, was that his strength was scarcely adequate for the amount of wear and tear which such a tour involved.

Dr. Appleton was a man to whom it was very difficult to rest, and yet to whom rest was becoming a real necessity. It was not that he did not get plenty of what is called "change." He entered largely into society in London and Oxford, and his inclination, as well as his duty to the *Academy*, led him to journey far and wide. But all this was not repose. He excelled in conversation, and was fond of breaking a lance in argument with some worthy antagonist; but a visit or a dinner party, even when it was not a prelude to business, or when it did not involve, as it did perhaps at Lord Houghton's[1] or Sir J. Lubbock's, a gathering of literary and scientific men, was, however enjoyable, yet often somewhat of a mental strain. It certainly was not rest.

There were, no doubt, a few houses where he could thoroughly unbend—at Canons Ashby, for instance, with Sir Henry Dryden, at Cheltenham, Sydenham, and, I hope I may add, at my own country vicarage, and at Brighton. But it was hard to get him, and harder still to hold him; though one of his great characteristics was the ease with which he could make himself thoroughly happy in the simple routine of uneventful home-life. One who knew him well writes:—

His readiness to enjoy and to be pleased with everything—a quiet afternoon in the garden, a country walk, a chat by the fire, no matter how unexciting the company—made him always a welcome guest. "Whom can we get to meet him?" never needed to be a matter of anxious deliberation, when he

---

[1] Lord Houghton writes: "I much enjoyed your brother's society, both from his freedom of thought and from his real sympathy with every thing good and great. . . . . It is a very fine nature lost to mankind."

wrote to ask if he might come and "bring his bag with him." He fell so naturally into our ways that we ceased to regard him as a stranger. His tender consideration and reverence for the elders, and his delight in children, always made him a pleasant addition to our home circle.

To us he knew that he was always welcome, and sometimes we really thought that we had caught him for a long and thorough holiday. But although he had come to us because he was overworked, we often found that he had brought a bag full of papers with him, and it generally ended in his returning to town on some pressing business before the proper term of his visit had expired. There was an intensity, moreover, in almost everything he did, even when he was supposed to be taking a holiday. If he went to a concert, it was as a student of music, of which he was passionately fond; if he read a novel, he analyzed and annotated it. I well remember a tour I took with him in Germany and Switzerland : he was, of course, a charming companion, but to get in his society the repose that we both required was indeed a difficult matter. To see everything, to go everywhere, with a complete disregard of distance or fatigue—this was his daily programme. And he was certainly unwell at the time, and quite unfit for the amount of exertion he wished to undergo. His indomitable energy carried him through everything; but it was a source of danger—it began to wear him out.

In the course of the year that followed his visit to America, Dr. Appleton began to suffer some inconvenience with one lung, and in February, 1877, he consulted Dr. Evershed, of Hampstead, on the subject. He was told that there was evident weakness, not, however, amounting to actual organic disease. This opinion determined him to try the effect of a short sojourn in a southern climate, and he left England early in the following month. He was at first very unfortunate in weather, for on arriving at Marseilles he found the "mistral cutting like a knife;"

and at Cannes he was laid up with a severe cold. This attack of "influenza," as he calls it, must have served to develop "weakness" into a condition of positive disease; for, on consulting Dr. Bennet, and subsequently Dr. Frank, at Mentone, he was told distinctly that the apex of the left lung was consolidated. The climate, however—though he found it somewhat relaxing—coupled with complete rest, produced, in a comparatively short time, a decided change for the better : " the progress of the mischief was stopped," he was pronounced " a good case," but warned that the cure would take two years.

I am sorry I have no records of this absence from home which admit of being quoted in this place ; but, in spite of anxieties, he evidently enjoyed his exile. He met many friends, and had the pleasure of spending some part of the time under the hospitable roof of J. B. Andrews, Esq., at Le Pigautié. After a short tour in Italy, he returned to London on the last day of May.

It was, I think, on Sunday, June 10, that, while wandering with me over the hills near Brighton, he told me, for the first time, about the state of his health. He was, no doubt, anxious not to give us pain, and so had hitherto spoken only of a troublesome cold, which he had found it difficult to shake off. I well remember the shock the present announcement was to me. He said, however, that he had placed himself, since his return, in the hands of Dr. Andrew Clark : his trouble was called "*fibrosis*," the area affected was very small, it was perfectly curable, and was in fact in process of cure. As the dreaded words *phthisis* or consumption were not used in our conversation, and as he had so much to say which served to allay my apprehension, I ended by believing that I had been alarmed too hastily. When he returned to London, and seemed to work on as usual, this favourable view appeared to be confirmed.

But notwithstanding ill-health and Dr. Appleton's

manifold engagements, the years 1876-7 were not unfruitful in literary work. In November and December, 1876, he contributed two articles to the *Contemporary Review*, entitled "A Plea for Metaphysic:" these papers, in conjunction with an article published in the same review, in July, 1874, on "Strauss as a Theologian," were intended to form chapters in a forthcoming work on the "Ego," to appear as a volume of Trübner's "Philosophical Library." A fourth chapter, on "Development," was occupying him when his health broke down more rapidly at the end of 1878. In the present volume, which may be regarded as in some sort a fulfilment of my brother's arrangement with Mr. Trübner, the three completed articles are reprinted, together with a considerable amount of unpublished matter, excluded before by the exigencies of space. They appear, moreover, under the title that the larger work was meant to bear, "What is the Ego?"

Dr. Appleton, also, still continued to give much attention to the important question of Copyright, his interest therein having been greatly quickened by his intercourse with the leading American publishers and literary men. He gave evidence before the Copyright Commission in January, 1877, and in the following month contributed a paper on "American efforts after International Copyright" to the *Fortnightly Review*. This article, which is included in this volume, excited a considerable amount of interest at the time of its publication. A careful analysis of its contents appeared in the *Times* of January 31, and on February 3 the *Athenæum* printed a long and elaborate comment by Mr. Moy Thomas. There were also important notices in the *Pall Mall Gazette*, *Academy*, *Examiner*, &c. It must, however, be borne in mind that the article is now reprinted—with additional matter formerly excluded from the *Fortnightly Review*—simply on account of its historical interest in a volume like the present. The question of International Copyright has considerably advanced since the date of Dr. Appleton's paper, and mainly on the lines he foresaw. The American point of view is now very generally recognized in this country; and further, in March, 1879, Messrs. Harper and Brothers issued an important circular on the question,[1] modifying their original position, and making the following proposal:—That full copyright in the United States shall, on reciprocal terms, be conferred on English authors, upon the condition that their works shall be manufactured and published in that country, by a citizen thereof, within three months after publication here.

On Nov. 1, Dr. Appleton left England for Egypt, in accordance with the recommendation of his medical advisers. He went, as he expresses it, "as a robust invalid," with sufficient strength and energy to enter fully into the charm of visiting such historic ground, and also with a firm belief that his wanderings in the sunny south would indeed be so many steps on the road to complete recovery.

After a pleasant journey he arrives at Alexandria,

Which looked most brilliant on this splendid afternoon, with the whole port covered with little boats filled with Arabs in their various colours : there was also a goodly assemblage of ships both of war and merchandise. I was met by Cook's tourist boat, with rowers in bright red, with the magic name of Cook on their jerseys, and the Maltese agent in the bows. I at once beckoned to him, and he came on board, got off all my luggage, for which the Arabs struggled like wild cats, and saw me safely through the custom-house with only the opening of my hand-bag. . . . .

Already I have found it necessary to learn some Arabic, but at present can only say a few sentences, the most important of which are " Go," and " I do not want a donkey." . . . . The donkeys in Alexandria disappointed me, being depressed animals, such as one sees in England ; but in Cairo the white donkey is a beautiful creature, holds up its head, looks happy, and is worth a good sum.

---

[1] See *Academy* of April 5, 1879, and of Oct. 23, 1880.

He halts for a time at Shepheard's Hotel, Cairo,

Where I have a comfortable room looking into a garden with two pelicans and some swans in it. My things are unpacked; Kant and Hegel are by my side, and I am quite happy. Captain Burton, the traveller, is next door but one: he is an old acquaintance.

After a few weeks at Cairo he goes on to Helouan-les-Bains, where he, at first, planned to remain quiet for the winter:—

This is quite a little place, an hour's ride, by a very rickety railway, from Cairo, and between two and three miles from the Nile. I was charmed with it at once, and now have stayed nearly three weeks with great pleasure, and, I hope, some profit. . . . . I have a splendid room (at the Grand Hotel), nearly twenty feet high, with two windows, through which I look out upon the Pyramids. . . . . To-day we had an influx of soldiers from Cairo to take care of Tewfik Pasha, the heir-apparent, who is come here to visit one of the princesses, who is taking the baths. She is called "Princess No. 2"—that is, she is the second wife of the Khedive, and is said to be his favourite. The harem is here in the different houses, which have trellis screens and sail-cloth coverings in all the balconies and verandahs, and even on the top of the house, to prevent any of these precious creatures from being seen. The place is full of lanky, black eunuchs, as conceited and insolent as they can stand: every morning they come past the hotel in carriages to take the sulphur baths. The Khedivial bath-rooms are a curious mixture of luxury and bad taste—yellow damask curtains and the most hideous carpets, that might have been made in Halifax.

There is not much to do at Helouan, but

Amongst other diversions are the shooting of the Nile geese; the catching of cobras, which abound in the neighbouring mountains; and lastly, the collection of flint flakes and desert plants. Of the latter there are a number of species: I saw a collection made by Schweinfurth, the African traveller, at the house of Franz Bey, containing nearly 250 examples.

He was at length advised by his doctor to take the Nile voyage in a sailing boat, if possible to the Second

Cataract; and so, leaving Helouan with some regret, he joined a party in the dahabeyah *Minnehaha*, and is charmed with his new experience:—

We have now been three weeks together, and pleasanter companions it would be difficult to find. There is a dining-room and a drawing-room, the food is excellent, and we have not had a dull, much less a disagreeable half-hour the whole way. The mode of life suits me thoroughly. The air is, of course, splendid—sunshine every day and all day, and not a drop of rain since we left Cairo. The perfect quiet and the ever-changing scene are more like a dream than anything else. There is no mode of travelling in the world that can be compared with it. . . . . We are now 450 miles or more S. of Cairo, and the weather [in January] is like an English July; we sit on deck all day with an awning over our heads, on comfortable sofas, with oriental rugs under our feet, and here we read and write and talk. There is always a little excitement, for three of our party are sportsmen, and there is generally a vulture, or a flamingo, or a crocodile-bird, or more rarely a wild duck or teal, to be had. Pigeon and turtle-doves we don't count: they may be shot by the hundred, and we get them for lunch or dinner every day. . . . . Then, I do a little work daily at philosophy, and am dabbling in Egyptian antiquities, besides French and English novels.

We have made it a rule, in view of the different nationalities on board, to talk English at breakfast, Arabic at lunch, and French at dinner, and we pay a small fine of one piastre for using our mother-tongue at forbidden hours. The lunch is generally uproarious, as none of us know more than a few words of Arabic—just enough to ask the servants for what we want. In the evening, after dinner, we take it in turns to read out a story from the "Arabian Nights," and finish up with whist. . . . .

Then, again, there is the doctoring of the crew; and this generally falls to me, as, from hearing me called "the doctor," the Arabs have got the idea into their heads that I am a Hakim, and I have now the still more honourable title of Hakim Pasha. Their ailments are simple: generally cuts in their hands and feet, or indigestion; for the first we give cold cream and sticking plaster, and for the last, castor-oil copiously. I have also two patients with bad eyes, and one with a boil on the top of his head, which I have duly poulticed.

.... We have nearly twenty of these Arabs on board, including a dozen for crew, three cooks, two waiters and a dragoman; and they are all very grateful for the slightest kindness. .... The dragoman is a very handsome Nubian, and a great favourite with ladies; he has spent two years in Paris, and speaks English also a little. Amongst other qualifications, he belongs to the order of howling and dancing dervishes, and this is a sort of certificate of respectability and honesty, as none but upright, straightforward men are admitted into these orders. He dresses in the most gorgeous manner, and for the most part in good taste: this morning I see he has put on a brilliant green satin waistcoat, but he generally appears in delicate, faded greens or yellows, admirably harmonized, and a red fez on his black head. ....

On Sunday we have a nice little service in the morning: the Major says the prayers or litany, the lady and her maid start a couple of hymns, and I read one of Robertson's sermons. One of the Frenchmen, who speaks English, asked to be allowed to attend—he is a Catholic; and now the captain, who is a Coptic Christian, attends also. He does not understand a word of anything but Arabic, or, it may be, Coptic also; he sits, however, in his turban and black cloak, a picture of oriental humility and attention, and no doubt says his own prayers.

The letter from which the next extract is made is dated "Cook's Hotel, Luxor, Feb. 28, 1878." He had now been as far as the First Cataract, and was on his way back.

There is not much to see till you get within about ten miles of Assouan, when the whole landscape changes, and, instead of the flat bank of drab-coloured mud, you have, on one or both sides of the river, mountains of black rock covered with the most beautiful golden sand. In fact, Nubia has already begun and Egypt has ended. ....

At Esneh we stopped for a day to bake bread for the crew: it is said to be the finest air in Egypt, and I spent the whole day on land, visiting the temple and walking under the palm-trees. The climate is certainly very balmy and beautiful; but as soon as you enter the Nubian region the air is much crisper, and, judging from its effect upon myself, I should say it is as much better than the climate of Egypt as that of Egypt is better than any in Europe.... We are just on the bend of the world, and already begin to see the stars of the Southern Hemisphere, while the constellations of the North assume a drunken, topsy-turvy appearance. Juvenal was a lucky fellow to be exiled to this delicious region....

The nearest approach to a crocodile we found and shot at opposite the island of Philæ, above the cataract, and just across the Nubian frontier. He was a vast lizard about three feet long, and, after receiving a shot from one of the Frenchmen, he bolted among the rocks and we lost him....

One day we visited a dahabeyah whilst in the act of passing up the cataract. We were on donkeys, coming from Philæ, when we first saw the boat battling with the rapids, and 150 struggling and screaming Arabs on shore dragging it up with ropes. It seemed to make about a foot an hour, and to go back two whenever the rope slackened. The sheikhs of the cataract, who organize all this pulling, were sitting quietly on their heels and smoking.... We went on board to see how it felt..... Even with every window shut, the water gets into the boat; but there is no danger in going up and not much in coming down, as the people on the spot are thoroughly used to it.

The following is an incident of the return voyage to Luxor:—

It was a windy day, and we were moored up against the bank between two villages, with nothing but sandy desert within sight. Presently two men in the Bedawin dress rode up on donkeys, carrying guns, and with a wretched little black girl walking beside them. Her feet were cut about dreadfully, and she was a miserable, crouching, and, in the face, perfectly hideous object.

This poor creature was purchased by the dragoman for £15, "the price of a cow," and was to be taken to Cairo as a servant to his wife. The story goes on:—

I raised a feeble objection to the transaction, on the ground that the Egyptian Government had given England an understanding to stop the sale of slaves, and it was now a crime by law, rendering the purchaser liable to fine and imprisonment. This was overruled by the acquiescence of the majority of the passengers, and Marisilla, much against her will, came on board. We gave her dates, which she duly ate, and put the stones on the carpet: she was as black as jet, with splendid white teeth, thick lips, and no nose appreciable. After a day or two she was washed, and a new dress made for her by the lady's maid under the directions of the captain of the boat; she began to smile and look happy, instead of sitting all of a heap, and at last answered to her name, and made the oriental salute by touching the lips and then the forehead. The sailors were very kind to her, and she slept below decks among the wine bottles. When we got to Luxor she was taken on shore, and had a bath and her hair cut; after which she returned gorgeous in a red chintz gown and a gauze coif, which made her look about fifty and a great swell. The poor thing had gained immensely in self-respect by being made decent, and stood up to be admired, and kissed our hands. This is my first experience of the traffic in human flesh.

Dr. Appleton now determined to leave the *Minnehaha*, and to retrace his steps. Those five days on the Nubian frontier "seemed to do me more good," he says, "than all the rest of the trip;" and further, the English doctor at Luxor advised him not to return to Cairo till the end of March; so he arranged to take the steamer to the Second Cataract. Fortunately, moreover, he found a congenial companion for the journey in the person of an old friend, Professor Blackie of Edinburgh. A few more quotations shall be made from the letters we received from my brother while in Egypt. In all my extracts it will have been observed that I am avoiding descriptions of temples and other antiquities, which are now so familiar from guide-books and other more formal and scientific works on Egypt; and even Abou Simbel must not tempt me from the rule.

On March 4 we found ourselves once more at Assouan, and again visited the bazaars, the quarries, and the beautiful, green island of Elephantine. Here we saw two wonderful things—a Nubian having his head shaved, and a chameleon with a tongue as long as his body. Afterwards, I found a number of chameleons, which are very common about here:

they are bright green, but, if you rub them and put them in a bad temper, they turn black. Mine, however, refused to eat their proper quantity of flies, and languished and died.

Five miles on donkeys through the desert brought us to Philæ, where we found Cook's steamer, which plies between the First and Second Cataracts. It can only be got up or down the falls when the Nile is very full, in the rainy season, and so it is kept above the First Cataract all the winter. .... From March 5th to the 16th we were in Nubia. .... The climate is beautifully warm, without being heavy or sultry: my thermometer marked from 68 up to 83 in my bedroom. The atmosphere, too, is deliciously clear; everything, even to the details of a temple, seems quite near and distinct. .... The sand is golden-coloured, and there is a good deal of black igneous rock, but scarcely any vegetation; though sometimes you come across an acre or two of the castor-oil plant, which is much prized by the women, who smear their hair and the whole of their bodies with this delightful unguent. We saw quite big girls of twelve or fourteen with absolutely nothing on but castor-oil and a fringe of hippopotamus hide round their waist. ....

At Korosko, one end of a caravan route down to Khartoum, we met the oriental merchant, gorgeous in yellow silk and with silver-mounted pistols; but there was little or nothing to buy that we wanted, except gum. ....

At Dakkeh, on our way back, all the women of the village turned out to sell their necklaces. I bought four or five: at present they all smell of castor-oil, and must be washed and restrung. ....

When we got back to Philæ, we took a boat to visit the First Cataract, and see the men and boys shoot the rapids on logs of wood. There were seven in all—one or two without logs, simply treading water. Those on the logs seemed to be able to turn out of the current at will, and one, quite an old man, put into land when half-way down. This exploit, which seems a very dangerous one, and cost an Englishman his life a few years ago, has been performed by the inhabitants of these villages for at least two thousand years. .... Between the island of Philæ and the island of Biggeh we saw little girls swimming across on logs, with their long blue dresses tied in a bundle on their heads, and on the top of all a quantity of clover for their cattle. They let down their dresses again before landing; so that the whole was a very decent operation.

[Near Abydus, on the way back from Luxor to Cairo,] I saw what I had never seen before, a mirage. To the right and left of our route were groves of palms, and, at about eight in the morning, these palms, though really standing in a sandy plain, seemed to be planted by the side of a refreshing lake or river; and we could even see the reflection of the trees upside down in the imaginary water. . . . . At Assiout we heard and saw the priest go up to the gallery of the minaret, close to the water, and call the faithful to prayer—an oriental sight not to be missed, which I had never before witnessed. Unfortunately, an execrable band made an effort to play Italian airs at the same time, which rather destroyed the effect.

On arriving at Cairo my brother was again examined by the doctor, and the result was far from encouraging. "He says I may be infinitesimally better, but must still come abroad in the winters for a year or two." He, however, endeavoured to take a cheerful view of his case, and to impress the same upon his friends. "In general health I am very well, though I find I have lost several pounds of flesh. This I shall probably make up on my return to England, and it is then rather than now that I expect to find evidence of improvement." Important business, moreover, was then claiming his presence in London, and I fear he was much harassed by the conflicting duties of an immediate return and of gradually changing the climate of Egypt for that of England. I wrote, I remember, to implore him to delay, and he yielded so far as to give himself another five or six weeks, which he spent in the Levant and Italy. I am glad to be able to resume my quotations.

After finishing my letters . . . . I went into Alexandria to look out for the other two members of my party, Professor Blackie and Mrs. Heygate. By four o'clock we were all safely on board the "Messageries" boat, and steaming away for Port Said. . . . .

The boat had come from Marseilles, and was full of French pilgrims and their priests, on their way to the holy places in

Palestine. (I heard afterwards that an English party went to Gethsemane the night before Good Friday, *armed with pistols*, and sang the hymn "Go to dark Gethsemane," after paying sixpence at the gate. This to my lay mind seems to partake rather of the nature of *bathos*.) .... The principal things we had to complain of in the French pilgrims were loud talking and fleas; and we were very glad when we got to Jaffa and saw the backs of almost all of them.

At Port Said, on Sunday, we went on board the English gunboat keeping guard at the entrance of the Canal, and had a very nice service and sermon. They were very warlike; and that same afternoon received a despatch not by any means to leave until two other gunboats had arrived.

As we approached Jaffa the most delicious odours of orange blossom came over the sea: it is a great place for oranges, of an enormous size, but very good. When the crowd had left we went on shore and spent an hour in the reputed house of Simon the Tanner. .... The smells are bad, but the walls are covered with hyssop in bloom; and from the top we get a beautiful view over the sea—just such a view as would have suggested to the Apostle that Christianity was meant for a larger world than Palestine. ....

All night long—after we had filled the ship chokefull of oranges—we steamed along the Syrian coast, seeing only the light at the headland S. of Tyre, for it was rather misty; but at six in the morning, Mount Lebanon, with its cap of snow, burst upon us, with the rising sun shining obliquely upon it. ....

Passing Tripoli — where we took on board a cargo of sponges—we got to Iskanderûn, or Alexandretta, the ancient Issus, in the corner between Asia Minor and the Syrian coast, and here we stayed lading for three whole days, till we were deep down in the water with 2,000 bales of cotton, besides oil, grain and oranges. This is the dirtiest and most unhealthy town I ever came across, but it is important commercially as the port of Aleppo, through which the produce of the far interior of the Turkish Empire comes to the sea. At the back of the town is a belt of marsh about a mile broad, and the sewage stands ankle-deep in some of the streets. There has lately been an extensive visitation of fever, and we saw a great many pale faces. Lately, since the Peace of San Stefano, the Circassians expelled from Bulgaria have begun to be deported here, on their way to the valley of the Euphrates. A thousand or more had already arrived, and 150,000 are expected ultimately. This is pleasant for the inhabitants, especially as they have brought small-pox with them, which is very bad at Constantinople.

Notwithstanding these drawbacks, Professor Blackie and I determined to make a little excursion into the interior. So on the second day, we got a couple of very bad horses from the English Vice-Consul, and the loan of his cavass, who rode, with a sword and a big knife, on a third beast. We rode for six miles across the marsh and up the mountain, on a fearfully bad road, taking three hours for our six miles: it gave one an idea of what travelling in Turkey is like. All along the road we met people coming with produce, and armed with guns; we met also the Circassians and their families, armed to the teeth, with rows of cartridges on each breast of their tunic. It was difficult to say which looked the greater scoundrels, the Circassians or the population who had armed themselves against them. At the inn at Beylan, the village we rode to, the yard was full of Circassians; their wives, sometimes exceedingly beautiful, rode on horses astride, with babies in boxes on each side of the saddle. . . . . In the curiosity shops here, and at Smyrna, you are offered brooches and trinkets, some of them still spotted with blood, which were taken from the Bulgarian women by these men.

We have taken on board a great man, a Pasha, going to Constantinople, formerly, I believe, the governor of Bagdad, with ten horses and a white donkey, besides servants. He doesn't eat with us, but has his salad and his olives after we have done. He has with him his private chaplain, a Ulema, with a green turban and a very nice mild face, who says his prayers on the deck, turning towards Mecca, with great regularity.

Every inch of the deck vacated by the pilgrims is now occupied by Turks, whom we have taken in at all the little ports on the way, and who are bound for Constantinople, changing at Smyrna. It was a very picturesque sight after dark to walk to the fore part of the ship amongst all these Mussulmans, sleeping or preparing to sleep. Each side, against the gunwale, oriental carpets were spread, and boxes and bundles disposed to windward as a protection. Some hedged themselves in nearly all round with their luggage, and then began gravely to change their daily dress of many-coloured coats and tunics for a nightly dress of nearly as many pieces and as much variety; afterwards, they smoked their hubble-bubble pipes, and went to sleep. In the fore part the hatches over the two entrances to the hold, and, at one time, the hatch over the aft entrance, were quite covered with men in white and yellow, sleeping and snoring under the starlight. . . . .

The coast of Asia Minor is exceedingly beautiful, as fine all along the southern edge as the Syrian coast is under Lebanon. At Mersina, Professor Blackie went off by himself to Tarsus, to see the house or birth-place of St. Paul, fifteen miles off. The reputed house is occupied by the American Consul, who showed a Greek inscription beginning ΟΙΚΟΣ ΠΑΥΛΟΥ; but I am afraid I am sceptical about the whole thing, except the beauty of the wide plain, with the snow-capped range above it, and a little Crusader's castle, like a mushroom, by the shore. . . . .

Smyrna, the northern limit of our journey, is a disappointing town after Cairo and Alexandria; the bazaars are not so good, and the oriental character not so marked. . . . . We just escaped a heavy fall of snow and came in for all the chilliness of the day after it: the bay, however, is warm—one of the great bays of the world; so, while the Professor and some Americans scamper off to see the ruins of the Temple of Diana at Ephesus, Mrs. H. and I go out for four hours of tossing and warm sunshine in a little boat. . . . .

We only stayed three hours at Syra—the ancient Scyros—a kind of Charing Cross in the Ægean, where all roads meet, and whence you can go anywhere. The town is finely situated, rising up the mountain in a pyramidal form to its acropolis. Then on we went through a labyrinth of misty islands, the wind dead ahead of us, but the sea not rough. . . . .

With the exception of Syra, the Greek islands showed but little signs of habitation; but very different was it when we began to near the Calabrian coast, after a fairly smooth run across the stormy Adriatic; all round the Italian sea-board were numberless towns and villages, almost continuous with one another from Spartivento to Reggio. . . . . At Messina we took on board 50,000 live quails for the London market; and, sublimely unconscious both of Scylla and Charybdis, between which we passed in the dark, we got to Palermo on Tuesday last (April 30) after seventeen days at sea.

Here (at Palermo) I have been for nearly a week, seeing the interesting Norman churches, the museum and the surrounding country. . . . . To-morrow I go to Catania, the Professor to Naples, and on Tuesday Mrs. Heygate starts, by Cunard steamer, to Liverpool ; so our pleasant trio, which has lasted, off and on, since the end of February, is broken up at last. After a few days at Catania, and a visit to Syracuse, I shall hope to get to Capri for a week, and then home by the 1st of June.

Dr. Appleton realized his programme in less time than he anticipated, for I see he was staying with us at Brighton on the day appointed for reaching London. We were glad to be able to congratulate him on his appearance; he was perhaps thinner, but he looked brown and well, and was in excellent spirits. He told us that the sea had done great things for him since he left Alexandria; his chest had cleared in a most satisfactory way, and he felt wonderfully better. He said so much about the effect of sea air that we were tempted to regret he had not had more of it, and hoped his advisers might let him, next winter, try the experiment of a voyage or of a quiet sojourn on some sheltered coast. The wear and tear of travel and its occasional vexations always told on him even when in health, and the great variations of temperature in Egypt had, we knew, given him many a cold. He himself was in favour of spending the next winter in the Bay of Naples, and, with a view to this, had made a complete circuit of that coast on his way home.

On his return to London he plunged into work with characteristic energy; he was told he "need not consider himself an invalid," and I fear he availed himself to the full of this implied permission to exert himself. But the mistake was soon discovered. It was a miserable June, with almost constant rain for the first three weeks; and before this period was over, a condition of fever set in, which remained constant for seven months; it was, in fact, the beginning of the end. In the second week of July he broke down so completely that he was prevailed upon to take a ten days' rest at Margate; and here again the sea air proved a friend, and he returned to town refreshed and stronger. Early in August we went to stay with him at Netley Cottage, and were distressed to find him looking ill and evidently very weak. Yet he was cheerful about himself, and explained his illness by a chill which he had experienced one night: he was returning to Hampstead from a friend's house in evening dress, and was caught in a heavy shower. He told us, too, of the worry and anxiety, which certain business affairs connected with the *Academy* were causing him. Moreover, the doctors spoke assuringly.

At this time nothing was decided about future movements, and I think he suffered from the uncertainty and from the divided counsels of his advisers. In this condition he came down to us at Brighton on September 1: his symptoms had for some time past suggested the idea of chronic malarial poisoning, and he was instructed to leave his pretty home at Hampstead without delay. He stayed with us for about three weeks, and fortunately the weather permitted him to be for the greater part of the day in the open air; after a short time given to work, he used to spend hours on the pier, lying on the shingle, or driving slowly up and down from Sussex Square to Cliftonville. He was very cheerful too, full of his usual keen interest in all around him; his voice was clear and strong, and he had scarcely any cough. I confess we shared the delusion with so many of his friends that all might yet be well.

He returned to town on September 19, and became the guest of Henry Holiday, Esq., of Oak Tree House, Hampstead, where he remained almost continuously until he left England in the following month. Here he received every attention that the most devoted friendship could suggest, but though he went manfully through a great deal of trying business, it was with obviously declining strength. But still the medical report was very encouraging; although the general bodily condition was not so good, the local trouble was certainly better; there was a tendency, he was told, to go back to the state in which he was when he returned last June. And, moreover, there seemed enough to account for a general disturbance of health in the work which he had been compelled to undertake—the removal of his books and furniture to his rooms at Oxford, and the final settlement of the *Academy* on what he believed to be a sure and prosperous basis. And so the weeks passed on, and at last, on October 16, the doctors decided upon Egypt as the place of his approaching exile—" Cairo, Thebes, and, if possible, Nubia"—and the die was cast. Dr. Appleton left Southampton on October 31, in the Peninsular and Oriental steamer, *Nepaul*, for Suez.

The following extract is from a letter I received from him dated November 4, 1878, off Gibraltar.

You will be glad to hear that I have passed safely through the formidable Bay of Biscay, and am now in warm air and calm water. I write this on Sunday night, off the Coast of Portugal, between Lisbon and Cape St. Vincent, with a piano going, and about a dozen people singing Hymns Ancient and Modern. . . . Maitland, as I think you know, follows me to Egypt, giving up his project of a winter in Rome. He is such a delightful companion, that this will be a great boon to me. . . . .

You will be pleased to know that my appetite has come back; I eat ravenously at all three meals, and have milk frothing and warm from the Peninsular and Oriental cow, at six in the morning and in the afternoon. The whole day, as far as possible, I spend in the open air, either walking on deck or esconced in a chair lent me by Miss Raven. We have had a N.W. wind hitherto, fresh and rather cold, but the best for the Bay, and now we have a simoon from Africa and a Scotch drizzle.

He arrived at Cairo on November 13, and took up his quarters at the Hotel du Nil. " It was excessively hot," he writes, " and the floods were out all round the city. The pyramids can only be visited by water." There were also "fogs every morning, in the English style." He soon became very unwell, and was most kindly nursed by Mrs. Loftie, who fortunately was staying at the same hotel. In the latter part of December, he determined, as he had been advised, to get on, if possible, to Luxor, where he knew by experience there was an excellent hotel, and an English physician in whom he had great confidence. In the steamer he suffered grievously. The accommodation was, of course, inadequate for an invalid, and the wind was bitterly cold.

He reached Luxor on January 1, 1879, "with bronchitis, increased chest trouble and loss of voice," and, although he received unremitting attention from Dr. Maclean, yet, on the whole, he got slowly weaker. The long continued fever was wearing him out, even more than the progress of the disease in the lungs. He was, however, always able to get out and sit on the verandah and chat with the friends who used to gather round his chair, and then "he was very cheerful—even merry." And he happily suffered no pain, and retained his intellectual powers in all their keenness. One day an old friend expressed a fear that the days were long and wearisome to him: "they are too short," he replied, "for what I have to do."

It soon became necessary for him to have the attendance of a servant, and a visitor at the hotel, Colonel Alexander, M.P., who had previously yielded to the invalid a large and sunny bedroom, now very considerately placed his valet at my brother's service. This was a great boon, and Henry Ireland proved a kind and experienced nurse. Madame Pagnon too—whom he had described, on the occasion of his former visit, as "a charming hostess"—did her utmost to make him comfortable.

On January 23, three travellers arrived, who had just completed a riding tour from Sioot to Luxor, all acquaintances of Dr. Appleton, one of them the friend of whom he speaks in his letter of November 4. Their coming was a great delight to him, and, weak as he was, he entered with characteristic interest into all they had to tell. He even discussed the feasibility of a summer expedition to Beyroot, in which he had agreed to join, adding, however, "but it is more than probable that I shall lay my bones in Thebes."

He sent off six letters on January 31; the one to myself, containing full instructions in the event of his decease, had evidently been written some time before; but there was a long postscript added, no doubt, on this last day of his life. Though still speaking of recovery as possible, he writes as one who is face to face with death, and, I am most thankful to say, with perfect calmness, and a mind absolutely "at rest." He was simply waiting for the revelation of "God's will," ready to stay or to depart.

Mr. Loftie, the historian of the ride to Luxor, shall tell the rest:—

In the morning (of February 1) we returned to the hotel . . . . and, as we were lingering in the porch, Appleton's servant came down with a pale face. His master was breathing very hard, he said, and did not seem to recognize him. We ascended to his chamber and summoned the Doctor in haste. But there was nothing to be done. The rays of the morning sun entered the open window, but the darkness of death had already shadowed our friend's face.

We had little time to give to sorrow. In that southern land burial follows death within a few hours, and, before many of the sojourners in the hotel knew he was gone, they were summoned to attend his funeral. . . . . He had died at a quarter before nine. By half past three all was prepared, and we wrapped him in his plaid and laid him reverently to rest. The landlady covered the coffin with a white sheet, on which wreaths of lovely flowers had been arranged, and four stout Arabs took up the light burden, followed by his three friends and many of those who, but the day before, had conversed with him as he reclined in his chair on the shady side of the terrace.

The Coptic Church at Luxor is a quaint building, entered

from a narrow lane by a court, over the door of which is a wooden cross. It has five aisles, supported by pillars, and the apse is shut off by a beautiful screen of carved woodwork, over which hang an old " gold ground " picture of two saints, and a modern German lithograph of the Holy Family. The body was borne into the sanctuary,[1] and while a kind clergyman from the hotel (the Rev. Henry Majendie, of Holy Trinity, Barnstaple) read the solemn English service, the Coptic priest and his assistants swung the censer round the coffin, and stuck long candles at the four corners. The scene was strange but very impressive, and tears were not wanting among those who stood amid the shadows of the dimly-lighted church.

We next took our sad way[2] through the outskirts of the town to the summit of a little knoll on the road towards Karnac, whose colossal pylons and lofty pillars were visible through the groves of palms. Here is a little enclosure in which rest the bones of those few English people who have died at Luxor. In one corner was a vacant space, and here the grave was dug, and when the last words had been said and the last blessing pronounced, we left the body of our friend departed in charge of the priests and officers of the old Jacobite Church.[3]

As Dr. Appleton maintained his manifold activities up to the very day of his departure from England, the news of his decease came with something of a shock of surprise upon many of his friends. I am glad, therefore, to have Dr. Maclean's permission to publish the following, which will serve as a reply to many inquirers:—

The cause of death, in my opinion, was exhaustion, dependent on a fever of seven months' duration. The patient undoubtedly suffered from phthisis, and, as undoubtedly, a portion of his fever was due to that disease, but another portion, and by far the larger, was due to the presence in his constitution of some malarial taint; as is evidenced by (1st)

---

[1] The enclosure in front of the iconostasis.

[2] The procession was headed by the scarlet banners of the Coptic Church with their white embroidered crosses. See Mr. Greville Chester's account in the *Academy* of February 22, 1879. The ready kindness and sympathy of the Coptic clergy are worthy of record.

[3] "A Ride in Egypt," by W. J. Loftie (Macmillan and Co.), pp. 352-4.

the slight and limited amount of lung mischief in comparison with the amount of fever, (2nd) by the daily occurrence of chills, and (3rd) by the immense influence of quinine, given as it should be given in malarial fevers, in reducing the temperature.

To Dr. Maclean my warmest thanks are due, both for his attention to my brother at the last, and for much trouble taken on my behalf in superintending the erection of a suitable monument over Dr. Appleton's grave. There are many others also, whose help and sympathy were a great support to the invalid, when those who would gladly have fulfilled the sorrowful task could not reach him in that distant land: to these, known and unknown, I am glad of this opportunity of acknowledging with gratitude their kindly service. To the three travellers I owe many thanks, and especially to "the Scot," who, in the hour of need, proved himself a true friend to him who is gone, and to myself.

The following letters are the result of a request that I made to a few of those with whom my brother was, from time to time, brought into close contact, that they would put on paper for me some reminiscences of his life and work. They seem to combine to form an interesting analysis of Dr. Appleton's character from independent points of view, and will, I am sure, be read with the attention they deserve:—

From Shadworth H. Hodgson, LL.D.

I know not whether I can add much to vivify the picture of my friend C. E. Appleton, by recording the impression left on me by our occasional but not infrequent conversations on philosophical subjects in the last ten years or so of his life. Philosophical our conversations usually were, for to that subject all others seemed naturally to lead, when circumstances allowed them to take their own course. In this at least we agreed that both of us regarded philosophy, properly so called, as the region where all the divergent streams of thought had their source and watershed.

Two traits were very marked in Appleton: his perfect fairness in argument, and his tendency to postpone details and consequences to the establishment (or refutation) of the principles which governed them; this last a trait by no means universal in Englishmen. So that, being agreed, as I have already remarked, on so much of the preliminaries, we generally found ourselves joining battle on Hegelianism, of which Appleton was an ardent disciple.

Then, there was a courtesy and a gentleness about his whole manner of arguing, which rendered a discussion with him a real pleasure. He would try to see your position in its best light and its strongest points, and do full justice to it. Then he would state his own case in the same way. I speak of cases where he was arguing for victory. The laws of fairness in discussion are different according as you are arguing for victory, or for eliciting truth by a common effort. In the latter case you are bound, in the former you are not, to state for the common benefit whatever difficulties may occur to you as important, against the view which you are maintaining. Appleton's fairness and courtesy, combined with what I shall presently notice, his subtlety, made him a powerful advocate. He had the rare art of persuading by argument. He was a born diplomatist, in the true and honourable sense of the word.

Another of his prominent traits was one which, it sometimes occurred to me, might be a source of his Hegelianism, I mean his generally sanguine temperament. If an idea was at once consistent, tenable, and desirable, then, to him it seemed that it *could* lack no condition of realization. Sooner or later it *must* take its place among actual facts.

Add to this sanguine temperament an artist-like delight in elegance and congruity, in the constructions of thought as well as in æsthetics proper; add, further, another trait not very usual in Englishmen, nor perhaps anywhere, at least in a high degree, I mean subtlety of intellect as distinguished from acuteness; that is to say, a fineness and keenness of the perceptive as distinguished from the discursive powers; and you have, it seems to me, a character predisposed for Hegelianism, if other circumstances favour.

Circumstances did favour, at Oxford, in Appleton's time. There was and still is going on there a series of events, which repeats on a small scale what has already happened on a larger theatre, in the history of philosophy itself. On the larger theatre, we have the sequence of Hume's eighteenth century naturalism, Kant's criticism, Hegel's absolutism. On the smaller, we have the dominance of Mill's or nineteenth century naturalism, inaugurated with the University Reform of 1851; then the Kantian re-action, led by the late Dean Mansel; then the Hegelianism, which still continues. Of course I speak only of the Oxford world which is affected by such topics. Theological Oxford, scientific Oxford, classical Oxford, æsthetic Oxford, and so on, are different matters, though of course not unconnected.

Appleton belonged to the Hegelian development. I well remember the vividness with which he pictured, in one of our conversations, his weariness of that dreary method of "pigeon-holing everything," which, by some imaginative process of his own, he identified with the Aristotelian logic, and the philosophies which are based upon it; not seeing that, though any system whatever may be frozen into formalities by incompetent expounders, yet, of all systems that have ever been promulgated, none so lends itself to such an ice-bound state as the Hegelian; a system in which all explanations, all theories, in every branch of knowledge, consist of giving the exact position of the subject in hand relatively to its neighbours, placing it in its precise niche in the particular "stage of development" to which it belongs in the great thought-process. But Appleton had eyes only for the life and motion of that process. To him the Hegelian logic revived what the Aristotelian stifled, the life and freedom of the universe. No dead abstractions, but a concrete idea developing endless articulations, matter and form, in one living union governed by thought. No logic but this could be commensurate to the boundless variety, the unfettered energy of existence.

I used sometimes to tell him (sure that he would not misconstrue me), that, with all his subtlety, he seemed to me to lack the one essential condition of philosophy—a determined spirit of analysis. He courted philosophy for what it could give—(I do not mean its temporalities)—for the freedom and amplitude of its outlook, the basis it afforded for intellectual activity in all directions, the intellectual dignity it lent to culture, in short as an adornment and instrument of the higher life. Perhaps he might with some plausibility have replied, that to do otherwise was to make philosophy itself a "pigeon-hole." But he did not accept my criticism. It was his continual regret that his multifarious engagements, especially as editor of the *Academy*, prevented his devoting his time more uninterruptedly to philosophical study, as he always hoped, some day or other, to be able to do; a wish unhappily not destined in this world to be fulfilled.

The bearing of philosophy on religion was one of its fruits in which he was most deeply interested. He had no sympathy with those who, from mistaking the deeply seated character of those feelings and cravings of human nature, which have never yet been satisfied without some form of theological creed touching the invisible world, and from thus misreading the facts of the case, are led on first to identify religion with creed, and then to consider creeds either as the mere guesses of antiquated science, or as the arbitrary creations of a self-indulgent fancy. Hegelianism is in no sense open to this reproach. It is a philosophy eminently compatible with religious faith in unseen realities, and performs in this respect all that religion can legitimately demand at the hands of philosophy (supposing philosophy has the power), namely, that it should secure for it a ground, in the unseen world, whereon its anchor can fasten, and hold for it, so to speak, against all comers, the intellectual *right* to believe.

I speak mainly from the recollection of a long talk with Appleton, in later years, but the exact date of which I cannot recall, on the subject of a future life, and the mutual recognition of friends therein. He strongly maintained our logical as well as moral right to believe, and not merely to wish, the affirmative of both points; though admitting the danger there was, and the consequent necessity of being on our guard, lest we confounded a belief, obtained as these are on the ground of a moral prompting, with a belief of facts which are in no way motived by desire and will, such as are the data and conclusions of science. A belief, which is a hope matured, cannot be inspired in others except by implanting the hope which is its seed. To teach it as if it were a fact of science, to teach it *dogmatically* as science is taught, is superstition. This is the difference between the two kinds of belief which it is important to observe, without giving up the right to believe in things sincerely hoped for and morally approved; the maintenance of which right was the object of Appleton's earnest contention in the conversation which I am recording. He refused to admit that man's hopes, and if his hopes then also his beliefs, either could be or ought to be confined within the limits of his merely scientific knowledge; that his reason should consent, as if mesmerized, to imagine herself a convinced and hopeless prisoner in the dark cavern of Plato's allegory.

I remember that the conversation contributed not a little to clear my own conceptions, at any rate, of these matters, as well as to strengthen my conviction of the reality of the unseen. On such talks it is a pleasure to look back, mixed though it be with the inevitable regret that they are to be enjoyed no more.

From Robinson Ellis, M.A., Senior Fellow of Trinity College, Oxford.

My first introduction to Appleton was in 1860. In the October Term of that year, and the Spring Term of 1861, he read with me for Moderations, and, during the remainder of his undergraduate course, I had frequent opportunities of seeing and talking with him. He was at all times an interesting companion; though a hard reader, he was never so absorbed in books as not to be keenly alive to all that went on about him. Moreover, he was by nature an innovator, and as it was his fortune to be at a College which was supposed to be strongly opposed to innovation, he was rarely in want of some fresh grievance, real or imaginary. At such times, he would project schemes of reform which were amusing from their hopelessness. He obtained a second class in the final schools in 1863, having before this time succeeded to a Fellowship at his College. Thenceforth, throughout the time that we were at Oxford together, Appleton never lost sight of me. I was at that time working at my edition of Catullus, and he was always interested in hearing and talking about it. Meanwhile, his own studies, as I learnt from him, had taken a new course; he was devoting himself to modern languages and history. Not that he ever gave up his philosophical reading; philosophy was indeed the subject in which his chief interest lay, and I remember his subsequently interrupting the laborious routine, which his editorship of the *Academy* imposed upon him, to devote a month to the assiduous perusal of Hegel with a friend at Brighton.[1]

[1] Namely, in the autumn of 1872, with Dr. Arnold Ruge, formerly Professor of the Hegelian Philosophy at the University of Halle, Editor of the *Hallische Jahrbücher*, and Member for Breslau in the First German Parliament at Frankfurt.—J. H. A.

From 1866 to 1869 I had few opportunities of meeting Appleton, already well-known at Oxford as an uncompromising reformer. But in the latter year the *Academy* was projected, and I was asked to become a contributor. Those who remember the *Academy* at its first starting, will not deny that it set up, and to a great degree fulfilled, a really high ideal. The Reviews were not only written by men of the highest eminence in their several departments, but with special attention to completeness and accuracy. The principle of signed articles made negligence impossible, and gave a significance to even short communications. None who knew the character of Appleton can doubt that the design, as well as the successful execution of the design were mainly, if not wholly, due to him.

At the close of 1869, I was elected Professor of Latin at University College, London. Appleton was one of the first to congratulate me on the appointment, and, from that time till my resignation of the chair in 1876, was in frequent communication with me. Partly through this connection, partly through the Savile Club, he established a tolerably wide acquaintance with the Professors of University College: and that Institution has ever since made the *Academy* one of its chief advertising mediums, to say nothing of the contributions which members of the professional staff of the College have added to its pages.

It was in 1870, that the question of reforming the pronunciation of Latin was started by the conference of schoolmasters. The question was taken up by the philological societies of Oxford and Cambridge, and the result was the formation of a syllabus drawn up by Professor Munro and Professor E. Palmer. My intimacy with Professor Key, a scholar at all times profoundly interested in every point of Latin philology, and through him with Mr. Roby and Mr. A. J. Ellis, would have sufficed to make the question one of special interest to me, if I had not already been attracted to it by the great work of Corssen. Hence, when Appleton opened the pages of the *Academy* to a discussion on the pronunciation of *c*, in Latin, between Max Müller and Munro, I felt that I could not remain a mere spectator, and contributed to the controversy an article on the pronunciation of *v*. An animated discussion ensued, which, if it did not settle the question, aroused public attention not only in England, but America. Soon after, I obtained the consent of University College to the introduction of the new pronunciation in my classes : and this was followed by Professor Key's introducing it into University College School.

At this time Appleton was residing at Hampstead. The noise of London had begun to affect my health, and I was beginning to apprehend a serious illness. He insisted on my joining him for a time, and the air of Hampstead, seconded by my friend's kindness and attention, soon restored me to comparative health. He was already planning a fixed residence there, and often counselled with me between conflicting spots. He was much taken with a cottage in the Vale of Health, but finally fixed on a smaller one in a higher situation. He was, I think I may say, very happy in this little home of his, and whatever time he could spare from the *Academy*, was devoted to the entertainment of the numerous friends his editorial position or social tendencies attracted around him. No guest of his can have failed to observe his extreme fondness for a very amiable cat, which was the habitual companion of his meals. Not content with a quiescent position at his side, she would mount his chair and seat herself upon his shoulder. If the weather was fine, he would take his friends into the little garden which surrounded his cottage, and allow them to inhale the wonderful air of Hampstead.

The necessity of reconstituting the *Academy* on a wider and more general basis, obliged Appleton to be constantly on the move. He traversed England to advertise the new Company he was forming, and was very successful in getting his shares taken. On one occasion I accompanied him on a fruitless visit of this kind ; but one repulse did not frighten him; and, if I remember rightly, he was not allowed to retire baffled from his second visit. I am persuaded that the excitement of these perpetual journeys had an injurious effect upon his health ; especially a prolonged visit, which he made in 1875 to the United States, where he was welcomed with a cordiality which he always spoke of with pleasure. It was after this visit that I first heard the alarming news that he was believed to be consumptive; but I was in the habit of seeing almost daily a consumptive patient in a far more dangerous stage of the malady, himself a friend of Appleton's, the lamented W. K. Clifford ; and comparing the two, I never could believe Appleton to be in any serious danger. I was wrong; both succumbed to the malady, but the earlier was "the more robust and hardy to the view," and it was not till a year after Appleton's death in Egypt, that Clifford died in Madeira.

I must say a few words as to the general impression which Appleton's life and character left upon me. I have never known anyone who was more determined. As soon as he had fixed upon a plan, he set about realizing it. The difficulties with which he had to struggle in the re-creation of the *Academy* were prodigious; I may safely say I knew none amongst my own friends who would have attempted to confront them. Two years after the first publication of the paper, everybody prophesied its decease; decease it did: but only to enter upon another and more prolonged existence. This was entirely the work of Appleton, and I know, from many conversations which we had on the subject, how laborious a work it proved. But he never flagged; and so great was the confidence in his ability, that, on his proposing to resign the editorship, the shareholders unanimously insisted that he should retain it. He was equally determined in the cause of research. Those who know Oxford best will probably admit that its highest rewards are too often bestowed on successful teachers, that education has to a great extent supplanted learning, and that investigation, whether of the laborious and minute, or brilliant and ingenious kind, finds but scant if any recognition. This, which since the publication of Mr. Mark Pattison's book on the University, has been more and more felt to be true, was realized to the full extent by Appleton. He saw that the University, with its vast machinery of examinations and class lists, was too well satisfied with this practical and palpable result to care much for its equally important function of guiding and stimulating inquiry in new and unexplored fields.

Among the many tutors and lecturers who filled the University, how few could be said to make any real use of its resources! How few frequented the Bodleian! How rare to find any one who examined or collated manuscripts! Our national treasures, the envy of foreigners, were almost ignored by ourselves. Within my own memory, the Austrian Gomperz had unearthed from its forgotten hiding-place in the Bodleian those admirable transcripts of the Herculanean papyri, which, thirty or forty years before, the Etonian Hayter had executed with religious care at Naples only to be mislaid and lost at Oxford. Facts like these pointed, as Appleton saw, to the necessity of organizing research. The spirit of research though dormant was not extinct; something might be done by merely enforcing and preaching it. He therefore attempted —with no great success perhaps, but still with an earnestness and enthusiasm which produced their effect—to create a society, which should have for its object the promotion and facilitation of research. He convened meetings in London, and preached the doctrine wherever he went. Finally, he edited a volume of Essays on Research, which included in the list of its contributors the distinguished names of Pattison and Sayce. The opposition which this movement of Appleton's aroused, proved to me its reality. The name of *researcher* was invented to stigmatize the holders of the unpalatable doctrine. If you wished to please the dominant party in common-rooms, it was only necessary to sneer at research and researchers. Even now the case is very little altered, and it was not without some difficulty that, when recently the new statutes for my own College were under discussion, I succeeded in getting admission for the obnoxious word.

Short as was our friend's career, it certainly was not unsuccessful. His creation of the *Academy*, and the wide diffusion which he gave to the idea of research, were more remarkable achievements than were attained by many much older men among his contemporaries; and for these, if for nothing else, he deserves the gratitude of all, who aspire to see the Universities take a higher position in Europe.

From T. K. Cheyne, M.A., Fellow of Balliol College, Oxford.

I feel some difficulty in putting down my recollections of your brother, on account of the exceedingly personal character of the friendship which united us. I was not acquainted with him in his undergraduate days, but I think our relations were as intimate as if they had been formed at an earlier age. Our paths lay together at a very interesting period, both to him and to me. Afterwards they diverged, and we seldom met, but the feeling of intimacy remained; he was not one to break a bond, or lose a friend. It is only of this early period that I feel justified in speaking. We were at one in our keen interest in the application of a scientific method to all branches of knowledge. The principles so ably expounded by the Rector of Lincoln, in his book on Academical Organization, found nowhere a more enthusiastic reception than in my friend and myself. He was not content, however, with limiting the action of those principles to the Universities. His notion was, that academies of savants, working in unison for the same branch of science, were one of the most urgently needed institutions, and, failing them, it occurred to him that an *Academy* of another kind might serve as a useful *point d'appui* for scientific workers in all departments. How well do I remember the walk in which he first communicated this idea to me! I cannot even now help wondering at the ardour with which he matured and subsequently carried out this cherished scheme. He found friends and sympathizers, it is true; but none brought such zeal and energy to the work as himself. Many were the colloquies we had on this subject; for, among his other admirable qualities, that of inspiring others with his own faith was pre-eminent, and I at any rate was not reluctant to be inspired. I suppose that, owing to the abundance of my leisure, he made more demands upon me than upon his other friends: for doubtless, among the early contributors of the *Academy*, few of the really working scholars of the Oxford of that day were omitted. He could, therefore, easily have found other assistants; but I shall always remember with pleasure the fact that, to the not unlaborious share of editorial work which he imposed upon me, I owe much delightful intercourse with the most stimulating of companions. It was impossible to damp him; no difficulties dismayed him; like the English army, he did not know when he was beaten.

It was in October, 1869, that the first number appeared. A first-rate publisher had been secured. The prince of English critics had not only approved (as he was in consistency bound to approve) the general plan of the new paper, but contributed a characteristic article to the literary section; Dr. Lightfoot had opened the history; Professor Huxley and Sir John Lubbock, the science; and the other departments had been, if not so attractively, yet not at all discreditably, catered for. Yet the editor was not entirely happy. He had accepted a contribution to the Byron literature from Mr. Murray, which seemed like condescending to the ways and methods of ordinary periodicals. He declared himself convinced of the necessity of making a dashing appearance in the first number, but I know his conscience was as much wounded by it, as if some positive duty had been violated. He wished to set the literary world an example, and lo! he had yielded at the first onset of temptation.

But he did labour hard to realize his idea of an organ of scientific research. Personally or by letter, he or his friends applied to many of the leading scholars and "researchers," both in this country and on the Continent. He much disliked the insularity of English scholarship, though he was also of opinion that German scholars unduly disparaged their English *Fachgenossen*. To be international was therefore his great aim. And if both English and German science and scholarship is less narrow and more cosmopolitan than formerly, a share in the credit is due to the little known but not less meritorious labours of Dr. Appleton.

This is, I fear, a dry disquisition, but the period which I look back upon is nothing less than dry; it is lighted up by the recollection of cheerful humour and unwearinable energy. Has this type of humanity been broken for good? or has Providence raised up other equal representatives of this fruitful combination of rare qualities?

> *From F. A. Channing, M.A., late Fellow of University College, Oxford.*

As I look back on the too short career of which I have had frequent but too insufficient glimpses, I seem to recall several distinct phases in the development of the mind and character of the friend we all loved so dearly.

My earliest recollection of Appleton is about the time we both took our degrees. His earnest, eager face and genial manner marked him at once among the many. He was one of the few who brought originality and a real vital interest to the Oxford studies; but, like many others of original power, he was perhaps too impatient of the schoolboy accuracy as to detail, which generally secured the highest places in the class list. Next I recall him as the centre of a little group of pupils and admirers, who may claim the credit of having been the first to feel and recognize his powers.

Appleton had at once struck out boldly into the deep waters of German philosophy, and soon found in Kant and Hegel, especially the latter, the spirit for which he had instinctive kinship.

Appleton's mind was naturally synthetic rather than analytic. His sympathies lay with the great intellectual enthusiasm which affirms unity; that seeks to find and believes in finding a universal explanation, a complete solution, of all the great problems; rather than with the critical and sceptical spirit, which finds safety in nothing but the negation of error.

To some he might appear to be too hasty, too sanguine in his hopeful views of a unity of solution; but it was the bent of his being, which he could not alter, and it gave a warmth and a beauty to his intellectual character which are infinitely more attractive than the chill of the universal negative. This love of synthesis and unity led, also, to a singular breadth, generosity and appreciativeness of mind. Each view, however outwardly in discord, must have some inner congruity, which only needed interpretation to bring it into harmony with the whole onward-sweeping development of thought and being.

This wide power of appreciation, of finding some good in everything, coupled with his geniality, gave the peculiar charm to his conversation that all his friends must have found.

Connected with this period is my recollection of Appleton in the old rooms at St. John's, which King Charles I. occupied when at Oxford—deep-windowed, wainscotted rooms, with a softly-tempered light, and far from all the noise and bustle of University life—a fit home for a real student.

Next, I remember him after his return from Germany. His freshness of enthusiasm and fulness of his subjects were delightful to watch.

At St. John's learning such as he had acquired in Germany was perhaps not in its natural sphere at that time; but the real attainments of Appleton, his original and vital interest in philosophy, and the strong, warm, natural power that made itself felt in all he said and did, soon gave him his proper status in Oxford.

It was about this time that he began to concentrate himself on political philosophy. How far he really carried this study I have never ascertained; but he certainly read the great German specialists on this subject to a great extent.

One outcome of this special reading was a scheme, which went a little way, and then came to nothing, like many good schemes. Appleton had the idea that if the very best philosophical treatises of all ages—the cream and essence of thought, as it were—were edited and issued in a popular form, as a series adapted for the general reading of the masses, the baser issues of practical politics would disappear, and higher standards be applied by all men; thus leading to a thoughtful and rational progress of human development. Several of Appleton's friends undertook special books in this scheme, and, for some months in 1867, I think a good deal of work was done upon it. Professor Jowett also undertook the general supervision of the series.

How it fell through I cannot remember; perhaps it was the germ of the *Academy* idea which pushed it aside, at first for a time, and then permanently.

The next phase of Appleton's career was the start of the *Academy*, in its original idea a contribution to English culture, the value of which cannot easily be exaggerated. A critical record and estimate of real work by real students was a novelty in this country; and if it could have been carried out exactly as first designed, it would have been a permanent source of intellectual power.

That the *Academy*, by the force of circumstances, ceased to be a simple record of students' work, and assumed the ordinary literary type, is the more keenly to be regretted, because it was obvious to all Appleton's friends that the multiplied work, the constant anxiety, and the inevitable occupation of his time in pecuniary and other organization needed for the enlarged *Academy*, deprived the world, to a great extent, of what might have been the best fruits and most lasting contributions of a fresh and original mind.

Appleton's articles on philosophical subjects, about this time, were marked with a peculiar subtlety and delicacy of thought which, coupled with his equally peculiar breadth of sympathy and clearness of insight, gave an unusual promise of really great achievements in this sphere. They were not merely the productions of a cultivated follower of the Hegelian school, but, while they showed how much his mind owed to the great Germans, they showed also a peculiar mental temperament and attitude, which we cannot be wrong in thinking would have produced really great philosophical results—results which could be understood and sympathized with.

With the development of the *Academy* into its larger and literary shape, Appleton's life passed from Oxford to London, from the ideal enthusiasm of the student life to the practical life of the world and society, to thought in its concrete forms. There are losses and gains in all such transitions.

Those who knew Appleton when in the full tide of his London life, and who passed pleasant hours with him on summer afternoons under the soft shade in the little garden of Netley Cottage, and were delighted with him in the artistic completeness of his beautiful retreat, saw how all of this went together, and was the natural filling in of the harmony of a bright, joyous, expansive nature, as well as of a refined, delicate taste, and a fresh, overflowing sympathy with all that was akin to thought and culture.

To this time, it must be remembered, belongs Appleton's great contribution to the future welfare of Oxford in his suggestions of an endowment of research. This scheme, which was subsequently advocated in a volume of essays, is a logical necessity, and was a fitting practical development of the admirable original idea of the *Academy*.

Of the later days, when anxiety and ill-health had cast a shadow over the brightness and warmth which ever were chief characteristics of Appleton's nature, it is hard to speak; but the point that struck one most forcibly was the vigour and the intensity of resisting life, the resolute way in which he met and smiled away the coming evils, full of the same vivid interests, and full too of the same genial breadth and kindness as of old.

From Basil Champneys, B.A., Harrow Lodge, Hampstead.

You ask me to put in writing some recollections of your brother, who was for many years my friend and neighbour, and whose loss I, with so many others, sincerely and deeply deplore. Though I feel that I am, of all his more intimate friends, perhaps the least able to give an adequate idea of his intellectual character and attainments, my own pursuits lying, as they do, in a totally different sphere from that in which his life was mainly occupied, I should be sorry to disappoint your wish, or to fail to contribute some record of a long and much valued friendship.

I formed my first acquaintance with your brother, I think, in 1869, at a club of which we both were members, and, knowing him first only as an agreeable acquaintance, soon learnt to identify him with the main work of his life, the foundation of the *Academy*. It was some time before I ceased to look on him as considerably my senior, I suppose from the habit of associating important practical achievements with mature age. The *Academy* was just then making its way with considerable *éclat*, and it was, no doubt, hard to realize, as I did before long, how completely its foundation and success was due to the originating idea and unflinching energy of so young a man. I found later, or thought I found, the key to the success of his endeavours in this as in other schemes, not only in the talent which he brought to bear, but especially, too, in the great directness and simplicity of a nature, which neither saw nor cared to discover minor objections and difficulties, but which, by looking directly towards the end in view, abolished the obstacles which it ignored. This characteristic struck me as especially notable in one who had been long associated with a University, whose influence often has the effect of developing the instinct of negative criticism to the exclusion of practical effort.

I had many further opportunities of noting the same singleness of aim and directness of purpose with regard to other schemes in which his co-operation was enlisted, and proved him a valuable and energetic ally in any endeavour to which his assent was given.

It was not long—about two years, I think—after my first acquaintance with him, that he decided to come and reside in my neighbourhood, and chose the cottage which was afterwards known to so many as his home. I remember well the great earnestness which he brought to bear upon even the minor arrangements of the details of his house, attaching to them a real importance as the external framework of his life, and as a factor in, and expression of, his personal æsthetic training. During the years he lived there, and until his increased ill-health obliged him to spend a large portion of each year abroad, I had the most constant opportunities of intercourse and companionship with him—opportunities which, I am now glad to think, I duly cultivated, with the result of learning to understand his genius and character.

In addition to the qualities I have mentioned above, I found that he possessed in a remarkable degree a large tolerance for the opinions of others. He distinctly belonged to the liberal type of thinkers, but his liberalism had a special individual note, and was clearly distinguished from the more popular phases of that school of thought. His intellectual processes were eminently metaphysical, and into these regions, from a constitutional incapability, I was precluded from following him. Nevertheless, I found it most interesting to observe how, through his own medium of thought, he had arrived at conclusions which I held on other grounds.

It would scarcely give an accurate idea of the special nature of his largeness of view to represent it as tolerance. Rather it should be said that, under the influence of a wide sympathy, he discovered subtile, ideal affinities between apparently incompatible tenets. As an example, I may mention that for various reasons, personal and intellectual, I had long since been led to accord more sympathy to Catholic doctrine than is usual with modern liberals; but it was a new experience to me to hear the ultimate mysteries of the creed explained and justified by their coincidence with theses of the Hegelian system. It was certainly most interesting and refreshing to me to find in a liberal a complete freedom from the usual liberal dogmas and limitations, and to get a glimpse of a totally novel method of arriving at tolerant conclusions.

He extended the same geniality to persons as to opinions, and it was rare to hear him speak, unless *ex cathedrâ*, either severely or disparagingly of any one. A difference between his friends was a personal distress to him, and one which he spared no pains to remove. His good temper was imperturbable. I have frequently seen him, when led by his principles to represent a minority of one, display in that unenviable situation the unruffled equanimity, which is usually conditioned by perfect agreement with the general opinion.

Such qualities in one exceptionally versed, as he necessarily was, in the intellectual movement of the day, made his companionship equally pleasant and instructive; and I feel, with many other friends of his, what a privilege has been lost to us by his early death. Of all my friends he was probably the last for whom I should have anticipated such a fate, and it was only towards the end of his last summer in England that I felt any serious doubt of his ultimate recovery. Though prepared to some extent for evil tidings, the news of his death was a terrible shock.

I am glad to have had this opportunity of recording, though in, I fear, an imperfect and fragmentary way, the strong and abiding impression which his personality has left on my memory. It is pleasant to think that, short as his life was, he had already achieved enough to make him widely known and truly appreciated.

From Frances M. Owen, Cheltenham.

I think you know that in losing your brother we lost one of our truest friends, and the place which he filled in our hearts will always be his.

The times when I saw most of him were when he came to stay with us here; his visits were always a very real pleasure, bringing many new elements of interest into a life that has a tendency to become monotonous.

I think our affection for him was partly enhanced by the feeling that he "came out" to us more than he did to many people, and was thoroughly at home in our house.

He was my husband's friend before we were married: they knew each other well at Oxford. As early as 1864 he mentioned to my husband his desire to start some literary and scientific paper. They spent a month together at Heidelberg when your brother was attending the lectures of Bluntschli and Zeller, before he went on to Berlin. I well remember the landlord of the "Hotel de Russie" at Heidelberg, when he saw my husband again, inquiring with enthusiasm for "his friend" Dr. Appleton.

My first acquaintance with your brother was made at Oxford in 1870, when he was invited to meet me at dinner. He sat next to me, and one of my first questions to him was, whether he had seen the Academy? (meaning the pictures). I can recollect the laughter with which my question was greeted, and the kind way in which he explained the joke to me, for I did not then know of his connection with the paper. Our friendship began that evening and deepened with every year that I knew him. He often came to stay with us, and he always brought with him a large store of sympathy for all that he found going on, and claimed it in return for all that interested him. He had a pleasant genial way of taking for granted that because we were real friends we cared to know what he was doing and thinking about, and many a long talk we used to have over the work and prospects of the *Academy*, in which so many of his hopes were centred. But he was by no means absorbed in his own concerns. Everything had an interest for him; one subject after another would come up for discussion, and he was never at a loss for some interesting fact or new idea in connection with each. Metaphysics, ethics, books old and new, antiquities, music, painting—he had his thoughts about all, and told them well.

He had a habit, which I always felt to be characteristic of him, of drawing out the opinion of any one he was speaking to, on any special subject, before giving his own, and there was a humility in his way of receiving such opinions, which those who did not know him well might have imagined too conspicuous to be genuine.

His playing was always a great pleasure to me, and many of our happiest conversations were in the pauses of his music. He would sit at the piano, wandering on from one exquisite melody to another, remembering from time to time special favourites of my husband's or of mine, and turning round suddenly, as he finished one of them, to ask some question which drew us into interesting talk. I remember one evening particularly, when he had been playing in this dreamy fashion for some time, he turned to me suddenly with the question, "What is the secret of a happy life?" I said I thought it would be to have passed out of oneself into the life of others. I never can forget how his face lit up, and how earnest his voice became as he answered, "That is it; that is it—that is the keystone of all true philosophy." I think our friendship took a new start from the talk that followed.

Very often I did not agree with what he said, and when I told him so he used to smile and say, "Ah! but you are open to reason. I do not despair of you; I shall convince you yet." But I always noticed that his most earnest discussions were tempered with mildness and calm, and I never heard him say a sharp or unkind word of anyone.

He was staying with us once after I had been ill, and the patient care with which he thought of everything that could amuse or interest me, is amongst many grateful memories of him. I specially recall a large bowl full of fresh violets which he several times arranged for me before I came down, having been out early in the morning to get them. This may seem a trivial thing to mention, but it was part of the man to me. His love for artistic and beautiful things was another strong characteristic, and we spent many an hour together, hunting the old-fashioned shops for furniture, china, old prints, &c.

In all literary work, his friends found him ever unselfishly and appreciatively helpful. He would go through anything they had been writing, slowly and carefully, never hesitating to criticize, but never grudging encouragement.

The last time he stayed with us we felt anxious about him, for he had begun to be ill. It was arranged that he was to come to us in Yorkshire, where we were staying in the summer; but he was afraid of the cold winds, and I never saw him again.

His last letter to me was written the day before his death. "Tell J.," he wrote, "that ancient Thebes was about as big as London, and its hundred gates were not gates in the wall—that would have been an element of weakness—but its hundred pylônes standing in front of every temple. The pylon is an enormous triumphant gateway standing in front of, but separate from, the façade. 'Hundred-gated Thebes' would be like hundred-spired London, and would signify the number of temples there were. This is an appendix written in bed."

Even at the last he seems to have been uncertain as to his fate, for he says in this letter, "It is not at all certain that I shall not leave my bones in hundred-gated (pyloned) Thebes. . . . . Recovery is possible, but not probable. So, if it is to be so, farewell, and God bless you both and the children."

When I received that letter I felt sure he was dead, and two days afterwards I heard that so it was.

It will be thought right that some illustration should be attempted of the position of Dr. Appleton's mind with reference to Christianity, the Churches and the religious questions of the day. It is a matter on which it is naturally somewhat difficult to speak; for conversations on such topics between two near relations, one of them a clergyman, must generally be of too private a nature to be reproduced in a memoir, connected, moreover, as they frequently are, with times of sorrow, suffering and bereavement. The task, however, must not be entirely declined, especially as I am assisted therein by the testimony of friends, and by notes and fragments extracted from commonplace books and elsewhere.

The early religious influences to which Charles Appleton was subjected, at school and at his father's house, were of a very distinct nature, and he certainly carried the traces of them, to a remarkable degree, throughout his career. If they can be summed up in the personality of one typical man, it is in that of John Keble, scholar, theologian and spiritual guide. "A sound rule of faith," and a "sober standard of feeling in matters of practical religion,"[1] were the features of our training in the old Reading days, which stand out clear and strong, and they left their mark, defined and indelible, whatever may have been the destructive processes or the new constructions of later life.

He was confirmed at the age of fifteen by Bishop Wilberforce, and, soon after, became a regular communicant. This religious practice he carefully observed throughout his life: indeed, as years went on, the Eucharistic Service became the one of all others which he really cared to attend, whether as a worshipper only or as a communicant; and on these occasions his devout and absorbed manner was always very remarkable. He seemed to enter into what was going on with all the concentration of an unusually earnest nature: it was to him no mere survival of an old habit, but a privilege, which his intellectual growth was leading him increasingly to value. Of this strongly marked feature of his religious life it will be necessary to speak again as we proceed.

Before he left home he showed much interest in current religious questions, chiefly those relating to the schools of thought in the English Church, and her historical position with regard to the Roman Catholic and Eastern communions. To this, as time went on, and his powers matured, he added considerations of a more philosophical nature; so that we need not be surprised to find that, in his freshman's term at Oxford, he was prepared to attack and to press upon the acceptance of his friends so tough a morsel as Dean Mansel's Bampton Lectures on the "Limits of Religious Thought."

---

[1] Advertisement to the "Christian Year."

The evidence he gave in March, 1871,[1] before Lord Salisbury's Committee on the working of Tests, at the University, may be considered to reflect in some degree his own experience at Oxford, although the facts and opinions were derived, no doubt, from a wide induction. He was strongly in favour of the complete abolition of tests, both on other grounds and because he considered that the reconstruction of belief, after the period of criticism and scepticism which had been induced by the studies necessary for the final classical school, was unduly interfered with by the operation of the test. In answer to Question 490 he replies:—

I think it quite impossible for any man to throw himself into the system of education for the final classical school at Oxford at the present time—I mean, not only to study it *ab extra* as so much knowledge, but really to assimilate it —without having the whole edifice of belief shaken to the very foundation. At the same time, the agencies which are brought to bear on him, the philosophical ideas and modes of criticism, not only destroy but ultimately reconstruct belief; and what I should say with regard to tests is this, that the test intervenes with a definite proposition which a man has to subscribe, just at the time when he is beginning to re-construct the edifice of belief naturally out of the ruins which had been undermined.

After a comparison between Germany and Oxford in this respect, the question is asked:—

Your view is, then, that just at the time when he would be called upon to sign the test, he is in a state of mental soreness and sensitiveness?

I would not call it (he replies) by that name: I should say that all the ideas in his mind have been shaken: he has taken them one by one from their place and their associations, and he has been led by the books he has had to read, and by the methods of thought he has had to practise, to isolate them, to criticize them and to analyze them into their component elements. The process of re-construction, which

[1] See also pp. 23-24.

begins then, is a very slow one, and it is exceedingly important that it should not be interfered with whilst it is going on. Whereas now, when the process is at its height, the University comes in with its honours and emoluments, and says, "That which we have taught you how to question for the last five years, we now demand that you shall definitely and finally believe."

This "intellectual probation" relates, as he explains in a letter to the *Pall Mall Gazette* of May 16, 1871, not so much to "the material of opinion, that which is believed," as to "the form and manner of believing it," resulting in the substitution of "an edifice of independent and individual opinion" for that which hitherto had rested on hereditary and authoritative grounds: and he regarded such a process without apprehension. In answer to Question 524 he says:—

I do not think there is any danger in the process of negation itself: I think it is a process of discipline, which an educated man may wholesomely go through. But the danger arises as soon as you interfere with it and stop the process of re-construction: such a stoppage produces vagueness of mind on all questions connected with the foundations of knowledge and of religion.

And again, in a letter to the *Times* of May 9, 1871:—

But, after all, is there anything to be alarmed at in the fact that the young men of England are undergoing an intellectual probation, which has been held to be wholesome and necessary by almost every great writer on education of ancient and modern times? It were idle perhaps to mention Plato or Descartes or Rousseau, as they may be regarded as interested parties in the demolition and reconstruction of opinion. I will therefore content myself with quoting two passages, one from St. Augustine and one from Archbishop Leighton, both of them, I presume, authorities above suspicion. In the treatise "De Magistro" Augustine says of a young man:—

"*Dubitationem tuam non invitus accipio*: significat enim animum minime temerarium, quæ custodia tranquillitatis est maxima. Nam difficillimum est omnino non perturbari, cum ea, quæ pronâ et proclivâ approbatione tenebamus, contrariis disputationibus labefactantur, et quasi extorquentur e manibus. Quare ut æquum est bene consideratis perspectisque rationibus cedere, *ita incognita pro cognitis habere periculosum.* Metus enim est ne, cum sæpe subruuntur quæ firmissime statura et mansura præsumimus, in tantum odium vel timorem rationis incidamus, ut ne ipsi quidem perspicuæ veritati fides habenda videatur."

And Leighton to this effect :—

"Dubious questioning is much better evidence than that senseless dulness which most take for believing. Men that know nothing in sciences have no doubts. He never truly believed who was not first made sensible and convinced of unbelief."

That Oxford should, after centuries of torpor, be again becoming the seat of influences by which men are made, not only morally but intellectually, their own masters, is one of the most hopeful signs that she is beginning to fulfil anew her great vocation in the land. And I have the satisfaction of knowing that the testimony which I have given, to the effect that these influences do prevail, is regarded by the highest living authority on academical education . . . . as at once a temperate and veracious statement of the facts.

I observed above that this evidence was based not only on personal experience, but also on facts derived from a wide knowledge of the working of other men's minds. Charles Appleton had rare powers of sympathy, borne witness to, as with one voice, by a large circle of friends; and this important natural gift placed him in very intimate relations, both during his residence at Oxford and afterwards, with many who were passing through such a period of probation as he so graphically describes. It was helpful to speak with one who had gone through some such ordeal himself, who would listen without denouncing, who had breadth of view and clearness of expression, who evidently was in earnest in his own search for truth, and whose life, in its purity and unselfishness, had manifestly found some anchorage. It is certainly remarkable to what an extent he became a lay confessor (if I may use the term) in cases of this delicate kind; and, it may be added, to what an extent he was able to be of real and permanent assistance in re-constructing the edifice of belief. For the natural bent of Dr. Appleton's mind was eminently synthetic; although he had no fear of analysis and of the free action of destructive forces, yet he was himself distinctly a builder, not a destroyer. In the evidence from which I have already quoted he speaks strongly in favour of "the preservation of definiteness in the Christian doctrine," stigmatizing "a Christianity from which all definite statements have been eliminated" as an "evil" to be carefully resisted in the life of a University.

And here another characteristic may be mentioned, to which attention is specially called in several letters I have received. However authoritative he might be sometimes, when the occasion seemed to demand it, nothing was more striking than the humility with which he was wont to receive the description of any real experience, especially of one within the sphere of the religious consciousness. A mere acquaintance might have thought his manner at such a time "too conspicuous to be genuine," but those who knew him well, and were trusting him because they knew him, were never likely to fall into such an error of judgment. It was the sacredness belonging, in his eyes, to any true working of the human spirit which awakened spontaneously his deference and respect. The self-revelation might be, no doubt often was, meagre enough; yet, by whatever weakness it was characterized, it nevertheless *was* a revelation of the inner life, in the presence of which he took the shoes from off his feet, because, with the refined sensitiveness of an earnest and reverent nature, he knew that he was standing on holy ground.

One phase of modern religious difficulties, with which, no doubt, he often came in contact, I have heard him discuss with much earnestness. If to any the assaults of criticism had made the early history of Christianity uncertain or beyond belief, the question would arise, Need such persons cease to be Christians? To this he always answered emphatically, No. The great Christian ideas—those, for instance, of the Incarnation and Redemption—are, he would say, too precious and life-giving to be surrendered because the records that enshrine them have become dim. In bygone ages the history may have been absolutely necessary, but to us, at our standpoint, the truths are guaranteed by the very laws of the mind itself. To some in these days a *Noli me tangere*[1] may be spoken, but not, let us hope, to make them give up Christ; rather, it may be, to draw them on to approach Him after a higher and more spiritual fashion. To know Christ after the flesh no longer, was regarded by the Apostle as a token of spiritual advance.[2]

And, in maintaining such a position, his devotion to the Sacrament of the Altar suggested a ready illustration. Observe, he would say, how, by a wonderful instinct, the Catholic Church " has placed the Mass at the centre of the religious life."[3] Protestantism and the Reformation, much as we owe them, were a departure from the main stream of development and a return to the letter, the outward, the historical. "The Catholic Mass is not, like the Protestant Lord's Supper, mainly and pre-eminently a memorial of a particular past event, but, before all things, *itself a sacrifice* which is eternal—*i.e.*, of the Lamb slain before the foundation of the world."[4] Herein we become conscious, not so much of historical events, as of " the cardinal facts of the spiritual world permanently present and energizing here and now," of a cosmical process ever going on without us and within us, of God giving Himself to man and again receiving back unto Himself the creature of His hand; and this consciousness, he would add, is " eternal life," even to know " Thee, the only true God, and Jesus Christ whom Thou hast sent."[5]

[1] S. John xx. 17. [2] 2 Cor. v. 16. [3] "What is the Ego?" p. 137.
[4] "What is the Ego?" p. 137. [5] S. John xvii. 3.

To many persons the line of thought indicated above will seem to imply a leaning towards the Roman Catholic Church, and the impression will not be diminished by the tenor of some interesting and thoughtful fragments which shall follow presently. He certainly did not regard Rome with feelings in the least approaching those of the ordinary Protestant controversialist. He had a deep respect for her, though in many ways she repelled him, as, for instance, by her attitude, as he conceived it, towards knowledge: he was struck both by the enormous debt owed to her by European society, and by her present position and work in the world. Moreover, he considered that, in spite of many but not insurmountable difficulties, she contained in her a capacity, shared by no other Christian body, of adaptation to the advancing requirements of mankind; as, for example, through her doctrine of development and the importance she attaches to the living voice of her "best self" in every age. "I should have made a devoted member of the Roman Catholic Church," he used to say, "if I had been born within her communion; but to change one's religion is another matter." And, in view of what he said about the Mass, he did not recognize the need of such a change. For if he spoke of the Mass, as he often did speak of it, as "the one satisfying service," he undoubtedly did not exclude the celebration of it in the Anglican Church, which, in this country, he always attended. In this respect, though never identifying himself with any religious party, he appears to have symbolized completely with the advanced Catholic school in the English Church; his Hegelianism found itself in practical accord with the old home training of early days.

In recording remembrances of conversations I have endeavoured, so far as possible, to reproduce the exact words employed; but I am glad to be able to add the following extracts, chiefly from Dr. Appleton's common-place books, relating to the above and to kindred subjects.

After some considerations as to the possibility of Miracles he adds:—

Is the renunciation of the miraculous necessarily connected with the surrender of belief in the orthodox view of the person of our Lord? No. Assuming as granted that God was manifested in Christ in a way in which He is manifested in no other man, it is possible to have two theories (equally compatible with this doctrine) of the relation borne by the Eternal Word to the system of Nature in which He appeared as an Individual. We may say, with the Church, that He could only be manifested in the world by interrupting its order, both in His entrance and in His exit, and during His life: or, taking into consideration the Scripture doctrine that this same order of Nature is His immediate work, in which He is continually present, we may say that His entrance into and exit from such a world need involve no such interruption, and therefore may have been unequivocally real, without being attended by miraculous circumstances. Why may not the idea of such a manifestation have been present at the creation of the universe; and why is it unreasonable or un-Christian to suppose that the universe was framed so as to culminate in the Incarnation? If two theories are equally compatible with Catholic doctrine, and science disproves one, that is no disproof of the great fact that Christ *is* in the world.

To the objection raised by Emerson and Strauss, as to the impossibility of the Infinite being manifested in *one* individual adequately, and that for its manifestation an infinite series of individuals is postulated, we may answer that the Bible does not only exhibit Christ to us as an Individual. He is certainly therein represented as the Soul or Head, of which the Church (*i.e.*, all Humanity, for all are potentially Christians) is the Body; in a word, as the consciousness of Christendom. The Roman Church, identifying Christendom with itself, yet seems nearer to this conception, in the paramount value which it gives to tradition.

If the manifestation of the Eternal Word in man is to correspond to the manifestation of the same Word in nature, the statement of Emerson and Strauss will be true, but ceases to be an objection to Christianity. (July 26, 1867.)

Is Truth an end itself, or a means to the accomplishment

of some practical end, such as the beautifying and refining of life, the cultivation of the altruistic sentiments, &c. ? Are men to strive to know or to be ? Are they to know in order to be, or to be in order to know ? One of the points at issue between the Church and modern science is just that.

Supposing science to be true, can it show results in subduing and expanding the emotions like Christian institutions, or, *e.g.*, like the cultus of our Lady ? Cf. Spinoza, " Tract. Theol. Pol.," c. xiv.—" Theology has not to do with *vera*, but with *pia* dogmata."

The men of science know nothing but knowledge. The Catholic Church has always been identified with all that is disinterested and chaste and beautiful and refined in European society, with every good thing, within the last 300 years, except with knowledge.

The industrial spirit has already destroyed the beautiful, and is in rapid process of mutilating the good, and of amending the true.

That physical science should set itself up as the staple of the culture of the future is out of all question. It has no power of subduing the emotions.

The Church in the dark ages saved science by dogmatizing Christian belief, and thus bringing it into the sphere of the intelligence ; it saved society by itself becoming a great political institution : it preserved art by the ornamentation of courts of justice and their employment as temples for worship. See Ozanam, A. F., " La Civilisation au 5ᵉ Siècle."

Nobody pretends that the Romanist doctrines are true *as they stand ;* but they are true in the sense of representing or standing for truths which are too deep for definite utterance. And this representative function they seem to discharge much more completely than the Anglican.

Is not faith, in the Catholic sense, the participation of the individual in the common consciousness of the Church ? and is not its assertion of its own infallibility simply a phase of the Church's assertion of its infallibility ? Is not this the reason why men, who have, in their individual capacity, opposed the doctrine of the Immaculate Conception, have "submitted themselves" after the promulgation of the dogma? To them the infallibility of faith, *i.e.*, of the consciousness of the Church, has superseded the infallibility of their own individual reason.

The Catholic system of ideas forms a consistent whole, along which the mind, if it once get within it, can travel without let or hindrance, either downwards from the most primitive ideas to the most modern definition, or from the latter up to the former; just as you can run up or down the categories of Hegel. What Catholicism starts with in the present day is the Personality of God, because this has been called in question by philosophy. This idea occupies the place of Hegel's *being*; but Newman's starting-point (in the "Essay on Development") is much more concrete.[1]

The centralization of Church authority is a development of the true idea of the *Sacramentum unitatis*; it shows its prematureness by stereotyping the transitory condition of authority, and by forming an obstacle to differentiation, and so to ultimate synthesis.

The modern representative of the monastic life is study and literature; but what relation do these bear to the Catholic Church?

In assuming an ecclesiastical form in the Catholic Church, Christianity has shown that it has penetrated the European world, but not penetrated it deeply enough. Its destiny is to be the informing spirit, not of a society apart, copying the forms of European institutions, but of those institutions themselves.

The Catholic Church is the highest form yet assumed by Christianity; and all the sects, which have detached themselves from it since the Reformation, are only important in their negative aspects as critics of the insufficiency of this highest form.

The normal progress of religion is from the particular historical manifestation of a side of truth to its ideal and general enunciation as a part of a system of thought, which contains its evidence in itself as a whole, and guarantees the

---

[1] This note, as well as the two following, was made in connection with a study of Newman's "Development of Christian Doctrine."

truth of the part independently of the mode in which that part found its way into the human mind. You ask[1] on what do I base the idea of the Incarnation and Redemption? How do I know it to be true apart from the teaching of Jesus Christ? Historically, in common with the rest of the world, I learnt it first from the Bible; but if the Bible record and the authority of the Great Teacher is called in question on external grounds, as is the case, religious emotion demands some other evidence of its truth than such record and such authority. Otherwise we must fall into the common error of giving up Christianity because the records of its foundation are uncertain, and the Person of its Founder veiled in obscurity. . . . .

The principal intellectual characteristic of the human mind, which marks it off from the animals, is its capacity for gathering up into one idea the whole of existence *as a whole;* in other words, of forming a conception of the world, as distinguished from forming a conception of a part of it: by the world, I mean everything—mind and matter—which exists. This conception, as an integral part of the structure of man's mind, and as forming, so to speak, the background and distance behind every other thought, has grown with the development of the mind by a natural and necessary process of evolution, the law of which has been ascertained. . . . .

Now one of the conceptions which man, at a particular stage of his development, has been compelled to form of the universe, is that the totality of things consists of a package on an elephant's back, which elephant stands on the back of a tortoise, which stands on nothing. Another idea of the world is that it is an act taking place within an infinite intelligence; structurally, so to speak, a part of that intelligence, and yet distinct from it, in the same sense as our thoughts are distinct from ourselves. This act consists of two parts; it is, first, a blossoming out into an indefinite number of particular forms, inanimate, animal, and finally human, and culminating in an individual intelligence such as we civilized human beings have, in the course of ages, come to possess . . . . [and it is, secondly,] a winning back the

---

[1] The present extract is from a letter to a lady who had written to Dr. Appleton on the subject of his article on Strauss in the *Contemporary Review* of July, 1874. The first part of the letter is dated March 10, 1875; the second, commencing "What I have called," &c., February 1, 1876.

individual to the point from which the first part of the act [the projecting part] started. . . . . The infinite intelligence, which has projected itself in the individual, returns out of the individual back again to itself. . . . .

What I have called, in my article on Strauss, the "Christian consciousness," is the *being aware* of this double action, this systole and diastole of the spiritual heart, going on within us as parts of the great cosmos. The double action goes on, Incarnation and Redemption are real, whether a particular individual is aware of it or not; just as the circulation of the blood goes on, and is the condition of physical life, whether I happen to be aware that my blood circulates or am ignorant of the fact, as all the world was for many centuries. It is not necessary that I should be aware of the cosmical process going on in my life, for it to go on; and this is the reason why (to use an expression taken from popular theology) there will be many people in heaven who are not in the least religious. Many of the best lives are lived by the light of nothing more than a healthy instinct. But a man may become aware of the cosmical process in two ways: either from a view of his individual life, or from a view of the world at large. In the former case the consciousness takes the form of religious emotion; and in this form I regard Christ as having had it more continuously, unmistakably, and lucidly, than any other person with whose life we are acquainted. He gave no explanation of what He felt; He knew He came from God, and had to go back to Him; and this feeling was the central fact of His Being; . . . . and, so far as we can see at this distance of time, He seems to have meant to indicate this feeling when He speaks of "Eternal Life." We, or some of us, have this consciousness, fractionally, dimly, occasionally; Christ had it wholly, quite clearly, and at every moment, or almost every moment, of His life; . . . . and He has enabled us to interpret our own consciousness of the cosmical life moving with us.

But it is possible, as I said, to arrive at a knowledge of this circulation of the great life of the world through each of us, not from a consultation of our individual consciousness, but on general grounds; from our knowledge of the world as a whole, and of our relation to it. And an age whose philosophy has brought it, independently of religion, to the point of seeing and understanding [this two-fold process], which reaches to the extreme limits of all conceivable existence, is in a condition to dispense, if need be, with the historical proof . . . . just as in the case of the circulation of the blood [we are] in a position to dispense with the expedient of verifying the feeble indications of our own pulse by the help of somebody who has a strong one.

* * * * * *

You say, How revealed—externally or internally? The latter way (that is, from a view of the world at large) would be external, the former (the interrogation of religious emotion) internal. If we cannot have both, it is better to have one than none.

"He saw for himself, and hoped to aid others to see, the compatibility of a fearless philosophy with genuine Christianity;" this is the sum of an " eager talk late into the night," held with an old and trusted friend, on what turned out to be their last meeting, at the little cottage at Hampstead, and it is the key to a great part of Dr. Appleton's life. "He had long planned a work which should reconcile the conflicting claims of religion and of science, from a philosophical point of view." He lamented the estrangement; he thought it was cruelly accentuated by heated champions on either side, and, with the characteristic generosity of his nature, he threw himself between the two armies, at the imminent risk of being struck by the missiles of both.

And he had, no doubt, to a remarkable degree, the qualities which belong to a peacemaker.[1] That truth must be sought by a fearless presentation of all sides of a problem, and that it is the work of philosophy to find the reconciliation of contradictory phenomena—this was no mere theory to him, but a ruling principle of thought and life. It might make him appear inconsistent to many, who, involved in the heat of party strife, find it

---

[1] "I recognise in him an essentially reverent mind, which has grasped clearly and strongly the indissoluble connection which exists between faith in God and a living hold on moral truth ; and he is strong enough in this vital conviction to be able to treat its opponents with a tenderness and generosity which may appear at times to exceed the demands of critical justice."—*From a Letter from the Rev. H. P. Liddon, D.D., Canon of St. Paul's.*

difficult to appreciate this meeting of the old and the new, of faith and reason, of reverence and free handling of sacred things; and yet it is remarkable how little, on the whole, he *was* misunderstood. At the time of his lamented decease it was my great privilege to receive a very large number of sympathetic letters from persons of widely differing schools of thought: to some he was the fearless thinker, to others the devout Christian; but all bore a most affecting testimony to his purity of life, singleness of aim, and great fairness of mind; to all it was a career of rare promise cut short—one that seemed destined to bear rich fruit in harmonizing the discordant utterances of these anxious times. But,

> doubtless, unto (him) is given
> A life that bears immortal fruit
> In those great offices that suit
> The full-grown energies of heaven.

And these remarks may serve to clear the way for a few final quotations, which, as relating to personal religion, I greatly shrink from publishing, and certainly should not introduce, did I not feel that, by affording a glimpse into an inner chamber of thought to which very few were admitted, they will serve to complete the picture which I am endeavouring to draw. I will only add that these devotional fragments are a few out of many, and belong, not to the period of declining health, but to that of Dr. Appleton's vigorous life at Oxford—a period, as we have seen, of fearless analysis and criticism, when destructive forces were in full play, and every truth was sternly challenged before it was admitted into the new edifice of independent and individual opinion.

In spite of the perversion of the mind, in spite of the weakness and estrangement of our spiritual nature, the true home of our being is God. . . . . He is the One Reality to which the spirit can cling with complete satisfaction.

As an object of desire God moves us in the world of our

spirits, moves us to desire Him more abundantly, makes us fit to receive Him, moves us at last into that perfect unity of mind with Him whereby man stands, as it were, within the circle of the Divine Life, ... is transformed into the perfect image of Christ.

Does not the soul of every one of us shrink up into itself with a sense of unprofitableness before the glory of the Redeemed? None more than my own.

There is no Easter without Lent, no rising from the dead without entering through the grave of death; you will not find Christ unless you first humble yourself before Him.

However unprofitable the way of life may seem to be, this very consciousness is a ray of light, and, in the things of God, to desire with all the heart is to have what we desire.

The following words were written on the eve of a new year:—

Let us look upon the passing of the year, not as a mere lapse of time, but as the passing by of the Lord God Himself, —as once He swept by Elijah, so now sweeping by us, carrying us with Him into the boundless future, yet safe with Him, shielded, strengthened, cheered by Him.

The next extract is a translation into devotional language of a leading thought in the first chapter of "What is the Ego?"

I cannot presume to speak of the nature of our Lord's temptation, because, like the death of Christ, it is one of those awful and inscrutable mysteries attendant on the manifestation of Deity to the world, which no words can clear up, no thought can grasp, and which, I always think, are best left, as the Bible leaves them, to be brought home to our souls by the inspiration of the Holy Spirit. .... Our business is not to pry curiously into the details of what Christ endured for our sakes—putting our fingers into the print of the nails, and thrusting our unbelieving hand into His side—as if HE were not sufficient for us, as if we could not trust Him to bring us to the Father without knowing, without having a theory about all He suffered for our Redemption.

After speaking of the Blessed Humanity of Jesus Christ enthroned in Heaven, he adds, in words which seem almost prophetic of his own early death:—

Wondrous miracle of Divine Omnipotence, that this poor flesh and blood I bear about me, often pained, always decaying, *too weak, it may be, to bear up against the winters of threescore years and ten*, shall be so purified, strengthened, glorified, as never to decay. We shall be like Him, not in His own unspeakable glory, but still like Him. . . . .
Is not an eternity of even the greatest happiness a fearful thought? . . . . We can only lean upon the will of God, crying, with David, "My times are in Thy hand. . . . . Make Thy face to shine upon Thy servant, and save me, for Thy mercies' sake."

JOHN H. APPLETON.

30, ST. MICHAEL'S PLACE, BRIGHTON,
      October, 1880.

INTRODUCTION.

A YEAR has passed since my friend Dr. Charles Appleton breathed his last in sight of the long, low range of yellow Libyan hills, and among the shattered fragments of Egyptian greatness, where I now write. His life, short as it was, had been a busy and a useful one. Gifted with a more than ordinary power of organization and of bending the wills and wishes of others to his own, he had been a leader in movements which but for him would have long remained the mere dream of speculative thinkers and unpractical scholars. If the English public has been induced to believe that knowledge is something more than the answers to examination questions, and that learning and science should be pursued for their own sakes—nay, patronized and supported by the public itself —the result is in great measure due to him and his unwearying exertions. In season and out of season he was ever pressing home the great truth which our English people had too long forgotten—the truth that the extension of knowledge is one of the highest objects at which a nation can aim, and that no nation can neglect it without suffering the penalty of degeneracy and decay. If we do not progress, we must retrograde, and intellectual retrogression eventually brings with it material retrogression as well.

The task that Dr. Appleton set himself to fulfil was two-fold. He had, on the one hand, to concentrate into a single point the desultory and scattered efforts of scientific and literary men, and prove that England has no need of being dependent on Germany or other foreign countries for its science and philosophy; and, on the other hand, he had to show that funds already existed in our two great Universities sufficient for creating and maintaining an organized body of scientific workers. The foundation of the *Academy* was the means he adopted for effecting his first purpose; the movement in favour of the Endowment of Research for effecting the second. The success that has attended both these endeavours has been far beyond the hopes and expectations of the most sanguine of those who laboured with him, and bears witness not only to his practical character and organizing ability, but still more to the indefatigable pertinacity which bore the fruit of an untimely death.

Forced at once by his nature and the circumstances in which he was placed to devote himself to a life of almost ceaseless practical work, Dr. Appleton was nevertheless at heart rather a student than a man of action, a philosopher rather than a party-leader. It was his intense sympathy with all forms of intellectual activity that drove him, in the first instance, from the seclusion of his study, and made him the editor of the *Academy*, and the organizer of associations. But his natural inclinations remained keen and strong, and he was ever looking forward to the day when he could resign his more active and practical duties, and turn unreservedly to his favourite study of metaphysic. Time after time has he sketched out to me the programme of his future life, when he had handed over to others the work in which he was then engaged; time after time has he expressed his bitter regret at his inability to turn at once to the calm and uninterrupted pursuit of philosophy. It was the dream of his life to reconcile the metaphysic of Germany, which he held to have reached its final goal in the absolute idealism of Hegel, with the inductive science of his own country. He believed that philosophy was no less true than science, and that consequently there could be no real antagonism between them. It was for philosophy to supply the ideas, the contents of which were given by science, and to furnish the mould into which the ever-increasing body of science could at each successive period of its history be poured.

The realization of this belief was the object of the work whose unfinished torso is published in the present volume. Torso as it is, however, it contains the outline and essence of his philosophic faith, and it is easy for those who will to supply the rest. The thoughts of an honest thinker are always precious, and the best thoughts of a mind and life like that of Dr. Appleton cannot be without their value.

The first chapters of the projected work are published in their complete and finished form. They have already appeared as separate articles in the *Contemporary Review*, but are here given with additions and corrections which Dr. Appleton intended to be final. Every line they contain is the mature fruit of patient study and thought. Dr. Appleton worked slowly, but it was because he worked with Japanese minuteness and care. Whatever he wrote had first been thoroughly examined and digested in his own mind, and even when written was changed, modified and polished with astonishing exactness and labour. Nor did he write except when, as he expressed it, the fit of philosophic inspiration was upon him; so that much of his work was composed in detached fragments, which were afterwards welded together into a harmonious whole. Philosophy, he believed, had suffered more from crude and hasty writing than from any other cause, and no one was qualified to express an opinion on a subject until his mind had become, as it were, thoroughly saturated with it. But the subject must be dealt with in detail before it could be dealt with as a whole; in philosophy and science alike, analysis must precede synthesis.

It is for this reason that what would have been the most important chapter of his book, that on Development, consists only of detached notes and disconnected paragraphs. Illness and death overtook him before these could be formed into a literary unity. It is the more regrettable, in that it is just this chapter which is the key to his whole philosophic system, and the centre and crowning-point of his work. It is useless for another to attempt what the author himself has left undone, and I can therefore only quote *in extenso* the isolated notes he has left behind, arranging them in the natural order of the thought they presuppose, and supplying the links between them, partly from Dr. Appleton's conversations with me on the subject, partly from notes made for the chapters entitled "A Plea for Metaphysic," but never incorporated in them.

Briefly put, Dr. Appleton believed that the knowledge and experience of each age is summed up in one dominant idea, which it is the business of the metaphysician to discover, analyze and define. These dominant ideas form a series, connected together, not like the limbs of a chair but by a slow process of growth and evolution. The metaphysician may pause at any one point in the series, and regard all that has gone before as a single whole or organism, the development of which may be traced and determined. The dominant idea of any one age accordingly contains within itself the dominant ideas of the ages that have preceded it, and can best be studied in the works of a literary genius who represents and embodies the ideas and aspirations of his own time. The *Zeitgeist*, or spirit of the nineteenth century, breathes through the writings of men like Matthew Arnold or Renan; it has been clothed by them with literary form, and given, as it were, material shape.

"In Renan, as in Emerson and George Eliot, we have the results of the most advanced philosophy absorbed into the element of the ordinary consciousness, and translated into the language of literature." Hence it was that Dr. Appleton began the exposition of his philosophic system with an examination of Mr. Matthew Arnold's metaphysical conceptions, and an attempt to fix and determine them with precision.

The following notes will exemplify what has just been said :—

Unsystematized and popular metaphysical notions are our masters; it is only by defining and bringing them into relation with one another that we become theirs.

When we know the cause of a thing, and can explain how it came into existence, it ceases to be an object of reverence for us; because we can think of the time when it was not, or when it was small and unimportant; it is because of the reverence and awe which we have of the world that, as an effort after freedom, we seek to know its cause; and because we shall never be able to explain the *ensemble*, we shall always be compelled to reverence it.

Thought differs in kind according to its structure. There is, therefore, one kind of thought which is the thought of a polypus, and another which is the thought of a beast, and another kind of thought which is the thought of a man; and just as the same chemical ingredients of food and air, being absorbed into the structure of a polypus become polypus, and into the structure of a beast become beast, and into the structure of a man become man, so it is with experience. Man considered the world before he considered particular things—hence what has been called the "apparent immodesty" of early inquiries; he had a view of, a thought about, the *ensemble* of things before he began to think about things separately, and he thought of himself in relation to this *ensemble* of things before he thought of himself in relation to things separately; and the first way of thinking about things separately was to isolate them in the presence, so to speak, of his thought about this *ensemble*, which he had already related to himself, as a child puts a coin into the toe of a stocking.

What metaphysic has done in the past has been to exhibit the formula, the type of structure, the ideal skeleton, of the thought prevailing at a particular time. The structure is there in the *Zeitgeist*, as Mr. Arnold calls it, whether it is reduced to type by the thinker or not; just as the skeleton of a particular beast is *there*, whether or not Professor Owen has examined and determined it, whether or not it has been exhibited in a formula. There are times when consciousness is low, and when this prevailing thought of the *Zeitgeist* has not found any adequate scientific exponent; when it has to be gathered from the literature, from the history, from the oratory it may be, of the time.

Metaphysic analyzes the datum of the *Zeitgeist* freed from its sensitive tissue, as the early arithmeticians disengaged and analyzed the datum of number immersed in sensuous objects or things numbered.

Experience, Matthew Arnold's *Zeitgeist*, is not an invertebrate mass, but a highly articulated structure; metaphysic is the reduction of the different forms and stages of this structure to types, and the determination of the law of their evolution.

The Nemesis of not being a metaphysician is, that one may be haunted by some isolated metaphysical notion—isolated from its place in the general development or march of thought, and consequently a figment—and may lose one's way in a mirage of deductions from it. Whereas the one key to all these metaphysical ideas is development.

The concluding words of this last quotation bring us to the core and centre of Dr. Appleton's philosophy, to the formula under which our present knowledge and experience must be summed up. Metaphysic and science have alike reached a stage when it is possible to reconcile their apparently conflicting claims, and answer the questions and difficulties that puzzled the thinkers of the past. As the body of knowledge grows, so too do the ideas which serve to contain and bind it together. Ideas exist apart from the minds of the individuals who share in them, as much as the laws or generalizations of science exist apart from the phenomena which they explain. An idea, once acquired, is acquired for humanity in general, not for this or that particular individual, and each new idea is but the necessary development of an old one. It was the chief merit of Hegel to have discovered and formulated this fact. The "secret of Hegel" is the evolution of ideas as summed up and embodied in the dominant idea or spirit of an age. Hegel proved that philosophy—that is, the history and doctrine of the idea—is a process, a "becoming," and that the idea, like the tree or animal, contains within itself from the first all that it is hereafter to become. Each successive age marks a period in the development of the idea, conditioned by the knowledge and experience of the time. The philosophy of each age is therefore relative only; the formula in which it can be embodied is true for that particular age alone.

What Hegel did for metaphysic, Darwin has done for science. Development alone can explain the world of phenomena. Things exist as they are because they have become so, and we can be said to know them only in so far as we know the history of their growth and development. We can tell as little what they will be hereafter as we can tell what will be the idea or *Zeitgeist* of the next century. All we can determine with certainty is, that that *Zeitgeist* will stand in strict relation to the knowledge of the time. The development of organic nature is the counterpart and reflection of the development of the idea through which it is presented to the mind.

Dr. Appleton approached his chapter on "Development" after a careful study and analysis of Wigand, Günther, De Maistre and Möhler; Oxenham's "Catholic Doctrine of the Atonement;" Ward's "Ideal of a Christian Church;" Perrone, "De Immaculata Conceptione;" and Kuenen's "Religion of Israel." But it was more especially Cardinal Newman's works which he proposed to take as its text. The famous volume on the "Development of Christian Doctrine," along with the fifteenth of the "Oxford University Sermons" (1843), and the criticism to which Dr. Newman's theory was subjected by Maurice in the Preface to his "Epistle to the Hebrews" (1846), were intended to bear the same relation to the chapter on "Development" as Mr. Matthew Arnold's writings to the chapter on the "Reality and Use of Metaphysics." Unhappily the intention was never carried out. All that remains of it is a brief sketch of what Dr. Appleton wished to say upon the subject, the heads under which he meant to treat it, and a few isolated notes. Such as they are, they are here presented to the reader, who, in spite of their brevity and technical language, cannot fail to find them at once suggestive and striking.

"The development of ideas takes place as follows :—

(1) When the idea is the correlative of a need, its development is conditioned by the historical development of that need. The history of the Messianic idea is a good example of this.

(2) The development of ideas differs from that of species in this respect—the development of species is in the way of differentiation only; that of ideas is not only in the way of differentiation, but also in the way of synthesis following upon differentiation. Thus Cæsarism is a development of Royalty through Republicanism.

In nature, the species, when differentiated, do not affect one another, because the unity of Nature is unconscious; in mind, on the other hand, the ideas, when differentiated, continue to affect and modify each other, because, the mind being a conscious unity, differentiated ideas are held together in view (though unconsciously) of a coming synthesis. On the other hand, an eclectic process goes on; that is, some of the ideas obtained by differentiation are essentially sterile, and are discarded by the mental process. These only survive, like extinct species made known by geology, through becoming imbedded in language and literature.

(3) Development by systematization. J. C. Hare ("Mission of the Comforter," p. 208, note G) distinguishes (a) when the meaning of an idea (that is, its contents) is brought out more distinctly by its parts, when differentiated, being arranged in their mutual connection; and (β) when

viewed in its relation to the rest of our knowledge, all problems being, as the French would say, *solidaire*. Canon law and discipline may be taken by way of illustration.

(4) Development by corruption or the breaking up of a type. This happens when the true contents of an idea become manifest in its last stage before it disappears, just as the true theological character of the Roman idea of the State became apparent when it developed into the cultus of the emperors.

(5) Development by absorption, where each stage is absorbed into the following, as in the progress of metaphysics, the several stages being preserved as such in literature, but becoming sterile, and so possessing only a historical importance.

(6) Development by cumulative accretion, where each stage is preserved in the body of the developing medium, instead of being left outside of it. This is the peculiar feature of the development of Church dogma; the idea of infallibility, for example, does not admit of the stages being absorbed into their successors, and the result is a body of mutually contradictory propositions which can only be held together by faith accompanied by a discrediting of reason, or by a series of minute and sophistical distinctions, as in the scholastic philosophy.

The developing medium is an organic society—that is, a society founded upon the family, because only in the family do we get the true *ego*. In oriental societies we do not yet have the family as the unit, and these societies are consequently incapable of development. They approximate to the nature of mere aggregates. In the Church—which, however, according to the Roman theory, springs from the mind of Christ—the family was, from temporary circumstances, very soon discarded as the unit of organization; the principle of cohesion was not that of an organic society, but much more that of what we may call *an interest* (" die bürgerliche Gesellschaft"). Thus we speak of the shipping interest or the educational interest; meaning bodies of people connected together by a certain class of their actions. The idea of Apostolic succession was an unsuccessful attempt to give an organic unity to the Church; it was unsuccessful because it was incompatible with that necessary element in all development, free and natural differentiation. It is only by becoming a national Church—that is, identical with particular nations in their religious capacity, as distinguished from being European or Catholic on the one hand, and from being a sect within a nation on the other—that the Church can become an organic society. The Jewish Church was perfectly so, and the development of ideas in the Jewish Church is consequently a normal and natural one; whilst the development of ideas in the Catholic or European Church is artificial, and that within a sect is generally a corruption—that is, a disintegration of elements, and the continual erasure of some of them. The fact that the Church became European or Catholic instead of national was owing to the Roman Empire, and the reaction against it resulted in the formation, not of Churches, but of sects—that is, of interests and connections. Where national Churches have been formed, as in England, they have had two defects: they have arisen in the maturity of a nation's growth, instead of being coeval with its original development, and constituting one phase of it; and they have introduced from the European Church the obstruction of certain unalterable dogmas and the principle of infallibility, this attribute being given to the Bible instead of to the Pope.

(7) *Development of ideas by inheritance.* An idea evolved during the lifetime of a generation is always mixed with the ideas—in some cases quite contradictory—which it supplants in the minds of contemporaries who acquire it after middle age; but in the minds of their children the old ideas have generally dropped out, and the new one is paramount without the modifying influence of this mixture. This mixture produces two effects: in the lower intellects an imperfect grasp of the new idea, in the

higher a criticism of it; in the intermediate class of intellects an endeavour after reconciliation, and a series of intermediate ideas between the old and the new.

(8) Development of ideas by familiarity—that is, by their gradual adaptation to the mental structure, and of the mental structure to them. We may compare the adaptation of the physical organism to a new modification of its internal structure, as in the case of a chronic disease which becomes less onerous by time, or to a new modification of external conditions, or of conditions partly external, such as a change of food or climate.

So Darwinism is regarded by Wigand " as an indefinite and confused movement of the mind of the age," as distinguished from a united scientific effort.

(9) Development by a critical sifting process, by which the temporary and occasional elements in ideas drop off, and the permanent element remains. Of this, Jewish prophecy affords a striking instance.

(10) Development by generalization. This, as illustrated in the history of the idea of God, has been dwelt upon in the Essay on Strauss.

(11) Development by specialization.

(12) Development by re-stating the problem.

"The Covenant is in history an idea of the same structure as that of the Ptolemaic physics. The nation which possesses the Covenant is regarded as the centre of the world, the government of which is conducted with a view to the good of one nation only.

The ideas of the Covenant and of the Messiah met in the idea of the latter being a deliverer from the curse of the Law—that is, the Covenant lapsed if every jot and tittle of the Law were not fulfilled; and yet it was impossible to fulfil them. This is the view of St. Paul, and presupposes that the Covenant is no longer with the collective Israel, but with the individual soul, which, of course, universalizes the Covenant and gets rid of the notion of hereditary guilt.

"The sources lying at the root of the development of Christianity have been—(α) an excess of faith, which evacuated reason entirely, and took *literally*, without any capacity of criticism or interpretation, the *words* of the early records, 'credo quia impossibile,' or 'quia absurdum;' (β) the metamorphosis of the remnants of European paganism; (γ) the blind and uncritical use of tradition, the fact that a doctrine had been handed down in a variety of independent areas being taken as a proof of its truth, whereas it was only an evidence of the similarity of the operations of the human mind when playing freely without the restraint of reason upon an external *datum*; (δ) the growth of abnormal emotion, especially among the celibate orders, and the crystallization of these emotions into new doctrines, the intellect taking their utterances literally without criticism, as it had done with the Scriptures and tradition. Emotion towards an *unseen* religious object, such as the Madonna, may be paralleled in Provençal poetry.

If Christianity had become completely identified with the rising Teutonic nations, as Yahvism did with the rising Jewish nation, in each of these nations it would have had a series of differing organic developments, and a synthesis of the results thus attained would have been much less artificial than the actual synthesis of the European Church. It would, in fact, have been analogous to the synthesis of the principles of International Law, which have actually grown up in this way. And Christianity had a natural tendency to identify itself with the rising nations, and this was one of the anarchical tendencies in it, leading to break up the Roman Empire, which necessitated persecution. What it did identify itself with was the *idea* of the Roman Empire after that empire had ceased to be a reality. In the Empire itself Christianity began by being a sect—that is, infra-national; and from being a sect it was elevated by Constantine into the supra-national position of a religion of the Empire. This act of Constantine was the great hindrance to its having a normal and natural development. It was an act done in the interest of the Empire, not of Christianity; it was curing a bite by the hair of the dog that inflicted it. This is still more apparent in the time of Charlemagne: Christianity is thus accepted as the religious expression of Imperialism, the spiritual sword by the side of the temporal. The Nemesis of this was that when the abstract Empire died in the fifteenth century, the abstract European Church died with it. It survives now as a name, just as the Empire survived as a name. But it was too late for religion to begin a national organic life; the Reformation was not so much a reconstruction as a paring off of the peculiar features of the European Church, which had arisen partly through the needs of society, partly through the synthesis of ideas, partly through systematization, partly, again, through corruption. Its normal process, as I have elsewhere shown, culminated in the Deism of the eighteenth century. If Christianity had been national instead of imperial from the first, it would probably have taken up into itself a larger number of pagan elements, but it would have escaped the infusion of Alexandrian philosophy into its dogmas. The evacuation of reason, too, which arose out of the emotional *abandon* of the played-out Jewish nation trying in vain to keep the subtleties of the law, and taking blind refuge in the authority of an ideal person, then in the authority of traditions about him, after that in the authority of written records, and finally in the authority of priests and councils—this evacuation of the contents of reason, due in the first instance to the *decline* of the Jewish nation, would have naturally come to an end with the *rise* of the German nations. The same would have been the case with celibacy, and the peculiar emotions and ideas arising out of it. Celibacy was a phenomenon of the wasted and declining empire, only secondarily and adventitiously of the healthy Teutonic stock it belongs to old, not to new communities. It would never have played the important part in the evolution of Christianity which it did if Christianity had become national instead of becoming imperial. And, finally, the use of tradition would have been the rational appeal to factors within the common consciousness of the nation, as it was with the Jews. (See Ps. xliv. 1; lxviii. 7; lxxiv.; lxxvi.; lxxviii. 1–3; lxxx.; lxxxi.; lxxxix.; cv.; cvi.; cxiv.; cxxxv.; cxxxvi.) Theirs is the living and simple use of tradition; the Christian use of it is artificial and external, and full of subtleties—a body of indistinct echoes coming from afar.

"Newman's view of the development of ideas may be compared with the view of the development of species held by the older school of naturalists—namely, 'that all known variations follow definite directions and remain within certain limits, being determined by the nature of the particular type,' instead of being indefinitely variable. Wigand says: 'What in reality is hereditary—viz., specific character—is regarded by Darwin as indefinitely variable; what in reality is transitory—viz., variations—is regarded as transmissible.'"

The close relation believed by Dr. Appleton to exist between theology and metaphysic will be abundantly evident from some of the above quotations. It is in its religious faith that the mind of an age finds its highest and truest expression, and the conception of the Deity it forms is but the reflection of the idea in which its knowledge, its experience, its explanation of the universe, is summed up. The idea of God is the idea whose gradual development is watched by philosophy through the several stages of its growth. If we can once determine and formulate what is termed the spirit of the age, we can also determine and formulate its conception of the divine. Hence the interest Dr. Appleton took in the questions of speculative theology; hence the essays on

"Atheism and Doubt" included in the present volume, and the notes he has left behind on the same subject. Of the latter, the following will serve to show his point of view and contributions to the science of religion:—

On any hypothesis, there is a Supreme Being, if there are superior and inferior beings. Man reckons beings superior and inferior as they approach more or less nearly to himself. The best that we know, as Luther and Goethe after him, said, is God.

The reason why man instinctively personifies the objects of Nature, is that these appear to him higher than himself, in being more powerful, more dreadful, more beneficent, more inscrutable; but at the same time he cannot but recognize that his own consciousness of personality is more perfect, more excellent than all of them. It is, too, a prison from which he never escapes: if he climb up to heaven, it is there; if he go down to the depths of the earth, it is there also. It is always with him; it surrounds him on every side, and is the medium through which he views everything else, even the mighty powers of Nature themselves.

In saying that God is a Being, we mean that he is an indefinite object of consciousness.

The connection of metaphysic with religion consists in this, that metaphysic is a systematic treatment of the thoughts of mankind about the *ensemble*, and religion is an imaginative apprehension of the *ensemble*, touched, as every grand thought must be, by emotion.

The origin of the idea of God is to be found in the projection, not by the individual, but by the community, of its own likeness. The God of Israel is Israel itself projected during the unconscious stage, when language, law, &c., are originated. Hence the early fundamental laws of a community are regarded as divinely given, its kings as deriving their authority from God. But beyond this stage of national or tribal monotheism, when the Deity is regarded as moral, there is a more primitive stage, in which the physical individual, not yet civilized, not yet a social being, projects his individual likeness into every single object of Nature. This is the stage of natural and non-moral polytheism. The intermediate stage gives us the personification of relations either between man and Nature (such as Fate, Plenty, the Furies), or social relations, such as Justice, Peace, War, and the like. Lastly, when society and the individual have become self-conscious, there is always the tendency to clothe the idea of God with the appurtenances of the empirical consciousness; hence later anthropomorphism. Our idea of God is fundamentally the projected image of the community, modified by the natural theism which preceded it, and the individualism which comes with reflection. This idea, as projected, is a fiction—a mirroring: the reality is that which projects it, and learns for the first time by the act of projection that which is contained within itself—which stands behind our individual life, and of which we cannot become conscious except through religion. The religious consciousness is thus a reflection upon our own individuality of the shadow cast by that wide personality which stands behind it and forms its background. No man hath seen God at any time; neither has any one seen the back of his own head.

Mr. Matthew Arnold exaggerates the interested, ethical element in religion. Religion originates out of curiosity, and prevails largely in consequence of the desire to know the answer to the riddle of life.

One reason why religion cannot have arisen originally in attending to conduct is, that all religions are at the outset profoundly immoral.

The less organized a society is, the closer the individual is to Nature, the more he is alone with her: day and night, the sky, the heavenly bodies, the seasons, the fruits of the earth, the wild animals, the storm and the evening calm—these are his friends or his enemies; these make the events of his life, the relations of which he is conscious; their forms and aspects fill his imagination and give rise to the language in which he expresses his thoughts about the world and himself. There is nothing ethical in his relations with Nature, and therefore there is nothing ethical in his religion. So soon as we find any ethical elements in a religion, we know that man is beginning to draw around him the complicated web of social existence, and that his relations with his family, his tribe, his industry, his chieftain, are beginning to become more important to him than the aspects of the heavens. Society is beginning to compete with Nature for the possession of the imagination. The Hebrew, the Roman religions are social, and consequently ethical, religions. They think of the Supreme as the community personified—the community in view of which the individual man has no rights. To think of the Supreme as an individual man, as in Christianity, is only possible after the first tightness of the social bond is becoming relaxed; it is only possible in a period of social decomposition. To us God is Nature; He is Humanity, or, as I should prefer to say, Sociality; and He is Conscience.

The qualities which we fill in from Nature are not moral qualities, mere beneficence or the reverse; it is not until society and conscience are included in our view of Nature that we apply to God the qualities which we infer from the *action* of these.

We fill in the idea of God with characteristics derived from our observation of Nature. But we fill in our idea of a man also with qualities derived from our observation of Nature. We know nothing of these qualities apart from their results in action, even in ourselves; hence we are worse judges of our own character than others are. The difference between the two cases is, that we have an image of our friend; whereas of God we have only the idea of the *ensemble* inherited from the past, and embracing in it the débris of the thoughts of ages.

Positivism is founded on an abstract idea—that is, a *fixed* idea, half an idea, the phenomenon namely. Materialism, again, on the abstraction of matter.

The universe, as many, converges upon the individual thing, as if that were the only thing in the world. Contrariwise, the thing is what it is only in its place, in its connection, in the universe.

These two sides are a process (with which may be compared the ideas of a special and a general Providence). So that the universe may be regarded as an infinite number of individuals, just as an infinite number of triangles may be drawn on the same side of the same base. The place of the individual in the total of existence is called his *identity;* his separate existence, as that to which the whole of existence converges, is his *reality*—the isolated fact apart from its conditions, whereas it *is* merely the convergence of conditions.

The universe as a unity is the major premiss of every *notion:* thus—
>The totality as one;
>The sum of conditions as many; that is, everything in the universe regarded as converging upon the individual thing;
>The individual thing.

The notion is a process of three factors and three characteristics.

The last note introduces us to a new side of Dr. Appleton's intellectual activity. His ambition was to re-write and complete the Logic of Hegel, which the great German thinker had confessedly left unfinished. The work was an arduous one, demanding time and leisure such as Dr. Appleton's short and busy life prevented him from getting. I have found other notes on the same subject, constantly in his thoughts as I know it at one time to have been. But among the fragments of thought which he has left us, bearing on no one special branch of inquiry, there are a few which are worthy of record, even in this age of active speculation and many books. Thus we have the following :—

Metaphysical ideas are not untrue in themselves, any more than the bodily desires are evil in themselves. They become untrue when isolated.

Being, in the Platonic sense of the word, was to Descartes a survival, an hereditary idea, which he never consciously abandoned.

The mind does not enter into experience and form part of it, but is limited by it. This is what is called finite thinking. The infinite object is the total object which includes the mind.

Mr. Matthew Arnold does not recognize the fact that knowledge is equally a master-desire with men as happiness.

Matthew Arnold's statement, that happiness is the chief concern with all of us, leads to pessimism.

The mind can only pass from one attitude to another by traversing particular curves, just as you cannot jump out of bed without passing through every position in space between a recumbent position and a standing one.

Metaphysical ideas are not the ideas which have made history, except when they have been the vehicles of emotion; but they are the ideas which have determined the course of human experience.

But I must stop here, lest I incur the charge too frequently and with too much justice brought against the editor of a posthumous work—the charge, I mean, of publishing what the author himself would have wished to remain unknown. The contents of a commonplace book are not intended for public perusal, and a fastidious writer like Dr. Appleton would have shrunk from seeing his crude first thoughts or roughly-composed jottings exposed to literary criticism. It is difficult for a friend to distinguish between what should be preserved and what should be thrown away; to him, naturally, all is alike sacred, and he cannot put himself in the position of the unconcerned reader. But I feel sure that, if he err at all, it is better to err on the side of suppression and brevity. There have been writers and thinkers whose fair fame has been sullied or destroyed after death by the indiscreet admiration of their friends. No man would desire to submit the whole range of his thoughts and imaginings to public scrutiny, and there is no man who could stand the ordeal.

The pages that follow are mainly occupied by what were intended to be the earlier chapters of Dr. Appleton's work on the "Ego." They have been published in the *Contemporary Review* for July, 1874, November, 1876, and December, 1876. But they are here reprinted, with considerable additions, partly contained in the author's original manuscript, but omitted in the published articles; partly supplemented by himself after publication. The chapter on "Development" was to have followed them.

The other articles comprised in the present volume are evidences of Dr. Appleton's wide sympathies. That on "American Efforts after International Copyright," reprinted from the *Fortnightly Review* of February, 1877, is a valuable contribution to a subject of great practical importance, into which Dr. Appleton flung himself with his customary energy and enthusiasm. Lastly, two articles have been reprinted from Blunt's "Dictionary of Christian Theology," by the courtesy of the editor, which exhibit Dr. Appleton's research and line of thought in those theological questions in which he always took so deep an interest. It is a matter of regret that it has not been possible to introduce into the volume anything bearing upon the movement with which his name is connected in so special a manner—the movement, I mean, for the Endowment of Research.

A. H. SAYCE.

LUXOR, *January*, 1880.

WHAT IS THE EGO?

Chapter I.—Strauss as a Theologian.

„ II.—A Plea for Metaphysic.

„ III.—A Plea for Metaphysic—*continued.*

WHAT IS THE EGO?

CHAPTER I.

STRAUSS AS A THEOLOGIAN.

THERE are many reasons which make it probable that the nineteenth century may be named by future historians of theology after Strauss, as the sixteenth century is named after Luther. And this not because he has been remarkably fertile in original ideas; for the only part of his doctrine which can be claimed as peculiarly his own is the so-called mythical explanation of the primitive Christian history, and this view has been in some measure surrendered by subsequent criticism. Nor, again, would the charm and lucidity of his style alone suffice to give him a more permanent place in the history of thought than the author of "Ecce Homo." Nor would the fact that, for the last forty years he has been the most solitary and unpopular man in Europe, give him a claim to mark the epoch. But—and here lies the reason—he has been the most unpopular man in Europe for the same reason that the conscience is the least amiable and esteemed of all the human faculties. He has been the "evil conscience," "the candid friend" of a time of transition; he has spoken when men would willingly have kept silence; he has divided what successive schools have laboured to unite; he has ripped up every compromise, he has probed remorselessly every wound; and has exhibited all the nakedness and deformity of the Christian spirit during its period of decay.

And this peculiar relation to the age seems to be one reason, though, as I shall show hereafter, not the only reason, why Dr. Strauss, when writing of theological matters, always moves in an atmosphere of chagrin. His pages—especially the pages of his more recent works—are full of explosions of displeasure. What, then, has the age done to make appropriate so irritable a critic? Apart from a good deal of personal soreness, it is the "soothing equivocation," the inevitable disingenuousness with which men compose their minds to rest, in order to proceed to the daily work of life without the disturbing intrusion of disquieting thoughts; it is the spirit of conciliation which makes of two things one, which is obtuse in descrying differences between things, and quick to note and exaggerate resemblances, which halts on the journey, and endeavours to perpetuate a state of transition in opinion.

Whether, in the performance of this ungrateful task, Dr. Strauss has used the *suaviter in modo* as much as he might have done consistently with a due adherence to the *fortiter in re*; whether he has treated in a manner sufficiently tender the embarrassments which religious dissolution entails in persons of refined sensibility who have to deal practically with the prejudices of the public mind, need not be decided here. Neither do I propose to dwell upon the details of the uneventful, though in some respects tragic career of a German literary man, excepting so far as they appear to fill up lacunæ in the transition through which the mind of Strauss passed at different periods of his life—a transition, as he would have us believe, identical with that through which the European mind has passed also. Whether this identity be a fact, we shall inquire before we have done; but, even if it be only in part a fact, it supplies a sufficient reason for the assertion with which we began, that the nineteenth century will be reckoned hereafter as the age on which Strauss pre-eminently has set his mark.

From the year 1835, when he published the "Life of

Jesus," down to the time of his decease in the beginning of the present year, Dr. Strauss has appeared before the world three times in the character of theologian: each time advocating a different tenet, each time starting from a different point of view, and each time addressing a different audience. In the first period, 1835–1840, the period of the first "Leben Jesu," and of the "Christliche Glaubenslehre," his standpoint is that of Hegel's "Philosophy of Religion"—*i.e.*, a distinctly Christian position, involving the maintenance in their integrity of the great Christian doctrines of the Incarnation and the Atonement; and in insisting upon these he addresses himself as a critical theologian to critical theologians. In 1864, after a silence of a quarter of a century, so far as theology is concerned, he published a revised edition of the "Life of Jesus," in which, no longer addressing the learned, but "the people," he relapses into the rationalistic deism of the English school of the last century, which, in the "Leben Jesu," he had condemned as insufficient (*unzulänglich*), empty (*leer*), and unworthy of the nineteenth century ("Leben Jesu," §§ 147–8). And finally, in 1872, in his "Confession," he writes for a class of readers who are neither critical theologians nor "the people," but a group of restricted dimensions, which he calls *wir*, we—*i.e.*, people who agree with him in holding the positions to which, at the end of his life, he has at length attained. Those positions are neither Christian nor deistic, but may be roughly, though not inaccurately, denominated the positions of modern physical science or methodized common sense.

Now these transformations of opinion taking place within the area of a single life, would be in themselves sufficiently remarkable, and the explanation of them would present a psychological problem of no ordinary difficulty. But what is still more remarkable is, that these stadia, which the mind of Strauss passes through during his lifetime, are the same as those which the theological movement of Europe had traversed during the two preceding centuries, only, in spite of assertions to the contrary, *in precisely the reverse order.*

Let us see what that movement has been, and how it arose from the previous development of Christian doctrine. If we examine the structure of religious dogma, we shall find that it consists of two elements—a particular element, and a general or ideal element; and that the tendency of the general element is, in the course of the development of the religious consciousness, to become more general, and to absorb into itself the particular element. Thus, if we compare the ancient religion of the Jews with that of any other nation, we find that their idea of God contained within it these two mutually contradictory factors. On the one hand, Jehovah was the national deity of the Hebrew race, in the same sense as the heathen gods were national gods; and yet, on the other hand, unlike the gods of the heathen religions, Jehovah is the God of the whole of mankind. That is—the idea of Deity was to the Jews on the one side a particular, and on the other side a general conception. The element of generality, though latent from the first, even when Jehovah is spoken of as pre-eminently "our," "thy," and "their" God, in distinction from "other" and "strange" gods, only grew up with time. The comparison of "ours" and "strange" does not necessarily go beyond the particular. Even the command, "Thou shalt have no other gods *before* me," does not explicitly do so. But so soon as the Jews came to ask, "Who is there among the gods that can be compared with Jehovah?" it was needful to go only one step farther in the same direction to say, "The idols of the heathen are but silver and gold, the work of men's hands: they have mouths, but they speak not; eyes have they, but they see not; they have ears and hear not; neither is there any breath in their mouths." By this negation, then, the generality in the Jewish idea of God becomes complete.

Similarly, when we read of the ordinance of sacrifices to be offered at specified times and places, and consisting of specified victims, we feel that we are still moving in the region of the particular; but when the prophet says, "Sacrifice and burnt offering for sin thou wouldest not, but mine ear hast thou pierced"—*i.e.*, taken me irrevocably as thy servant; the generality involved in the idea of a permanent state of sacrifice in the moral and religious life, has absorbed into itself the multitudinous and recurring ordinances of the sacrificial cultus.

So Christianity in its primary aspect appears as a further generalization of the old religion, and as giving a meaning to it. The Jehovah of the Jew, as we have seen, had become, from being the God of a nation, the God of the whole of mankind: but he was not conceived as having definite relations with any nation outside the covenant; his relations to the rest of mankind were either non-existent or vague and indeterminate. To the Christian consciousness, on the other hand, this particular relation becomes generalized in a two-fold manner: it becomes not merely a relation to every nation and to every human being composing it, but it becomes a paternal and permanent, and no longer a merely covenanted and so precarious, relation, dependent upon conditions and upon the observance of the Mosaic law. So again with regard to the old sacrificial cultus, the Christian idea of one continual and all-sufficing sacrifice is the permanent generality which, while it gives a meaning to the particular ordinances, supersedes them by summing them up in itself.

An objection may here be made to this view of the development of religious dogma by successive expansion of its generality, that Christianity itself introduced into the religious consciousness a series of new particulars, in the shape of the historical events occurring at a particular place, under particular circumstances and in a particular year, which the paternal relation of God to the world and the supersession of the ancient ritual, is conditioned by, and made to depend upon. It is undeniable that the original Christian faith is immersed in the element of historical particularity; and that it was this element of historical particularity which, so soon as the Christian religion began to be preached, was found to be a stumbling-block to the Jews and to the Greeks foolishness. But it is none the less true that within the Christian community itself, before even the first generation of believers had passed away, the same process of generalization is applied to this very historical element, which we have already noted as expanding and ultimately bursting through the national and ceremonial constituents of Judaism. And the reason of this is, that an historical event, *as such*, is not a possible object for the religious consciousness at all. It may excite the emotions, but not the religious emotions. The specifically religious emotions are not excited until the minds of the community of believers have travelled away from the actual occurrences far enough to be in a position to reflect upon them. After the particular event has passed away, the *meaning* of it, the generality in it, appears above the horizon, and "dawns," as it is said, upon the mind. It is then this *meaning*, this general or ideal aspect of the event which is dwelt upon, and which excites the emotions and becomes the dominant factor in the religious consciousness. It is this *meaning*, as distinguished from a merely emotional recollection of the event, which by its generality serves to perpetuate the event to which it belongs, to bring it into definite relations with the permanent order of the world, and more especially to bring it home to the soul, to give it inwardness, and to make it authoritative over the conscience. Lastly, it is this *meaning* which, as so assimilated, constitutes the side upon which religious experience is ultimately brought into contact with science and with the other general ideas of mankind.

To take an instance. So long as the religious consciousness rests in the mere historical events, it cannot see in Jesus Christ more than a teacher, or in his crucifixion more than a martyrdom; but it was not as a teacher or a martyrdom that the person and death of Christ were assimilated by the religious consciousness of even the earliest Christians; it was as the Incarnation and the Atonement, conceptions of a greater generality and complexity than those which had marked the development of the Jewish religion, or its transition to the Christian. The person of Jesus Christ ceases to be that of a particular individual,[1] but stands for that of the whole human race, and his death ceases to be a particular event, and becomes "the slaying of the lamb *before the foundation of the world.*"

It was this abstraction of the religious consciousness from the historical and particular, this immersion in the idea, in the generality, which produced at once the primitive heresies and the early definitions of the Christian faith. The points at issue in the early Church are not questions about the actual occurrence of the recorded events as amongst ourselves, but questions as to their meaning, and about the nature and qualities of the Deity, or, to use the terms of the schools, they were not historical but Christological.

The same tendency was, if not developed, at least maintained in the Catholic Church of the Middle Ages; and while making it no sin to withhold the Bible from the congregation, it vindicated to the Church the right of developing doctrine, and placed the Mass at the centre of the religious life. The Catholic Mass is not like the Protestant Lord's Supper, mainly and pre-eminently a memorial of a particular past event, but before all things *itself a sacrifice* which is eternal—*i.e.*, of the "Lamb slain before the foundation of the world." Indeed, the whole

[1] Compare Ephrem Syrus ap. Photium Cod. 229. οὐ τὸν τινά ἄνθρωπον ἀλλὰ τὸν ὁλικόν.

distinctive quality of Catholicism is conditioned by the keen and unwavering appreciation of the cardinal facts of the spiritual world, as permanently present and energizing here and now as truly as any history has recorded them to have operated in the past. And it can scarcely be denied that this generality in the Catholic conception of Christianity has produced the most consummate flowers of the religious life.

It is of course easy to exaggerate this generality of form in the Catholic religion, and to shut one's eyes to the elements of historical particularity which still clung to it. The historical lurked in the *legenda* of public worship, though in a tongue "not understanded" of the congregation; it stirred up the warlike passions of Europe in the Crusades; it found a permanent expression in not a little of mediæval art. But it was not until the Protestant Reformation and the translation of the Bible into the modern languages of Europe that the written record of the *origines* of Christianity came definitely to the front as the authoritative standard whereby the now highly articulated structure of the traditional faith was to be judged. The Reformation, whatever else it was, was certainly an appeal from the spirit to the letter, from the inward to the outward, from the present to the past, from the ideal to the historical; in a word, from generality to particularity.

For those who embraced the Reformation, therefore, the centre of gravity, so to speak, of the religious consciousness, became displaced. With the appeal to the written record emerged also the private intellect, the "common sense" of the individual, as the sole guide to its interpretation, and, as a consequence, an endless *morcellement* both of feeling and opinion. Unity and centrality in development were lost; and with them much of the beauty and sweetness of the Christian life. We cannot stop to follow out the manifold results of this displacement in detail; but so far as our especial purpose is concerned, the appeal from religion as it had come to be after fifteen centuries of growth to the records of its foundation, gave rise—so soon as the immediate effects of the crisis itself had disappeared—to three very remarkable phases of thought, a brief explanation of which in their order will bring us down to the proper subject of the present paper, the original position taken by Dr. Strauss.

1. The new specific reference of the contents of religion to the historical circumstances of a distant age and the erection of "common sense" as the criterion by which those circumstances and the records of them were to be judged, landed, and could not but land, the Protestant mind in a negation. "Common sense," the intellectual phase of the eighteenth century, could not accept a miraculous history as miraculous. Missing, with characteristic want of tact, all the finer points, all the sentiment, not to speak of the speculative ideas involved in primitive Christianity, it invented the hypothesis of imposture to account for the miracles; and left the philosopher at liberty "to regard with a smile or a sigh" the obscurity of the founders of superstition and the ignorance or credulity of its votaries. This attitude, the characteristic standing-point of English Deism, and of the continental *éclaircissement*, carries with it, as will easily be seen, the surrender of a great deal more than the historical element in religion. It involves, as was proved by the event, the erasure of all the distinctive traits of the Christian consciousness itself; it involved an aversion from the whole Christian ethical view of life, and an establishment of the maxims and sentiments of prudential morality in its place. But it did not necessarily involve, as we may see in the case of Voltaire or Gibbon, a demolition of the more primitive and abstract elements of the religious consciousness, as, *e.g.*, the belief in the existence of God. The belief in an extramundane mind, remote, inscrutable, clothed, so far as it was clothed at all, with the attributes of its

worshippers, a kind of Supreme Common Sense, became fused with a more or less emotional and imaginative conception of the maxims of prudential morality under the name of Natural Religion. It is out of this abstract residuum that Bishop Butler attempts to reconstruct again the belief in Christianity upon the basis of the prudential motive, that it is conceivably true, and if true, the penalties for disbelieving it are severe. But no ingenuity can construe the idea of the Christian God out of the abstract Deity of Natural Religion; and for this reason. To the conception of the Divine Nature, as embraced by and constituting the Christian consciousness, the operations of Revelation, Incarnation, and Redemption are not accidental incidents, which can be let drop or set aside, leaving the idea of God in its integrity. They constitute it. God is nothing to the Christian, except as revealing himself in consciousness, as incarnate in the world, and as redeeming it. As it is somewhere happily phrased, I think by Mr. Picton, "a new race was born in Christ: the divine humanity to which God is not Object only, but Subject."

The God of Natural Religion, on the contrary, is not this spiritual process in and towards mankind, but a motionless point, which is the mere negation of the series of finite things. The idea is, as Feuerbach has conclusively shown, nothing more nor less than the apotheosis of the human understanding—*i.e.*, of the abstract logical centre of the reasoning faculties. The deduction of a sanction for prudential morality, then, from this abstraction, which is the God of Deism, although it may have been a necessity from a psychological point of view, was ethically superfluous as well as impossible. For prudential morality has a sufficient ground in itself, and is not advantaged by deriving its sanction from a transcendental entity; while, on the other hand, a vanishing point, which is the mere negation of the finite, such as we have found the God of Natural Religion to be, is incompetent to supply a sanction to prudential morality or to anything else.

2. The impotence and superfluity of Deism as the guide and sanction of life, or as a resting-place for the emotions, produced a reaction towards Christianity; and in Kant's "Religion within the limits of pure Reason," as in Butler's "Analogy," we may discern an attempt to recover some of its ideal elements. But in Kant there is no attempted return, as there is in Butler, to the historical factor which Deism had demolished. Rather, he strives to make out a compromise between the phraseology of those theological ideas which are compatible with his system, or which the emotions require as a supplement to it, and the phraseology of isolated parts of current religion. With Kant, as with Fichte, "nur das Metaphysische nicht das Historische macht selig; das letztere macht bloss verständig." But the reaction towards the Christian consciousness did not stop here; and in Schleiermacher's philosophical reconstruction of it we discern a partial recrudescence of the tendency towards the historical, though confined to the single case of the resurrection of Christ as a means of helping out the psychological method. This recrudescence, which is of the nature of a *purpureus pannus* in Schleiermacher, reopened the whole question of the historical factor in religion, and brought about that curious phase of conflict between a faith in bondage to the letter and a philosophy which had grown up in conscious estrangement from any form of Christian sentiment. This conflict has assumed a place in history under the name of Rationalism.

3. The point at issue between the Rationalists and Supernaturalists was no longer, indeed, that which had been raised by the English Deists—viz., whether or not the Christian religion was a tissue of imposture, unworthy of the consideration of reasonable men, the position confronted by Bishop Butler; and the line of defence no longer consisted in proving by forensic methods the good

faith of the Biblical writers. The hypothesis of imposture had worn itself out, without being exactly refuted, and with Voltaire seems to have fallen into disrepute through its own intrinsic improbability. But the rejection of the miraculous element in the records, which had been the latent motive of Deism, remained the latent motive of Rationalism. The Rationalists were thus enabled to take common ground with the Supernaturalists in accepting the Gospel narratives as history; while contending for the readjustment of their outlines, so as to read them as the history of natural events, as against the traditional mode of regarding them as a true history of supernatural intervention. It is not difficult to see that both the contending parties alike based their position upon the dualistic conception of God which, in common with Deism, banished him to an indefinite distance from the world; while in the conception of the Supernaturalists, the mechanical character of the supposed relation of God to the world was not materially modified by the theory of occasional interposition. Further than this, the long-continued conflict between the two views had the effect of hatching a numerous brood of minute, specialized, and intermediate points of view, some bearing a closer resemblance to one parent, others to the other, until at length, as Schwartz says, "Nobody knew any longer to which class he himself belonged, and still less in which class he should place others."[1]

At this crisis, just forty years ago, Dr. Strauss, at that time a young lecturer of twenty-eight years of age in the Theological College at Tübingen, and saturated with Schleiermacher and with Hegel, came forward with the sinister question: "You are disputing what sort of history the Gospels are: *are they history at all?*" Can you withdraw the miraculous element from a history claiming to narrate miraculous events, and leave behind any such residuum of natural history as the Rationalist

---

[1] "Geschichte der neueren Theologie," p. 5.

proposes to do? If you deny the possibility or the demonstrability of the miraculous, the question which remains to be answered is not "How do you reconstruct the narrative *without* the miracles?" but "How do you account for the origination of the narrative *with* the miracles?" This question was posed by Strauss with an entirely unmistakable directness, and ran like an electric shock through all the various schools of "soothing equivocation" with which Germany teemed. And the answer is equally unmistakable: given the Jewish expectation of a Messiah, and given the appearance on the scene of an exceptionally impressive personality, the application of the former to the latter will account for the gradual evolution of the mythus which forms the ground-work of the Gospel narratives. The working out of this answer in relation to all the main groups of evangelical narrative, occupies nearly the whole of the original "Leben Jesu" of 1835, which was translated into English by no less a person than Miss Marian Evans.

This, then, was the negative side of Strauss at that time; and it was epoch-making in the sense that it closed the episode of conflict between faith and common sense, which the appeal to the historical record, as the criterion of the contents of the religious consciousness, had initiated at the time of the Protestant reformation.

But this negation was not the whole of Strauss, although it is the side of his doctrine which has attracted most attention in this country, while in Germany it has formed the starting-point of the important modern school of evangelical criticism, and the subject of continual modification in accordance with the growth of knowledge. Neither was the ground idea of the myth originated by Strauss. It was an application of Hegel's profound diagnosis of the elements which go to constitute the religious consciousness. The ideas involved in religion are, according to Hegel, the same ideas as those which form the content of Philosophy; but that which specific to the religious consciousness is the imaginative conception of them, and the concretion of them into individual forms. The imaginative concretion of the idea of God, or of his operations in the world, what Strauss calls mythus, is thus not merely an hypothesis to which he is driven experimentally by the study of a particular record; it is a necessary quality of religion as such, which being taken away, religion would cease to be what it is.[1]

What, then, is Strauss's position in reference to the religious as distinguished from the historical elements in Christianity? Does he renounce Christianity in surrendering the latter? Assuredly not: and it is this which distinguishes his stand-point from the Deism in which the Protestant episode culminated. Here I will let him speak first for himself. In the concluding dissertation of the "Leben Jesu" he says:[2]—

The critic is intrinsically a believer. In proportion as he is distinguished from the rationalistic theologian and the freethinker, *in proportion as his criticism is conceived in the spirit of the nineteenth century,* he is filled with veneration for every religion, and especially for the substance of the sublimest of all religions, the Christian, which he perceives to be identical with the profoundest philosophical truth.

The object which the modern critic must set before himself is two-fold, "to keep the faith unmutilated, and at the same time to keep science unoffended:"[3] and it is

---

[1] "Leben Jesu:" Ein'eitung, § 14. That the Hebrew and Christian religions have their myths like all other religions " wird bestätigt," says Strauss, " wenn man vom Begriffe der Religion ausgeht, und fragt was zu deren Wesen gehört und also Bestandtheil aller Religionen sein muss, und worin hingegen die einzelnen Religionen sich noch unterscheiden können. Wenn man Religion im Verhältniss zur Philosophie bestimmt als das Bewusstsein desselben absoluten Inhalts aber nicht in Form des Begriffs sondern der Vorstellung; so ist leicht zu sehen dass nur unter und über dem eigentlichen Standpunkte der Religion das Mythische fehlen kann; innerhalb der eigentlich religiösen Sphäre aber dasselbe wesentlich und nothwendig vorhanden ist."

[2] Schlussabhandlung, § 144, "On the Dogmatic Import of the Life of Jesus." [3] Schlussabhandlung, § 148.

because it only attempted to perform the latter of these two functions that Strauss condemns Rationalism.

The insufficiency of Rationalism consists in its not doing what every theory of religion (*Glaubenslehre*) should do; that is, taking the complex of belief with which it has to deal, it should first give it adequate expression; and secondly, bring it into some relation, whether positive or negative, to science. Now, in the effort to make the faith agree with science, Rationalism has defaced the proportions of the faith. Thus to regard Christ as nothing more than a remarkable human being presents no difficulty to science; but this is not that Christ in whom the Church believes.[1]

And in speaking of Schleiermacher he praises him for having "sought to retain what Rationalism had lost, the essential part of positive Christianity, whereby he has saved many in these days from the narrowness of Supernaturalism and the emptiness of Rationalism."[2]

What, then, is this positive element to which Strauss attaches so much importance? It is the general or ideal factor in religion, the growth and expansion of which to ever greater generality and ever profounder meaning we have already noted in the Jewish community and in the Christian Church, until in the latter the process was interrupted by the appeal of the Reformation to the letter and the records, followed by what we have ventured to call the Protestant episode. The greatness of Strauss, then, does not so much consist in his negation of the letter, and in dealing thereby the death-blow to the controversy between the Rationalists and Supernaturalists which was eating away the vitals of religion, as in taking up the threads of the old development of doctrine, re-establishing centrality in the movement of ideas, and carrying on that development several degrees further.

I have already called attention to the way in which the idea of the person of Christ became generalized in

---

[1] Schlussabhandlung, § 147.   [2] Ibid. § 148.

the early Church, from the time when St. Paul said,[1] "Though we have known Christ after the flesh, yet from henceforth know we him no more," till we get in Ephrem Syrus the more technical conception of ὁ ὁλικὸς ἄνθρωπος—and how his work and sacrifice were conceived as an external fact beginning "before the foundation of the world," and, as set forth in the Catholic doctrine of the Mass, going on to the end of time. Now hear Strauss in a classical passage :[2]—

Spiritual existence in its truth and reality is found neither in God by himself nor in man by himself, but in the union of God and man (*der Gottmensch*); neither in the infinity of the one nor in the finitude of the other, taken by themselves, but in that process of self-surrender and recovery taking place between the two factors, which from the Divine side is revelation, and from the human, religion."

This new generality, like the ground-work of the Mythical Theory, is all to be found in Hegel; but Hegel's exposition of the speculative notion of the Incarnation and Atonement was sufficiently obscure and vacillating to lead the so-called "right wing" of the Hegelian school to attempt, and to suppose Hegel himself to have attempted, by means of this notion, a rehabilitation of the historical particularities of the Gospel record. That such was not Hegel's real meaning may be inferred from numberless passages in his works; and the necessity of proving that such a reconstruction of the historical was incompatible with his own system of thought, gave rise to the so-called "left wing" of the Hegelian school, and to the "Halle Yearbooks," to the early numbers of which Strauss contributed.

The question at issue between the two contending parties was this: Does the conception of the Incarnation and Atonement as an eternal process constituting the essential nature of spiritual existence, lead of necessity to, is it compatible with, the summation of this process

---

[1] 2 Cor. v. 16. [2] "Leben Jesu:" Schlussabhandlung, § 150.

in a single individual? Hegel had said, the important point for us is not that the summation did or did not take place in a single individual, but that it was part and parcel of the earliest consciousness of the Christian community to which we can penetrate, *to believe that it did*—to believe, that is, that the infinite and the finite spirits had actually confronted each other in their entirety within the area of a single mind. This is not a real answer to the question, although it cannot be denied that, for the religious consciousness as it exists imperfectly in the ordinary Christian, it is important to be convinced, that the consciousness of God, which in us is a dim and partial glimmering, attained only in rare moments of exaltation, cannot be explained away; because it has existed in an historical person with complete and uninterrupted lucidity, during a whole life-time. For this practical purpose of edification and encouragement, it may be said, the belief is everything, and the truth of the conviction of secondary importance. But, on the other hand, a firm emotional grasp of the generality, that the whole universe is framed upon the basis of the continual and uninterrupted intercourse of the Infinite with the Finite, supplies the same need, without being liable, as everything historical must be, to be called in question on the ground of insufficient external evidence.

However this may be, the question to be decided by the scientific theologian is not whether the doctrine of the summation of the spiritual process in an individual is edifying, but whether it follows from the idea of that process itself. And here the dry and ruthless Swabian intellect of Strauss comes in, as always, with an unmistakable answer:—

According to the conception of science, the infinite has its existence in the alternate production and absorption of the finite; and the *idea is realized only in the entire series of its manifestations*.[1]

[1] "Leben Jesu:" Schlussabhandlung, § 149. Cf. "Christliche Glaubenslehre," § 66, p. 220.

This generalization of the doctrines of the Incarnation and Atonement is the upshot of the instructive chapter on the "Dogmatic Import of the Life of Jesus," which forms the concluding dissertation of Strauss's original "Leben Jesu," and of the "Christliche Glaubenslehre," in which the previous stadia traversed by the development of Christian doctrine are subjected to the same searching criticism as the historical element had been in the previous work. During the whole of this negative sifting of dogma, the new generalization, which we have endeavoured to explain, forms the dominant conception, the background; and it is a noteworthy fact that the "Glaubenslehre," though it appeared after the "Leben Jesu," was planned before it; thus showing that it was the attainment of this new conception which motived the elimination of the historical, and not the elimination of the historical which precipitated the new generalization as its residuum.

Whatever, therefore, we may think of Strauss's speculative Christology as a doctrine capable of assimilation by the religious community, enough has been said to show that it represents the normal development of the Christian consciousness; that it is of a piece with the tendency to generalization which made of the old Mosaic religion a spiritual instead of a merely national or heathen religion: which made the doctrine of the Divinity of Christ the centre of European thought, and the Mass the hearth and home of Catholic worship.[1]

---

[1] That the generalization of the doctrine of the Incarnation in its most complete form, as it appears in Strauss as distinguished from Hegel, was not foreign to the thinkers of the Middle Ages, might be shown by plenty of quotations. I will content myself with one from St. Thomas Aquinas, which is as follows:—

"Cum Deo competat summa perfectio tanto magis est Deo simile aliquid quanto est magis perfectum. Sed totum universum est magis perfectum quam partes ejus, inter quas est natura humana; *ergo totum universum est magis assumptibile quam natura humana.*" Summa iii. 4, 1. Compare with this the almost identical import of Spinoza, Epist. xxi. "Dico ad salutem non esse omnino necesse, Christum secundum carnem

But the importance of the speculative Christology of Strauss does not consist solely in its normality as the latest term of a continuous development. Its special value, at the present crisis, is that it provides a basis for the religious and specifically Christian emotions, outside and independent of the dissolution produced by historical criticism. No one who is acquainted with the progress which historical science has made within the last half century, with the exactness of its method, and with the increasing internal agreement of its results, can sincerely propose to do otherwise than resign to it unreservedly the primitive records of religion. But it is impossible, in the long run, for the religious emotions to remain attached to the imagination of events which have been called in question, even though their historical truth may be ultimately established. What religious emotion demands is the eternal and indisputable, and no historical event resting upon external evidence which may become the subject of discussion can have this character of eternity and indisputableness. Whether we will or no, emotion must disengage itself from the mutable and uncertain, and take refuge in that inner sanctuary of general doctrine which is the organic growth of the collective reason of mankind, and which, in the progress of the individual life, may be brought to the test of religious and moral experience.

But it is time that we proceed to examine the second phase through which the mind of Strauss passed, and which was exhibited after the lapse of nearly thirty years in the popular revision of the "Life of Jesus," published in 1864.

2. The principal thing that strikes us in this revision

noscere; sed de aeterno illo filio Dei, h.e. Dei aeterna sapientia, quae sese in omnibus rebus, et maxime in mente humana et omnium maxime in Christo Jesu manifestavit, longe aliter sentiendum. Nam nemo absque hac ad statum beatitudinis potest pervenire, utpote quae sola docet, quid verum et falsum, bonum et malum sit."

of Strauss's great work is the alteration of tone apparent in the author as he approaches his subject.

His aim is no longer to construe a portion of past history into forms capable of assimilation by the modern mind (*eine vergangene Geschichte zu ermitteln*), "but to lend a hand in the eventual emancipation of the human mind from the galling yoke of belief."[1]

The criticism of the Gospel history has (he complains) during the last twenty years undeniably run to seed (*ins Kraut geschossen*), new hypotheses especially relative to the Synoptic Gospels, their sources, composition, and mutual relations, spring up fast and free; are set up with zeal to be knocked down with zeal; *als ob es um Nichts weiter handelte*, as if there were not a further question in the background. And the controversy is becoming so extensive in its scope that one may well begin to be anxious whether we shall ever get clear on the main question, if its solution is to be postponed until the critical problem is settled.[2]

What, then, is this "main question" which agitates Strauss to such impatience? On this point his characteristic plainness of speech does not desert him. In the dedication of the book to his brother he congratulates him on having given his life to commercial pursuits, and thus avoided all the vexations and persecutions which beset the career of the theologian; and on having the insight to perceive "that *political progress*, at least in Germany, can never be secured until means have been taken to emancipate the popular mind from the religious illusion (*von dem religiösen Wahn*), and substitute a purely humanistic culture."

It will be seen at once that the ground of aggression against popular religion which is taken here is an entirely different position from that which Strauss had occupied thirty years before. Not less trenchant than now, he was content then to say, "We leave the believer his belief, let him leave us our philosophy."

[1] Vorrede, xiv.   [2] Ibid. xv.

And his main endeavour was, as we have seen, to draw a line of demarcation between the ideal and permanent element and the historical creed with which it had become interwoven. In the revised and popular "Life," on the other hand, this permanent element, although not overtly abandoned, is let drop by the author, with the unsatisfactory explanation that he will not trouble the popular reader with conceptions which it may be difficult for him to grasp; and, with the exception of a few isolated passages which recall the earlier work, but have no pretension to be called in any sense a Christology,[1] the revised "Life" is largely occupied with modifications of the negative results arrived at previously.

One thing, however, is very remarkable, as indicative of the new stand-point taken by the author—namely this, that Strauss now attempts what he had not attempted before, a positive reconstruction of the historical Christ, from the residue of record which remains after the miraculous events in the Gospel history have been eliminated. This, it will be remembered, is precisely the attempt which Rationalism had made, and which Strauss had in his first work condemned, in the strongest terms, as *unzulänglich* and *leer*, and as unworthy of the state of knowledge in the nineteenth century.[2]

What, then, it may be asked, were the intermediate steps by which Strauss travelled from the speculative

---

[1] As a typical passage in Strauss's second manner, I may give the following from the Preface to the "Leben Jesu," of 1864 (Vorrede, xvii.) :— "We live in a crisis like that of the Reformation, the difficulty of which consists in the fact that a portion of the dominant Christianity has become as intolerable as another part is indispensable. To the Reformers the intolerable element was the ecclesiastical, to us it is the biblical. . . . . The indispensable and indeed imperishable element which remains to us of Christianity is that by which it rescued mankind from the sensuous religion of Greece on the one hand, and from the Mosaic law on the other; the belief, namely, that there is a spiritual and moral power governing the world, and that the service we have to render to this power is, like itself, spiritual and moral." &c.

[2] Cf. p. 235.

Christology of the first "Leben Jesu" back to the point of view of the old Rationalism? Are there any logical elements inherent in the first position, the development of which necessitates the second? As he gives no explanation of the mental procedure himself, I have most carefully considered—with a view of doing, so far as in me lies, complete justice to Strauss—what dialectical movement of ideas is conceivable from the speculative Christology to Rationalism; and I have found none. I have found no mediation of the two stand-points but a biographical one; a "mediation" made up of the circumstances of Strauss's life during those thirty years which intervened between the publication of the two "Lives." And although, until a complete biography of Strauss is published, my explanation may be called in question, I offer it to the consideration of the reader for what it is worth. The first effect of the publication of the first " Life," even before the appearance of the second volume, was the dismissal of Strauss from his tutorship in Tübingen. The whole theological world of Germany was up in arms against him. His teachers disclaimed the "Life" as in any sense a deduction from their principles; many of his friends renounced his acquaintance; those who stood by him became at once suspect, were passed over in promotion, or dismissed. He retired to a mastership in the Lyceum of his native town of Ludwigsburg, and lived with his parents. But here again a fresh trouble was in store for him in the displeasure of his father, and the uneasiness of his mother at the continual bickerings which took place between the two men.[1] After a year, in the autumn of 1836, he took refuge in Stuttgart, and occupied himself with the preparation of the second, third, and fourth editions of the "Life" which were speedily demanded. For the book had made a prodigious success, and had become the centre of a

[1] Zeller, "David Friedrich Strauss in seinem Leben und seinen Schriften geschildert" (Bonn, 1874), p. 44.

vigorous and embittered controversy, which raged from one end of Germany to the other. Into this controversy Strauss plunged with ardour: his opponents obtained small mercy at his hands, and he asked none from theirs. But the speedy result upon his own mind and temper was the beginning of an aversion to the subject with which he had been dealing. In December, 1837, he wrote to his friend Eduard Zeller, that so soon as he should have finished the third edition of the "Life," "he would wipe his hands of theology altogether."[1] And for the next two years he wrote nothing but literary reviews for the newspapers. The profound exasperation at the treatment he had received on all sides seems during this interval to have partly subsided, and he again returned to his old studies. Two little works, "Selbstgespräche über Vergängliches und Bleibendes im Christenthum," and an article on Kerner, which he subsequently (1839) united under the title "Zwei friedliche Blätter," were the product of this altered mood, and represent the nearest approach that Strauss ever condescended to make to the point of view of the ordinary believing Christian. This sympathetic overture he afterwards, when other causes of exasperation supervened, condemned as a morbid outcome of the "horror of feeling himself alone in the world, which penetrated into every limb."[2] In the same year he received a call to a Theological Chair at Zürich, but before he could enter upon it, a popular *émeute*, excited by the appointment, had removed the Ministry which made it, and left Strauss without further hope of getting a Professorship. Fortunately he does not appear to have ever suffered from that cruellest penalty which attends the expression of unpopular opinions—pecuniary embarrassment. But his life-long exclusion from an academical career, for which he was adapted by tempera-

---

[1] Wolle er sobald keine theologische Feder mehr anrühren. Zeller, "D. F. Strauss in Seinem Leben," u.s.w., p. 48.

[2] Zeller, *op. cit.*, p. 51.

ment, and which by its regular succession of duties would probably have subdued a certain restlessness of character observable in him—this life-long exclusion, Professor Zeller tells us,[1] weighed very heavily upon him. In the parallel case of Arthur Schopenhauer there can be little doubt that the exclusion from a congenial sphere of duty conditioned to some extent the more extravagant pessimism of his writings: and I am disposed to attribute the altered tone in Strauss towards religion, in default of any other explanation, to these external circumstances of his career. In 1839 his mother died, after a prolonged illness, increased by worry; in 1841 his father followed. Strauss plunged with energy into his old studies again, and brought out the two volumes of the "Christliche Glaubenslehre," which he had planned before the "Leben Jesu," and anticipated to some extent in the "concluding dissertation" of that work. The "Glaubenslehre" was not a success. It appeared, at least the second volume of it, simultaneously with Feuerbach's "Wesen des Christenthums," which took possession of the public mind, as Strauss's "Leben Jesu" had formerly done, but left little chance of popularity for a continuation of a less startling kind. And now at length Strauss seemed determined to keep his resolution to write no more theology. His interest had cooled, and as a theologian he was silent for the next twenty years. "I can only write when I am in a rage," he said to a friend; and his rage had fallen with the decay of opposition. But these years were not destined to be more fortunate. In 1842 he married an actress of remarkable personal attractions and culture, but after a brief period of happiness, spent in the neighbourhood of Heilbronn, a growing alienation of sympathy between man and wife culminated at the end of five years in a voluntary separation. This was a terrible blow to his sensitive nature; and, in speaking afterwards of his

[1] *Op. cit.*, p. 53.

mother's death, Strauss "rejoices that she did not live to see his life wrecked by a convulsion far more fatal than any of those theological persecutions whose virulence used to be such an affliction to her."[1] The lady retired to her friends in Stuttgart, where she remained till her death in 1870; and Strauss began a vagrant life, unable to settle in any place for more than a few years. He read with diligence, as he always had done; but he found it impossible to write. No one subject could chain his attention; but was dropped for another. He turned himself to politics, and at length to the editing of the letters of the Swabian poet Schubart, which had been committed to him.

In 1848 came the Democratic movement and the Frankfort Parliament; and Strauss, at the urgent request of his friends, though much against the grain, allowed himself to become a candidate for his native township of Ludwigsburg. But his ill-luck continued to attend him: his election failed in consequence of the country votes. However, he was soon elected to represent the same town in the Wurtemburg Chamber, the country electors having in this case no vote for the town member. In the Chamber he became sensible of his entire want of sympathy with the movement which was rife in Germany: he set his face steadily against the stream, and voted consistently with the small nobles and the clerical party. The Radicals were exasperated; even his own friends deserted him; and a requisition was conveyed to him to give up his seat. He refused; but a few weeks sufficed to convince him that his position was untenable. One day, on the urgent demand of the Radical members, he suffered the indignity of being called to order in the Chamber,[2] and he at once wrote to his constituents and resigned his seat.

[1] "The Old and the New Faith." Translated by Mathilde Blind. 'Memoir of Strauss,' xli. London: Asher, 1874.
[2] This was, according to Zeller, undeserved. *Op. cit.*, p. 72.

It was at this time, apparently, that he first came to entertain the opinion—which he afterwards expressed in the dedication of the popular "Life of Jesus," which we have already quoted—that political progress in Germany was impossible until "the religious illusion" was dissipated.

Nothing can possibly be worse (he writes) than the condition of Germany at the present time. My position is clear. If I have to choose between an aristocratic and a democratic despotism, I say, without hesitation, I prefer the former.

One can see that in this sweeping condemnation there is not a little of personal chafing under unmerited injuries. And the experience of every one will bear witness that nothing is more easy than to construct a generality of this sort out of the circumstances of one's own private sphere. A man quarrels with his architect, and relieves his feelings by writing a paper to prove that the extinction of the whole class of architects is an indispensable condition of modern progress. My grocer serves me with some adulterated commodity, and in my righteous indignation I feel that I am at one with all that is sound in European thought in inveighing publicly against the powerful and predatory class of licensed victuallers. Many a man who has groaned under the tyranny of the clerical majority at our English universities has been permanently alienated, not only from the Church but from all religion.

In this respect Strauss is not very unlike those idolaters who were accustomed to chastise their deities on an access of misfortune. But it remains to ask why Strauss should have selected the distinctive tenet of eighteenth century Rationalism as the speculative accompaniment of his chagrin. That his mind had been tending in that direction is shown by the character of the biographies which occupied his pen during the latter part of the interval between the two "Lives of Jesus." In Ulrich von Hutten he had found the hero of theological conflict. The contentious, irreconcilable character of his subject was congenial to him. At the time of the concordats with Rome he asks himself what would Hutten have done:—

"*Damals rief ich : ist denn kein Hutten da ?*" "And because I found none among the living, I undertook to renew the image of the dead Hutten, and present him before the eyes of the German people."

Later again, the feeling of his own isolated position leads him to seek intercourse with kindred souls in the past. In this mood he turns to the unpublished papers of Reimarus in the Wolfenbüttel library, from which Lessing had already drawn; and Reimarus becomes a hero, as Hutten had been—the hero of negative evangelical criticism. So Strauss, by following his varying moods, is brought back again to theology, but he returns to it no longer as a speculative theologian of the school of Hegel, but as a Rationalist. The metaphysic *welche selig macht* has evaporated along with the sweetness of the Christian temperament; Strauss is himself scarcely conscious that it has done so; it does not occur to him to explain how it went. He even talks still, in the "Life" of 1864, about the *ächten Heilswahrheiten*, the genuine saving truths, as if these were still a part of his mind: but when we look for them, we come only upon the jejune trace of Deism. The place of the *Schlussabhandlung* of the earlier "Life" is occupied by a new positive factor, in the shape of a reconstruction of the evangelical history, with the miraculous threads of narrative drawn out of it; precisely the feat which thirty years before he had pronounced impossible from a critical point of view; and inasmuch as the result is "not the Christ in whom the Church believes," but merely an *ausgezeichneter Mensch* whose lineaments should give no offence to science, we must quote Strauss against himself, and say that this is the criticism, not of the nineteenth century, but of the eighteenth.

Upon Strauss's last publication, "The Old and the New Faith," it will not be necessary to dwell at any great length. Its contents are known in this country, and are fresh in the memory of all who care for these things. Unlike the second "Life," it is not a *provocatio ad populum*, but an esoteric "confession" addressed to the unknown "we" who have arrived at the same opinions. The opinions are not new or strange; they exist sporadically wherever philosophy is in decay or has not yet formed a part of education, as amongst the present generation of men engaged in physical science. They have no especial interest in themselves; but their combination, and the fact that Strauss, who had once attained the commanding heights of philosophical speculation, should, at the end of his career, have relapsed into them, present a curious problem, but *distinctly a problem in individual biography, not a stage in the march of ideas in the world*. Here again the immediately preceding condition to this latest phase seems to have been the study of Voltaire, as the immediately preceding condition of the mood represented by the "Life" of 1864 was the study of Reimarus.[1]

In "The Old and New Faith," the last vestige of the original Strauss, who made an epoch and will live in the history of thought, is swept away. In the "Life" of 1864 the Christological element is allowed to drop, but the critical remains. In "The Old and New Faith" the critical falls to the ground also. What, for instance, can be conceived more entirely at variance with the nicety of the true critical touch, than to take the crudest and most materialistic forms of early popular belief, and bluntly ask—Do we believe them? Of course we do not; but what has become of the long march of doctrinal development, by which we have arrived at the religious

[1] Zeller, *op. cit.* 98.

consciousness of to-day? Is that to count for nothing? Are we to be judged by the most primitive conceptions? What was the object of the "Christliche Glaubenslehre," if not to show that the development of the Christian consciousness is a reality, capable of specific description?

All this is, however, let drop without a word; and we are confronted with the *schroffer Gegensatz* of the modern and the primitive mind.

It would seem a remarkable inconsistency that Dr. Strauss, after having thought himself out of every belief in development as applied to ideas and to the religious consciousness at large, should find so much repose in the contemplation of the evolutionary doctrines at which modern physical science has arrived. If there is continuous development in the inorganic and organic worlds, why not, as Hegel insisted that there was, in the world of thought? The diremption of the two kinds of development may be possible to the individual, but in the long run, as a diremption in the consciousness of mankind, it must ultimately eliminate itself.

It is on this subjective and individual point of view that Strauss, hunted, *destitué*, systematically tarred and feathered by fortune and the theologians, came during the latter half of his life more and more to stand. And as marking the relapse, the speculative decay, if I may use the expression, I will quote in conclusion a passage from the "Glaubenslehre," which cuts away any objective and philosophical value from the second and third phases of Strauss, and leaves his original position, the position taken by the first "Life of Jesus," as the only historical one that he ever took, and the only one by which he will probably hereafter be known:—

The subjective criticism of the individual is like a hose which every child can handle for a time; but the criticism which consummates itself in the course of centuries, rushes down like a mountain torrent, and against it every barrier is powerless. The true criticism of Dogma is its history.[1]

[1] "Glaubenslehre," I. x. 71, quoted by Zeller.

CHAPTER II.

A PLEA FOR METAPHYSIC.[1]

IN reviewing the theological works of the late Friedrich Strauss I abstained from discussing the truth or falsehood of the particular tenets which Strauss held during different periods of his life, and tried to confine myself to an appraisement of the various philosophical points of outset which he successively occupied, and of the methods which he successively used in operating and going forth from these standing-points. I now propose to employ somewhat of the same purely formal method in the case of Mr. Matthew Arnold, who appears to me to be quite the most important constructive intellect in the domain of politics and religion that we have had in Europe since Strauss. Not that Mr. Arnold has the scientific equipment of Strauss, or anything like Strauss's familiarity with the historical course of human thought. He is a man of letters, not a strict thinker; he plumes himself, as is allowable in a man of letters, on not understanding what is meant by accurate thinking; and he congratulates himself, not unfrequently, in his two later books, on the incoherence and inconsistency of his ideas, as on an Englishman's privilege. And thus his works, admirable, enjoyable, and important as they are, have still this one note of insularity—that, while he cheapens philosophy before the great public by putting its enunciation dramatically into the mouths of absurd personages, he is himself nearly always under the influence of metaphysical ideas of one kind or another, and as he is unconscious that he is so, he uses them at

[1] "Culture and Anarchy," by Matthew Arnold, 1869; "St. Paul and Protestantism," by the same, 1870; "Literature and Dogma," by the same, 1873; "God and the Bible," by the same, 1875. Published by Smith, Elder & Co., London.

haphazard; in his first two books, "Culture and Anarchy" and "St. Paul and Protestantism" (as it chances), well and fruitfully; in his two later books, "Literature and Dogma" and "God and the Bible," blindly and without result.

I will now try to explain and justify this criticism, and it will be convenient to do so under the following heads:—

1. The standing-point of Mr. Arnold's negative criticism of current ideas in politics and religion.
2. His assumptions and method when he leaves this standing-point, and proceeds to the positive part of his theme.
3. His criticism of Descartes' and other philosophical ideas.
4. His new religious construction, "The eternal not-ourselves that makes for righteousness."

In the course of this inquiry, and by means of it, better perhaps than in any more systematic way, I shall try to show what modern metaphysic is, what are the facts with which it deals, what it has done, and what are the problems still outstanding which it may hope to grapple with successfully in the future.

And in conclusion I shall try to ascertain why it is that Mr. Arnold, beginning as he does to philosophize well, goes on to philosophize badly, and ends by not being able to manage and control his philosophical thinking at all.

1. The great merit of "Culture and Anarchy" is its having translated into the language of literature the metaphysical idea, "the notion, so familiar on the Continent and to antiquity, of the State,"[1] as the "organ of our collective best self."[2]

We want an authority, and we find nothing but jealous classes, checks, and a deadlock; culture suggests *the idea of the State*. We find no basis for a firm State-power in our ordinary selves; culture suggests one to us in our own best

---
[1] "Culture and Anarchy," p. 51.   [2] Ibid. p. 80.

self.[1] .... By our every-day selves .... we are separate, personal, at war; we are only safe from one another's tyranny when no one has any power; and this safety in its turn cannot save us from anarchy. .... *But by our best self we are united, impersonal, at harmony.*[2]

There is, we are told, a kind of philosophical theory, "a peculiarly British form of Atheism," current amongst us—

that there is no such thing at all as a best self and a right reason having claim to paramount authority, or at any rate no such thing ascertainable and capable of being made use of; and that there is nothing but an infinite number of ideas and works of our ordinary selves.[3] But elsewhere this is certainly better understood.[4]

Elsewhere, on the Continent for instance, this idea of the collective as distinguished from the individual reason, and standing above it, as conscience is distinguished from and stands above desire, has long been familiar under the names of the *Ego* (*Ich*) or common consciousness (*Gemeingeist, Gemeinbewusstsein*); in our own Hobbes we had something like it in the "Great Leviathan;" but since the seventeenth century till now, with perhaps the single exception of Coleridge, this idea of the better self has been erased from English thought. Let us see how one of the greatest of American writers describes it :—

We grant that human life is mean, but how did we find out that it was mean? What is the ground of this uneasiness of ours—of this old discontent? What is the universal sense of want and ignorance, but the fine innuendo by which the great soul makes its enormous claim?

* * * * * *

In all conversation between two persons, tacit reference is made to a third party, to a common nature. And so in groups, where debate is earnest, and especially on great questions of thought, the company become aware of their unity, and that the thought rises to an equal height in all

---

[1] "Culture and Anarchy," p. 83. [2] Ibid. p. 80.
[3] Ibid. p. 116. [4] Ibid. p. 124.

bosoms, that all have a spiritual property in what was said as well as the sayer. It arches over them like a temple, this unity of thought, in which every heart beats with nobler sense of power and duty, and thinks and acts with unusual solemnity. All are conscious of attaining to a higher self-possession.

And again :—

What we commonly call man, the eating, drinking, planting, counting man, does not, as we know him, represent himself, but misrepresents himself. Him we do not respect, but the soul whose organ he is, would he let it appear through his action, would make our knees bend. When it breathes through his intellect, it is genius ; when it breathes through his will, it is virtue ; when it flows through his affection, it is love. And the blindness of the intellect begins when it would be something of itself. The weakness of the will begins when the individual would be something of himself. All reform aims, in some one particular, to let the great soul have its way through us ; in other words, to engage us to obey.[1]

This collective *Ego*, this best self, this element of common consciousness in man as a member of society, standing behind and operating through the ordinary individual consciousness, is precisely, and from first to last, and nothing else than, the subject matter of Metaphysic as it has been understood since Kant. As Biology is the science conversant with life, its manifestations, its kinds, and changes, and formulates the laws of them ; so Metaphysic is the science conversant with the collective consciousness of man as a member of society ; it investigates the manifestations, the kinds, and the development of those ideas which, as Mr. Arnold says in another place, "gradually and on an immense scale discover themselves and become, instead of being ready-made in precise and reduced dimensions to suit the narrow mind of the individual."[2] And I have quoted

---

[1] Emerson's "Essays, Lectures, and Orations" (London: Orr, 1851), pp. 121, follg.
[2] "Literature and Dogma," Preface, xiv.

these passages from Mr. Emerson at some length, because in spite of their rhetorical character, they state accurately, and with considerably more detail and distinctness than Mr. Arnold ever does, and moreover, in perfectly intelligible language, what is meant by the collective consciousness, and how it acts upon and through the ordinary and undeniable experience of everybody.

Let us now see how a great French critic describes this common consciousness:—

Le plus grand progrès de la physiologie moderne a été de montrer que la vie de la plante et celle de l'animal ne sont qu'une résultante d'autres vies, harmoniquement subordonnées et aboutissant à un concert unique. La vie du vertèbre est la résultante centralisée de l'individualité de chaque vertèbre ; un arbre est la consonnance de milliers de bourgeons. *La conscience est de même une résultante de millions d'autres consciences concordant à un même but.* Le cellule est déjà une petite concentration personnelle ; plusieurs cellules consonnant ensemble forment une conscience au second degré (homme ou animal). Les consciences au second degré, en se groupant, forment *des consciences au troisième degré*, consciences de villes, consciences d'Eglises, consciences de nations, produites par des millions d'individus vivant d'une même idée, ayant des sentiments communs. Pour le matérialisme, il n'y a que l'atome qui existe pleinement ; mais pour le vrai philosophe, pour l'idéaliste, la cellule existe plus que l'atome, l'individu existe plus que la cellule ; la nation, l'Eglise, la cité existent plus que l'individu, puisque l'individu se sacrifie pour ces entités, qu'un réalisme grossier regarde comme de pures abstractions.[1]

[1] Renan : "Dialogues et Fragments Philosophiques" (Paris, Calmann Lévy, 1876), p. 90. Compare p. 164, where he speaks of this common consciousness, coeval with language, as "la constitution des groupes d'idées qui devenus le patrimoine de chaque race, dominent encore aujourd'hui la marche de l'humanité." On what may be called the natural history of these groups Comparative Philology and Anthropology, and what is called in Germany "Völkerpsychologie," the Psychology of Peoples and Races, are daily throwing important light. What metaphysic does in regard to these ideas is not so much to describe the external circumstances of their origin, nor the modes of their manifestation, as to determine their typical forms, by comparing those of greater with those of less complexity ; and by decomposing each into its constituent elements, to discover the relation they bear *to one another*, and the laws of their

That the common or social consciousness is more real than, *existe plus que,* the individual and empirical consciousness, is a statement which to English modes of thought savours of the unmeaning; and it is into this "réalisme grossier" of English thinking that Mr. Arnold lapses at pp. 67 follg. of "God and the Bible," when he tells us that to say, as Descartes says, that some things "have more objective reality," "partake in more degrees of being," "have more reality, more being," than other things, is to use words which "have absolutely no force at all, we simply cannot follow their meaning" (p. 69). Yet in "Literature and Dogma" we find him never tired of saying, with as great distinctness as M. Renan, and with more iteration, that the "impersonal" self which we share with others (p. 264) is "real," whereas the individual self is "apparent" (pp. 63, 259, 359); that it is "true and permanent" (p. 88), whereas the ordinary and empirical self is "lower and transient" (p. 202). Well, this more permanent reality is what we are thinking of —this and nothing else is our subject-matter—when we speak of metaphysic; it is the higher self, the common consciousness, which culture extricates from the lower and individual self, and which, as having "claim to paramount authority," we are recommended by Mr. Arnold to organize and embody in the State.

But there is another aspect which Mr. Arnold seizes in this higher and impersonal self, as he proceeds. In "Culture and Anarchy" he is arguing against "the mere doing as one likes, affirming one's self, and one's self just as it is,"[1] which we prize so much in this country, "the Englishman's heaven-born privilege of doing as he likes," marching where he likes, meeting where he likes, bawling what he likes, breaking what he likes;[2] and by con-

---

development. Metaphysic may be called the morphology, as distinguished from the natural history, of this "third degree of consciousness."

[1] "Culture and Anarchy," p. 80.   [2] Ibid. p. 95.

fronting these individualist and anarchic claims with the claim to authority of the best self by which we are all impersonal and at harmony, he is naturally led to assign to the social consciousness an exclusively moral or practical operation, and not any authority or even importance in confronting the intellectual anarchy which we no less prize in this country, the heaven-born privilege of the English Protestant of *thinking as he likes*. Indeed, he goes so far as to affirm positively in one place,[1] " Now thought and speculation is an individual matter ;" and on the next page that " man philosophizes best alone." I shall have to return to this admission hereafter, and to show how much of the unsoundness of Mr. Arnold's later speculations in " Literature and Dogma," and in " God and the Bible," is due to the fact that he sets himself to carry out this maxim. At present it is enough for my purpose to note that philosophizing alone, is incompatible with Mr. Arnold's idea of culture as that which brings us into contact with " the best that is known and thought in the world," with the "main stream of man's advance . . . . towards knowing himself and the world, things as they are ;" and has been the fruitful parent of all the " stock notions" and intellectual " petrifactions"[2] which it is his aim in recommending culture to " bathe" and " float" with " a fresh stream of disinterested consciousness," and by this means to dissolve. It is obvious, too, that at this stage at least of his progress he is using an *argumentum ad homines*; for the collective thought with which the individual philosophizing is contrasted is not the collective thought of society or of the world, to which culture appeals, but the collective thought of the various sects of Protestant Dissenters. He says : " A free play of individual thought is at least as much impeded by membership of a small congregation as by the membership of a great Church. . . . Thinking by batches of fifty is to the full as fatal to free thought as

---

[1] "Culture and Anarchy," pp. 185, 186. [2] Ibid. p. 184.

thinking by batches of thousands;"[1] and he commends the utterance of the *Daily News* to the effect that "the common reason of society ought to check the aberrations of individual eccentricity," adding that "this common reason of society looks very like our best self or right reason to which we want to give authority, by making the action of the State or nation, in its collective character, the expression of it."[2] "Without society," he adds afterwards emphatically, "there can be no human perfection;"[3] and his constant objection to "the dissidence of Dissent" is, that it cuts off Nonconformists from "the stream of the vital movement" of the world's thought; so that we may be justified in supposing that when he contrasts thought with conduct, and suggests that the first is the proper function of the individual, while the latter depends, in order to be right, upon the recognition of the paramount authority of the "common reason of society," he is confronting them, as he himself says when he confronts Hebraism and Hellenism, "with what I may call a rhetorical purpose,"[4] and that the great aim of culture is not to make us follow the authority of the best self in matters of conduct only, but to bring us into relation with "the *whole* play of the universal order,"[5] with the *whole* intelligible law of things.

But we are not long left in doubt as to Mr. Arnold's real meaning. In "Culture and Anarchy" he is seeking a cure for rowdyism, "doing as one likes," in practice; in his next book, "St. Paul and Protestantism," he is seeking a cure for the intellectual follies and narrowness of Dissent, and here he evidently feels that his maxim about "man's philosophizing best alone" must go to the wall, for it is in fact the very principle of private judgment upon which Protestant Dissent is founded.

[1] "Culture and Anarchy," p. 187. [2] Ibid. p. 120.
[3] Ibid. p. 227. [4] Ibid. p. 130. [5] Ibid. pp. 132, 184.

In "St. Paul and Protestantism" he says, as he said in "Culture and Anarchy," "The law of the moral order stretches beyond the private conscience; is independent of it and absolute;"[1] but not, it would appear from "Culture and Anarchy" at least, the law of the intellectual order beyond the eccentricities of private judgment. Yet as early as on page 12 of "St. Paul and Protestantism" we get, from the exigencies of the author's polemic against Dissent, a new position taken up. The resistance of the Church to the one-sidedness of Puritanism was, we are told, "as favourable to the growth of thought and to sound philosophy as it was consonant to common sense." It is, then, the national intelligence, and not the individual, which we must confront with the eccentricities of sectarianism. Why—if it be true that thought and speculation is an individual matter? Let us hear what Mr. Arnold has to say in praise of the National Church and of its ministers :—

And thus (*i.e.*, by not separating for differences in opinion) they do homage to an ideal of Christianity which is *larger, higher, and better than either their notions* (he is speaking of the Dean of Ripon and Bishop Ryle) *or those of their opponents*, and in respect of which both their notions and those of their opponents are inadequate.[2]

This "larger, higher, and better" intelligence which the nation has in its collective capacity, instead of tying itself to narrow and fixed ideas, as Puritanism does, is continually undergoing that law of transformation and development which obtains in a National Church.[3] We then have Dr. Newman's "Essay on Development of Christian Doctrine" quoted to show how this transformation and development takes place. It takes place, as Mr. Arnold commends Dr. Newman for saying, not as "an effect of wishing or resolving, or of forced enthusiasm or of any mechanism of reasoning, or of any subtlety of

---

[1] "St. Paul and Protestantism," p. 117. [2] Ibid., Preface, vii.
[3] Ibid. viii.

intellect," but "*of its own innate power of expansion* within the mind in its season, though with the use of reflection and argument and original thought, more or less as it may happen, with a dependence on the ethical growth of the mind itself, and with a reflex influence upon it."[1] This example of Dr. Newman emboldens Mr. Arnold to say of the social consciousness in its intellectual aspect and operation, as standing above and having authority over the private reason, what he had hitherto only ventured to say of it in its moral and political aspect, as standing above the private conscience:—

Thought and science follow their own law of development; they are slowly elaborated in the growth and forward pressure of humanity, in what Shakspeare calls

"the prophetic soul
Of the wide world dreaming on things to come;"

their ripeness and unripeness, as Dr. Newman most truly says, are not an effect of our wishing and resolving; rather do they seem brought about by a power such as Goethe figures by the *Zeit-Geist* or Time-spirit, and St. Paul describes as a divine power *revealing* additions to what we possess already.[2]

"But sects of men are apt to be shut up in sectarian ideas of their own, and to be less open to new general ideas than the main body of men;" and thus it was by maintaining the solidarity of the Christian consciousness that the Catholic Church followed, Mr. Arnold (apparently still on the track of Dr. Newman) tells us, a true instinct: "but the right *philosophical* developments she vainly imagined herself to have the power to produce, and her attempts in this direction were at most a prophecy of this power, as alchemy is said to have been a prophecy of chemistry."[3]

This, so far as I am aware, is the first appearance in Mr. Arnold's theological writings of the *Zeit-Geist*, or Time-

---

[1] "St. Paul and Protestantism," p. 30.   [2] Ibid. pp. 35, 36.
[3] Ibid. pp. 35, 36.

spirit, which plays so important a part in "Literature and Dogma;" and we see how he is driven upon the idea of it gradually, and away from his notion of thought and speculation being an individual matter, by the exigencies, as I have already noted, of his polemic against the eccentricities of Puritanism. Here, then, we have the counterpart in the sphere of science and intelligence of the "best self," which, as we have seen, in matters of conduct, has the *rôle* of regulating the insubordinate desires; and whose organization in the State would have the effect of harmonizing the conflicting classes and tendencies of society.

Shall we say that Mr. Arnold has here two principles or one? that he means to keep his "best self" in one pocket and his "Time-spirit" in another, just as a psychologist of the Scottish School might put the "intellectual faculties" in one imaginary pigeon-hole of the mind, and the conscience and "moral faculties" in another equally imaginary pigeon-hole? He never, so far as I have seen, explicitly combines the "best self" and the *Zeit-Geist*; he never says in so many words, the "best self" is the common consciousness of social man in so far as it influences practice, and the *Zeit-Geist* is the common consciousness of social man in so far as it controls thought and speculation. But in speaking of the one-sided enthusiasm for ideas characterizing certain nations, and notably the Greeks, which he calls Hellenism, and after contrasting it with the one-sided enthusiasm for practice characterizing certain other nations, and notably the Jews, which he calls Hebraism, as if to obviate the inference that he is here dealing with two principles which are ultimately diverse, he says—

> And yet the lesson must perforce be learned that the human spirit is wider than the most priceless of the forces which bear it onward, and that to the whole development of man Hebraism itself is, like Hellenism, but a contribution.[1]

---

[1] "Culture and Anarchy," p. 142.

And just as he says elsewhere that "the law of the moral order *stretches beyond the private conscience* of the individual," and is independent of it and absolute ;[1] so here he says, speaking of a specific question, that of immortality—

Above and beyond the inadequate solution which Hebraism and Hellenism (here) attempt *extends the immense and august problem* itself, and the human spirit which gave birth to it.[2]

This common consciousness which Mr. Arnold has thus brought so vividly before us as the "best self" and the *Zeit-Geist*, and less felicitously perhaps, because more vaguely, as "the prophetic soul of the wide world dreaming on things to come," is, then, the fundamental principle of modern metaphysic since Kant. It is the "Ego" of Fichte and Schelling, and the "Absolute" of Hegel. And the transition from the standing-point of individual thinking to the standing-point of the common consciousness, which we have seen forced upon Mr. Arnold by the exigencies of his polemic against the Dissenters, is compared by Kant, in an often-quoted passage[3] in the second supplement to the "Critique of Pure Reason," to the revolution in astronomy made by Copernicus.

It is with us (Kant says) as it was at first with the idea of Copernicus, who, dissatisfied with the theories of the heavens, on the assumption that the starry host revolved round the spectator, tried whether he could not succeed better if he supposed the spectators to move and the stars to remain at rest.

This, then, is what I mean when I say that Mr. Matthew Arnold is differentiated from the main and characteristic body of English thinkers by having the metaphysical point of view, and that *he builds his negative criticism of current politics and religion on the*

---

[1] "St. Paul and Protestanism," p. 117.
[2] "Culture and Anarchy," p. 143.   [3] "Werke," vol. ii. p. 670.

same intellectual area as Strauss built his constructive edifice of doctrine upon. Mr. Arnold has the true and fruitful standpoint in metaphysic, and (*exempli gratiâ*) the late Mr. Mill had the wrong and sterile one, in the same sense as Copernicus had the true and fruitful point of view in astronomy, and Ptolemy had the wrong and sterile one. And it is this elevation in his point of view which forms the real justification of Mr. Arnold's comparison of the metaphysical developments of the mediæval Church to alchemy :—

The right *philosophical* developments she vainly imagined herself to have the power to produce, and her attempts in this direction were at most but a prophecy of this power, as alchemy is said to have been a prophecy of chemistry.[1]

It is because the mediæval Church worked from the wrong metaphysical point of view, the point of view of the individual, instead of that of the social consciousness, and not because its point of view was metaphysical at all, that justifies Mr. Arnold in saying—

Every one who perceives and values the power contained in Christianity must be struck to see how, at the present moment, the progress of this power seems to depend upon its being able *to disengage itself from speculative accretions which encumber it*.[2]

For "it was," he tells us, "inevitable that the speculative metaphysics should come"[3] and develop the Biblical data, inasmuch as "the Bible raises many and great questions of philosophy and criticism ;"[4] but "for the adequate development of Christian doctrine, so far as theology exhibits this metaphysically and scientifically," the Church, whether Ante-Nicene or Post-Nicene, "has never yet furnished a channel."[5] It is therefore "of capital importance" that the Church of England has "left her mind comparatively open . . . . for the

---

[1] "St. Paul and Protestantism," p. 36. [2] Ibid. p. 56.
[3] Ibid. p. 39. [4] Ibid. p. 36. [5] Ibid. p. 35.

admission of philosophy and criticism as they slowly developed themselves outside the Church and filtered into her."[1] It is of capital importance for two reasons — 1st, because "what essentially characterizes a religious teacher and gives him his permanent worth and vitality is, after all, just the scientific value of his teaching, its correspondence with important facts, and the light it throws on them;"[2] and secondly, because "philosophy and criticism have become a great power in the world, and inevitably tend to alter and develop Church doctrine so far as this doctrine is, as to a great extent it is, philosophical and critical;" and whatever "hinders their filtering" into Church doctrine from the secular world without, "and becoming incorporated, hinders truth and the natural progress of things."[3] For the scientific sense in man, the sense "which seeks exact knowledge," "never asserted its claims so strongly" as at the present time; and "the propensity of religion to neglect those claims, and the peril and loss to it from neglecting them, never were so manifest."[4]

We see, then, from the foregoing pages, what is the basis of Mr. Arnold's negative criticism—we see the ground which his thought covers, and the place where he stands—first, when he confronts the social anarchy, the doing each as we like, which is so much prized in this country, with the "better self" by which we are at one and impersonal; and secondly, when he confronts the religious "Philistine," his private judgment and his "stock notions," with the *Zeit-Geist*, or perpetually transforming influence of a larger social intelligence. We have seen that this "best self" and this *Zeit-Geist* are only two aspects of one and the same fact—namely, the common consciousness of social man; and that this common consciousness has been the specific subject-matter of metaphysic since the time of Kant. We

---

[1] "St. Paul and Protestantism," p. 51.   [2] Ibid. pp. 71, 72.
[3] Ibid. p. 35.   [4] Ibid. p. 72.

have seen that the change from the point of view of the individual in philosophizing to the point of view of the common consciousness, is that which differentiates metaphysical inquiry since the reform of Kant from metaphysical inquiry before Kant. We have seen that this change is the specific characteristic of Mr. Arnold's procedure in assailing anarchy, whether in society or in opinion; that it is the change from the private spirit to "that universal order which the intellect feels after as a law and the heart feels after as a benefit;"[1] and that this change is one of the same importance and of the same kind as that which Copernicus made in the point of view of the old Ptolemaic astronomy. Let us now try to understand, with Mr. Arnold's help, something more about this common consciousness—what it does, and how it works.

And here it is very important to remember that we must beware of hypostatizing this common consciousness of society too much; of thinking of it as a thing which is kept in the House of Commons, or in the Archbishop's Palace at Lambeth, or in the office of the Board of Works. It is safer not to hypostatize it at all, but to speak only of its operation. As Mr. Arnold says when speaking of God, *what* God is we know not—we are simply aware of his operations; so indeed we may say of the individual man, *what* he is we don't know, but we know his thoughts and we know his works. Of these we can speak, and from them infer his character. Now what are the operations which this *Zeit-Geist*, this "best self," this common consciousness of society, performs? What are the organs through which it acts? Well, we are all its organs. "A man," says Emerson, "is the façade of a temple in which all wisdom and all good abide." It is when *we*, each of us, act and think in a particular manner that the common consciousness is acting and thinking through us. What, then, is this particular manner?

---

[1] "St. Paul and Protestantism," p. 73.

"From within and from behind," to quote Emerson again, "a light shines through us upon things, and makes us aware that we are nothing, but the light is all." When does this happen? How is it to be distinguished from our manner of operating as individuals?

It will be convenient, for the sake of clearness, if we confine ourselves to the thinking aspect of this common reason, and neglect, for the present at least, its acting aspect. And we shall not be thereby making again an arbitrary distinction between the two aspects, which we saw before that Mr. Arnold does *not* make, because, as we shall see presently, the ideas which the common reason has, are not, like the ideas which the individual reason has, *merely* theoretical, but are ideas which are themselves operative and influential in transforming practice and knowledge alike. They are what we sometimes call *principles*, meaning by principles not merely something which is true or untrue, but something which lives and moves and operates. In speaking of the operations of the common consciousness as ideas, we mean, then, to present in one view both its acting aspect as the "best self" and its thinking aspect as the *Zeit-Geist*.

What is an idea of the common consciousness of social man, or, as we may call it shortly, a metaphysical idea? I say "metaphysical," because these ideas *are* metaphysical in the same sense as the "best self" and the *Zeit-Geist* are metaphysical—that is, not "non-natural" as Mr. Arnold says in his most recent work, "God and the Bible," but beyond the natural, in the sense in which conscience is beyond and above the natural desires, and society is beyond and above a "state of nature," and a conception scientifically adequate is beyond and above the "stock notion" of "the practical man," "who is apt to scrape the surface of things only."[1]

We are all familiar with the comparisons which have been instituted between society, or the "body politic" as

[1] "St. Paul and Protestantism," p. 83.

it is generally called, in this connection, and the animal body. Both are organisms—*i.e.*, both are composed of parts which act upon and are reacted upon by the centre of the structure. In this simple and abstract sense of the word "organism," some thinkers have maintained that the solar system is also an organism. But this general similarity of the social and the animal structures, the recognition of which marked an important advance in social science, has tempted philosophers from Plato downwards to work out all sorts of minute resemblances between the two, which are often merely imaginary. We find Mr. Herbert Spencer, for example, after comparing the "currents of merchandise" flowing through the community to the blood, going on to compare the gold and silver coinage to the round discs or corpuscles in the blood.[1] More important to notice, perhaps, for our present purpose, are the false judgments of historical events which are founded on another comparison of a similar kind. I mean the assumption that the moral duties of a community are the same in kind as the moral duties of an individual. Governments representing free communities, for instance, are blamed for not acting towards one another, or towards the individual citizen, according to the same ethical principles as those which guide the actions of individual citizens towards one another. Machiavelli perceived the distinction between the two classes of actions clearly, though under the influence of the ideas of antiquity he perhaps expressed it paradoxically. The resort to force which belongs legitimately to communities, both in their dealings with one another and with their own citizens, but not with the same latitude to citizens in dealing with one another, is an instance in point. One reason for this distinction would seem to be that the duties of individuals to one another are conditioned by their having a moral superior in the community to which they belong; whilst communities, whether in relation to one another or in

[1] "Essays Scientific, Political and Speculative," vol. i. p. 414.

relation to their own citizens, have no such moral superior. However this may be, the distinction is one which is obvious to any one attending to the question, and has led thoughtful writers to speak of the "inherent immorality" of society as they speak of "the Machiavelism of nature :"—

"La nature," says M. Renan, " est d'une insensibilité absolue, d'une immoralité transcendante, si j'ose le dire. L'immoralité de l'histoire et l'iniquité inhérente aux sociétés humaines ne sont pas moindres. La société, quoi qu'on fasse, sera toujours dans l'impossibilité d'être juste."[1]

I should prefer to speak both in the one case and in the other in the spirit of the old Hebrew prophet representing the august centre of government in the community of Israel in His relation to the individual citizens : " For my thoughts are not your thoughts, neither are your ways my ways. For as the heavens are higher than the earth, so are my ways higher than your ways, and my thoughts than your thoughts."[2] Indeed the comparison of the structure of society to the animal organism, with which we set out, instead of leading us to the superficial conclusion that the ethics of the community are *therefore* the same in kind as the ethics of the individual, might have led us, on closer examination, to an exactly opposite result. If society be an organism, it would seem to follow that its normal action would resemble the normal action of its unit, the individual, *as little* as the normal action of the animal organism resembles that of its unit, the cell of protoplasm.

These considerations, if they be at all near the truth, will have prepared us to find that ideas of the *Zeit-Geist* or common consciousness, what we have called metaphysical ideas, differ widely both in dimension and in

---

[1] Renan, "Fragments Philosophiques," pp. 13, 41, &c. Cf. Mr. Leslie Stephen's "Confessions of an Agnostic" in *Fortnightly Review* for June, 1876, p. 852.
[2] Isa. lv. 8, 9.

structure from the ideas of the "ordinary self"—*i.e.*, of the individual mind. And this is the case—

(*a*) First as to dimension. We find Mr. Arnold saying of certain ideas that "they gradually and *on an immense scale* discover themselves and become," instead of being "ready-made in precise and reduced dimensions to suit the narrow mind of the individual."[1] The essential characteristic of a metaphysical idea is that it is an idea of the *whole* of its object; of *all* its aspects and conditions, and not merely of some of them. Now what is the character of the ordinary notion which a man has of a thing? It is not the whole thing he has in his mind, but a bit of the thing, or, in logical language, "an abstraction" from the whole thing. It is a kind of mental picture or illustrative image of the thing as it looks from a particular point of view, covering a bundle of attributes the selection and grouping of which has been determined by the same particular point of view, and registered by a name. Comparative philology has shown how these particular points of view were reached. It has shown that words, such as we know them, are a secondary formation; that the first significant speech of man was not a word describing an isolated thing, but a composite utterance, in which many words were embedded together, describing a composite scene. Then disintegration begins (I am compressing still further Mr. Wallace's excellent account of this matter given in his Prolegomena to the logic of Hegel[2]); and the elements of the composite utterance become independent words held together by the syntax of the sentence. These linguistic fragments then

---

[1] "Literature and Dogma," Preface, xiv.

[2] "Logic of Hegel," Prol., p. lxxxvi. See also the *Contemporary Review*, April, 1876, "The Jelly-fish Theory of Language;" Sayce's "Principles of Comparative Philology," 2nd ed. (Trübner), pp. viii.-x. (xii. xiii.), 136, 144, 151, 152, 159, 217, 234, 243 (215, 226); also Waitz, "Anthropologie der Naturvölker," i. p. 272, &c. (English Trans., p. 241); also Sweet on "Words, Logic and Grammar" in the Proceedings of the London Philological Society for 1877.

become fixed in speech as the names of the several objects which entered into the original scene; and represent the objects, not as they are in themselves, but as they appeared from a particular point of view—viz., as parts of the scene. It is just as if we were to take the well-known figure of the kneeling acolyte in Domenichino's "Communion of St. Jerome" out of his surroundings in the picture, and mount him on a blank canvas by himself.

This is the kind of idea that constitutes the medium of exchange in ordinary intellectual commerce. The Germans call it a *Vorstellung* or illustrative image. Mr. Matthew Arnold himself calls it "a mere notion of the understanding," and he rightly contrasts with it a "religious idea,"[1] and elsewhere "a rational idea" which is not only a part but a "*chief* part of our experience."[2] This contrast in the dimension of the ideas employed is the chief point in his comparison of the Epistle to the Hebrews with the genuine work of St. Paul.

We have seen then what the ideas of the "ordinary self" of the individual are like: we have seen that they represent *fragments* of experience, and not the whole of experience, abstractions from and aspects of the object, and not the object in its totality, not the *ensemble* of its conditions. Let us now see how M. Renan describes the springing up of one of these large-scale ideas of the common consciousness which are called metaphysical:—

L'homme allait inattentif. Tout à coup un silence se fait, comme un temps d'arrêt, une lacune de la sensation: "Oh! Dieu! se dit-il alors, que ma destinée est étrange! Est-il bien vrai que j'existe? Qu'est-ce que le monde? Ce soleil, est-ce moi? Rayonne-t-il de mon cœur? O père, je te vois par delà les nuages!" Puis le bruit du monde extérieur recommence: l'échappée se ferme; mais à partir de ce moment, un être en apparence égoiste fera des actes inexplicables, agira contre son intérêt evident, se subordonnera, à une fin qu'il ne connaît pas, éprouvera le besoin de s'incliner et d'adorer.[3]

[1] "St. Paul and Protestantism," p. 165.   [2] Ibid. p. 107.
[3] "Fragments Philos.," pp. 40, 41.

Observe that M. Renan here describes the emergence of the social consciousness, the "better self," and *along with it and constituting it,* the most simple and primitive metaphysical idea. Divested of emotional language, we have here a sense of aloofness, a certain posture taken up, a certain relation established; we have what is called a *synthesis,* a putting together of two elements—on the one side the thinking and feeling man, and on the other an indeterminate and obscure but immense object of consciousness—the universe around him, and of which hitherto he had formed an unconscious part. This relation, in which the two correlatives merely confront one another for the first time—nothing more, is what is called in philosophy "Being." Mr. Arnold says in his later works that he does not understand what "Being" means. It means this detachment which M. Renan describes, mere "over-againstness" to consciousness, or, as the Germans would say, "das reine Gegenüber." There is as yet no question as to *what* is over-against me, or *what* I am, or *what* is my relation to that which is over-against me, but merely the consciousness that I am over-against an immense indeterminate object, and that this immense indeterminate object is over-against me. It is merely "Est-il bien vrai que j'existe?" "Is it really true that I am standing aloof and alone over-against this immensity?" Experience is not yet born, this feeling of isolation is its birth-pang; and the outline which I draw round the terms of this primitive relation, so as to include them both, becomes the rude mould into which all my subsequent experience is poured. And mere outline as it is, we can see at once that it is more concrete than the *Vorstellung* or ordinary notion of the understanding, which serves to do the intellectual business of life, because it is an outline enclosing the *whole* of experience, and not, like the *Vorstellung,* a representative image covering a fragment of experience only. This larger idea, which emerges first at the birth of the social consciousness, is what is called in German philosophy a *Begriff*, which means what we have called "a synthesis."

Now we can see at once that this primitive synthesis of Being is not our synthesis; it is not the mould into which we of this age pour *our* experience. It would be more true to say perhaps that the dominant conception with us, our synthesis, is the idea of development. It is the idea of development which has been framing and moulding more and more of our experience since the time of Lamarck. Thus, we find Mr. Arnold, for instance, appealing to it against the Dissenters, with the same assurance as he appeals to the *Zeit-Geist*, to legitimate his assumption of the non-occurrence of miracles. To separate for opinions, we read, is worse than having, as we have in the Anglican "Articles of Religion," an inadequate and unsatisfactory synthesis, because it cuts the Dissenter off from the growth of the community; it leads him to give a finality and absoluteness to his doctrines which they have not; "it is to be false to the idea of development."[1] To appeal to the *Zeit-Geist* of our age, and to appeal to the idea of development, are, with Mr. Arnold, the same thing. The formula of our Zeit-Geist *is* development. We have only to read George Eliot's last two novels to see how every phase of many-sided thought, in our times, can be illuminated by this one idea. It has transformed, as we know, or is transforming, the whole field of knowledge; every science is being reconstituted by it; it has "turned its light" upon our old problems, and shown us, not so much the answers to them, as the ineptitude of putting the great questions of life in the way we have hitherto put them; our old distinctions and oppositions fall away of themselves, and a wholly new order of questions has arisen. What a distance between this complex synthesis in which we stand, and the simple "O Dieu, est-ce bien vrai que

[1] "St. Paul and Protestantism," p. 24.

j'existe?" with which human experience begins! What a distance from our synthesis even to the synthesis of "Substance and Accidents" which framed and moulded the experience of the men of the thirteenth century of our era! or again to the synthesis of expiation which occupied the mental field when the ancient societies were falling to pieces, and, as Mr. Arnold says, "the mind of the whole world was imbrued in the idea of blood."[1] How inadequate they seem! Yet, though inadequate now, they were once adequate, and in their own age they enveloped, as with a cloud, the whole horizon of thought.

(*b*) So much, then, as to the dimensions of metaphysical ideas, of the syntheses of the *Zeit-Geist*, or consciousness of the community; they include, each in its turn and for the nonce, the *whole* of the experience of an age. Now, secondly, as to their structure. In saying "structure," I am trying to find a word for that element of resistance which we experience in thinking of all kinds. We can only move in certain directions; and just as we cannot scratch the lobe of our left ear with the toe of our left foot, whereas a dog can, because his physical structure is different from ours; so we cannot think anything or anyhow we please. Aristotle speaks of the reasoning process being "bound"—δέδεται ἡ διάνοια. It is enclosed within the four walls, so to speak, of its thought; and this inclosure is due to structure. When, again, we get entangled in a paradox, and we find that thinking is for the moment stopped, what stops it? It is the resistance arising from the collision of structural elements in the ideas themselves, just as it is the interference of the structural elements in a skein of silk which stops our unwinding it. The structure of the *Vorstellung* or illustrative idea of ordinary thinking may be likened to that of a cone or convergent pencil of rays, having for its base the series of qualities in the object which are

---

[1] "St. Paul and Protestantism," p. 173.

appreciable together from a single point of view, and for its apex the name combined with a representative image of the object so appreciated. And whatever qualities there may be in the object which refuse to lend themselves to this convergence on a single focus, they simply disappear; or if they appear, they obliterate by their appearance those other qualities with which they conflict. This phenomenon we are familiar with in physics under the name of "interference;" in the logic of the notion it is thus expressed by Sir William Hamilton—"When an object is determined by the affirmation of a certain character, this object *cannot be thought* to be the same when such character is denied of it."[1] Such, for instance, is the structure of what Mr. Arnold calls "a mere notion of the understanding, and not a religious idea," in the Epistle to the Hebrews, where it is said that Christ's death was a perfect sacrifice which consummated the imperfect sacrifices of the Jewish law.[2] It is a fasciculus of that portion of the attributes of a great historical event, which can be grouped from a particular point of view, and from which all those qualities of the event which cannot be appreciated from, or which make against, this point of view, are excluded.

The structure of an idea of the *Zeit-Geist*, or common consciousness, as it is much more ample, is of necessity much more complex. It gets this greater complexity from two causes—from the nature of the common consciousness, and from the fact that it is the idea not of a part of the object, but of the whole of it. The consciousness of the community is not, like that of the individual, a single stream of thinking, but the convergence of many streams of thinking; just as society itself is a convergence and conflict of many opposite tendencies. These opposing tendencies correct each other, as we know, and give to society the means of

---

[1] "Lectures on Logic" (Blackwood, 1860), vol. i. p. 81.
[2] "St. Paul and Protestantism," pp. 164, 165.

developing, transforming, and improving itself, which the individual man has not. We may say of the community, as Aristotle said of Nature, it is "like a man who acts as his own physician."[1] The one-sidedness of one stream of thinking setting in a particular direction is corrected by meeting and mixing with another stream of thinking coming from the opposite direction; and the *Zeit-Geist*, or spirit of any particular age, is the synthesis or mixture of these opposing streams. We get the same result if we contrast the view of one side or aspect of an object, such as we get in ordinary thought, with the claim which the mind of man makes to see the object *as it is*, in all its aspects, on all its sides, to see the whole of it. The object itself is the result of the equilibrium of opposing forces: and *its process*, as we should now say in evolutionary language, is just the play of these forces, their conflict with one another. We cannot gather into a *Vorstellung*, or convergent pencil of attributes, this play of forces; to ordinary thinking the object is not a process; it can only be seized in one of its statical aspects; it must be *supposed at rest*. On the other hand, when it is said that metaphysic conceives the object as it really is in itself, we mean that it conceives the object, not supposed at rest, but, as it actually is, in process; not as a fasciculus of attributes, but as the point in which conflicting forces meet and make reality.

The metaphysical idea or synthesis of the *Zeit-Geist* will thus contain, in its very constitution and structure, those seeds of internal conflict and disruption which we find in all living things as distinguished from artificial products, bearing the mark of the workmanship and volition of the individual.

We shall see the nature of this synthesis of opposites best in a familiar example. Take the ordinary English or French notion of liberty. "What a Liberal means by

---

[1] Phys. Ausc., B. 8. μάλιστα δὲ δῆλον, ὅταν τις ἰατρεύῃ αὐτὸς ἑαυτόν· οὕτω γὰρ ἔοικεν ἡ φύσις.

liberty," says M. Renan, as Mr. Arnold quotes him, is
"the non-intervention of the State." It means a vacuum
created and jealously maintained round about the
individual citizen by a system of checks and barriers
against the interference of the community with his
private affairs. This was Mr. Mill's notion of liberty;
it is Mr. Herbert Spencer's: it is the ideal of the great
American Commonwealth. On the Continent this
enthusiasm for "the heaven-born privilege of doing as
one likes" has gone the length in Proudhon and his
followers of what is called the "Abolition of the State."[1]
This is a very natural ideal in old communities like
France or England, where from historical causes the State
is the embodiment of the power and authority of certain
classes, and not of the power and authority of the whole
people. But it is for this very reason an abstraction
of a part of the conditions of national well-being as
appreciated from a particular point of view; it is not a
synthesis of the whole of the conditions. Over against
it and in antagonism to it we have another stream of
thought, descending to us from the communities of
antiquity, in which the State was everything and the
individual had no rights against it. We have Divine
Right and the legal devolution of the supreme magistracy
on the principles which regulate the inheritance of a
private estate, and we have the theory of our Conservative
party that the suffrage is a privilege to be bestowed from
above and not a claim to be rightfully made from below.
This too is an idea of the understanding, an abstraction
of a part of the conditions of well-being made from
a particular point of view. It leaves out of sight the
undeniable fact of experience, that classes in possession
of power habitually govern in their own interest and not
in that of the people at large. But it is the historical
theory as against the theory of the European revolution.

[1] See a little book having this title by Dr. Engländer (Trübner, 1873).

It is the theory of the seventeenth century as against the theory of the eighteenth.

What then is the synthesis which shall hold together these conflicting abstractions? The Germans call it the *Begriff der Selbstbestimmung;* in English, the Synthesis of Self-determination. What is it that actually takes place in a community in which these counter-tendencies are operative? Mr. Arnold's view of the "best self," as extricated by culture and organized in the State, will help us to answer. What takes place is a process, a development, something like this. *The more* the State becomes the expression of the "best self" of an increasing number of its citizens, *the more* the highest liberty of the subject will consist in the application to his own individual life of an authority of which he is becoming in an increasing measure, and according to his culture, the author. As a citizen he is not at liberty "to do as he likes," any more than he is *in foro conscientiae;* but he is free in that he determines his own actions through the middle term of his "better self," as embodied in the community. The condition of self-determination is not, like that of liberty, detachment from, but identification with the community. His accession to it adds to its authority in the same measure as it adds to his liberty. The point to note about the synthesis of freedom or *self-determination through the community,* is that it is not, like the idea of liberty, the idea of a thing ready-made, and done in a moment—

> "Verterit hunc dominus, momento turbinis exit
> Marcus Dama"—

but a gradual process of political and moral development, of which no two citizens can be said to partake at the same time in exactly the same degree. Freedom is not a ready-made thing, a *datum;* but, to use Mr. Arnold's expression, "it gradually and on an immense scale *becomes.*"

The synthesis of self-determination I commend to the

attention of the reader, as a fair and easily understood specimen of what a metaphysical idea, an idea of the Zeit-Geist, of the common consciousness, is like. We see how its dynamical, its developmental character, enables it to hold in solution two conflicting streams of thought which, taken apart, assume the form of immovable and sterile abstractions mutually exclusive of one another. We see too that whilst the abstractions of divine right on the one hand and of liberty on the other represent two *theories about* a part of the object, the synthesis represents a real process which is continually taking place in the object as a whole. This is what, I take it, is meant by saying, as philosophers say, that metaphysical ideas have an objective existence, as well as an existence in our thoughts. They are objective in so far as they are principles actually at work in transforming the world.

Have I outstripped Mr. Arnold in this exposition of the nature of the metaphysical synthesis? No: the elements are all there. There is the element of the paramount authority of the State as we have seen throughout; and there is the liberty of the individual *in vacuo*. Speaking of Wilhelm von Humboldt, Mr. Arnold says: "He saw, of course, that in the end everything comes to this—that the individual must act for himself, and must be perfect in himself;" and then he seems for a moment to fall in with M. Renan's formula, and to maintain these two conflicting elements in their antagonism. "A Liberal believes in liberty"—he is here quoting Renan with approval—"and liberty means the non-intervention of the State. But such an ideal is still a long way off from us, and the very means to remove it to an indefinite distance would be precisely the State's withdrawing its action too soon."[1]

It would seem from this as if the ultimate aim is to be the eventual non-interference of the State. No: this

[1] "Culture and Anarchy," pp. 125, 127.

is only Mr. Arnold's provisional solution: for he asks—and here we see the lineaments of the real synthesis forming themselves around the two conflicting abstractions—"whether we should not try to put into the action of the State as much as possible of right reason or our best self, which may, in this manner, *come back to us with new force and authority?*"[1] But although his mind, as we see, tends towards this metaphysical form of thought continually, and in this particular instance strikes upon it, yet he handles the synthesis faintly and infirmly ἀμυδρῶς μέντοι καὶ οὐδὲν σαφῶς ἀλλ' οἷον ἐν ταῖς μάχαις οἱ ἀγύμναστοι ποιοῦσι.[2]

I said at the outset that Mr. Arnold's negative criticism of political and religious anarchy covered the same metaphysical area as Dr. Strauss's positive construction of religious doctrine; and we have already seen that the element in which he moves, is the element of the consciousness of the community as distinguished from the element of individual consciousness. Now let us compare the synthesis of freedom, which we have just elaborated and made definite from Mr. Arnold's faint and disjointed sketch, with a synthesis expounded by Dr. Strauss. He is speaking of the relation between God and man:—

> Spiritual existence in its truth and reality is found neither in God by himself nor in man by himself, but in the union of God with man; neither in the infinity of the one nor in the finitude of the other, taken by themselves, but in that process of self-surrender and recovery taking place between the two factors, which from the Divine side is revelation, and from the human side is religion.[3]

It will be seen that the structure of these two specimens of the metaphysical synthesis, although their

---

[1] "Culture and Anarchy," p. 120. [2] Arist. Met. i. 4.
[3] See this passage quoted on p. 142.

subject-matter is different, is precisely, point for point, the same; and their fluid or developmental character is the same also.

(*c*) This fluid and developmental character in the metaphysical synthesis brings us to another question. We have seen that internally—*i.e.*, in respect of its structure and of its contents—the synthesis is a process; and that its process is conditioned by the fact of its being the meeting-point of opposite streams of thought. But what as to its genesis? In other words, what is the relation between the synthesis of one epoch and that of the preceding epoch? We have seen what a distance there was from the primitive synthesis of "Being," mere detachment from the *ensemble* and the thought of aloofness from it, with which experience began, and the synthesis of "Development" which is transforming our own thought. How did the social consciousness traverse this distance? how did it get from the one standing-point to the other? how does the *Zeit-Geist* of one age pass over into the *Zeit-Geist* of the next? Does the new synthesis drop from the clouds, as an epoch in human history wears itself out and gives place to the next? as the different species of animals were supposed at one time— how long it seems ago and yet how short a time ago it really is!—to have been created separately and put into the world as they were wanted. Or shall we say that as our ancestor, the Ascidian, has become Man by minute and continuous processes of change, so the synthesis of Being has become the synthesis of Development by a series of growths similarly minute and continuous? We may perhaps with safety admit thus much upon the probable ground of the analogy of nature, now that we have such good reason to believe in the continuous evolution of species; without committing ourselves at present to the explanations which have been offered of the mode of the evolution. Mr. Arnold, for instance, says of these syntheses, "they gradually and on an immense scale *discover themselves* and become." They form themselves "insensibly," they come "almost of themselves," and displace the previous syntheses "easily and without any turmoil of controversial reasonings." "We are not driven off our ground—our ground itself changes with us."[1] All this is a little characteristically *nonchalant* and vague; but it shows that Mr. Arnold holds that there is an evolution in ideas as in species, whatever the mode of it may be.

We have already had before us a passage from Dr. Newman's "Essay on Development," in which he speaks of an "innate power of expansion within the mind in its season," and at the same time states a conviction that the evolution is not an effect of "any mechanism of reasoning." What he means by expansion he tells us in the following words. He is speaking of what he calls a "living idea"—*i.e.*, an idea which has operation, as we saw that the metaphysical synthesis had:—

Let one such idea get possession of the popular mind, or the mind of any set of persons, and it is not difficult to understand the effects which will ensue. There will be a general agitation of thought, and an action of mind both upon itself and upon other minds. New lights will be brought to bear upon the original idea, aspects will multiply and judgments will accumulate. There will be a time of confusion, when conceptions and misconceptions are in conflict; and it is uncertain whether anything is to come of the idea at all, or which view of it is to get the start of the others. After a while some definite form of doctrine emerges; and, as time proceeds, one view of it will be modified or expanded by another, and then combined with a third, till the idea in which they centre will be to each mind separately what at first it was only to all together.[2]

Dr. Newman adds further on:—

Its development then is not like a mathematical theorem

---

[1] "Literature and Dogma," Preface, xiv.
[2] "An Essay on Development of Christian Doctrine" (Toovey, 1845), pp. 35, 36.

worked out on paper, in which each successive advance is a pure evolution from a foregoing, but it is carried on through individuals and bodies of men; it employs their minds as instruments and depends upon them while it uses them.[1]

He ultimately arrives, and it is very remarkable that he should do so if we consider that the "Essay on Development" was written five-and-thirty years ago, at an explanation identical in its outlines with the hypothesis of Natural Selection:—

It often happens, or generally, that various distinct and incompatible elements are found in the origin or infancy of polities, or indeed of philosophies, some of which must be ejected before any satisfactory developments can take place, if any. And they are commonly ejected by the *gradual growth of the stronger*.[2]

How thoughtful and serious is this endeavour of Dr. Newman's to unravel the problem as compared with Mr. Arnold's light and airy way of saying that the ideas "gradually discover themselves on an immense scale and become?" Then again there is the explanation which in substance I take to be Hegel's, which we may put thus. The social consciousness, as it expands and grows more complex with the onward progress of society, becomes at length too large for the mould into which it has hitherto been poured. New elements of experience arise which refuse to be included within the dimensions of the synthesis as it stands; they form themselves consequently into groups outside the lines of the synthesis, and thus become a standing protest against its sufficiency. In time they acquire a coherence of their own, and begin to take the form of a second synthesis, outside the first, and negative of it. We thus get a counter-synthesis, exclusive of the traditional and habitual one. What follows? The traditional synthesis no longer includes the whole—

---

[1] "An Essay on Development of Christian Doctrine," p. 37.
[2] Ibid. pp. 46, 47.

it has become an aspect only of the totality, of experience; it has become an abstraction conditioned from a particular point of view, the point of view of the epoch which is exhausting itself and just passing away. Instead of being any longer a metaphysical idea, it has sunk to a *Vorstellung*, "a mere idea of the understanding," as Mr. Arnold would say. And the counter-synthesis which has arisen over against it is in like manner *an abstraction* conditioned from the particular point of view of the new epoch, of the new social forces which are beginning to emerge and assert themselves, *and not the whole of the fact;* it is an idea of the understanding, negative and exclusive of its predecessor in possession. Thus we are brought back to the formal position from which we started. We have again two antagonistic streams of thinking, coming from opposite sides, and meeting and mixing. Then a third synthesis, in whose process both can be harmonized, again emerges. The formula of this development may be thus expressed: *position* (the traditional synthesis in possession), *opposition* (the counter-synthesis), and, lastly, *composition* (the new synthesis, erasing the conflict by means of a richer and more widely working principle).

Hegel has named this perfectly intelligible mode of development (as it seems to me with needless paradox) the process of "absolute negativity." "Absolute negativity" means negativity which is itself negatived, and thus results in an affirmation: the existing synthesis is "negatived" by the counter-synthesis growing up outside it—excluding it and excluded by it, until the new and riper synthesis arising from the meeting of the two streams of thought "negatives" in its turn the opposition between them by absorbing them both into a larger and more complex process of its own.

As a hypothesis explaining the mode of evolution of social ideas, and standing upon the same footing as the hypothesis of Natural Selection explaining the mode of evolution of species, I conceive that this "absolute negativity" of Hegel's, in spite of its repellent terminology, is like Dr. Newman's principle of the survival of the stronger, worthy of attentive and respectful consideration. The question with the one as with the other is—Does it cover all the facts? But it is a mistake to say that modern metaphysic must stand or fall with this attempt on the part of Hegel to explain the evolution of the social consciousness. We can see that there are a number of subsidiary hypotheses which may complete or modify this formula of the "absolute negativity." There is the view, for instance, that there is a latent syllogistic process intervening between each stage of the evolution; the view dismissed apparently by Dr. Newman. Further, there is the view that a synthesis must be exhausted in its operation by growing into an extreme and impossible form, before a counter-synthesis can arise. An illustration of this may be found in the way in which what Mr. Arnold called Hellenism, the enthusiasm for perfection, wore itself down to the exiguous and at the same time the extreme and extravagant form of a crowd of spectators collected to see Phryne coming up out of the sea in the person of Venus Anadyomene. And in the exhaustion of Hellenism, the counter-principle of Hebraism, the consciousness of sin, rises into importance. "This obstacle to perfection," says Mr. Arnold, "fills the whole scene, and perfection appears remote and rising away from earth in the background."[1]

Once more, there is the subsidiary hypothesis that evolution in social ideas is sometimes brought about by the synthesis of one community, at a particular time, coming across the path of the synthesis of another contemporary community at a lower or a higher stage of development. The intercourse of nations would thus bring about the opposition of a counter-synthesis, and give rise to the effort to re-absorb the conflicting elements in a larger, more complex process.

[1] "Culture and Anarchy," p. 137.

But whatever be the value of these various hypotheses to *explain the mode* of evolution, the important qualities in a modern metaphysician are the recognition of the existence of such a thing as a social consciousness at all, a "better self" which is above the individual; and the recognition of the fact that this social consciousness, like all other living things, is in a condition not statical and fixed, but dynamical and perpetually developing. These two essential qualities of the metaphysician we have seen that Mr. Arnold possesses. He has, too, the flexibility and delicacy of touch which are required in dealing with a moving object like thought without interrupting or obscuring its movement. He has, moreover, an indispensable pre-requisite of the metaphysician, which Plato had to perfection, and that is *humour;* the gift " of imaginatively acknowledging the multiform aspects of the problem of life, and of thus getting itself unfixed from its over-certainty, of smiling at its over-tenacity,"[1] the gift which makes a man shrink from treating any idea " as too serious a thing, and giving it too much power."[2] *Humour*, in this sense, is indispensable to the metaphysician because he has to deal with thoughts which occupy at one time the whole field of consciousness and determine for the nonce all our mental operations, and then grow old and effete, and have to be frankly given up, as a new synthesis looms into view. It is to be lamented that Hegel had not this gift of humour: few Germans have: they are too serious; they think the results they get far too final; and it is a quality conspicuously absent from Hegel's followers.

But there is a not less indispensable habit of the metaphysician which Mr. Arnold has not, and that is strictness—sureness of touch in handling his ideas—what Aristotle calls σοφία. In the preface to his latest work Mr. Arnold makes himself merry at the expense of the German

---

[1] "Culture and Anarchy," p. 147. [2] Ibid. p. 229.

critics for their "vigour and rigour;"[1] and no doubt Germans have not that gift of imaginative detachment from their ideas which is required in a critic. They make too much of them, and carry them out to ridiculous extremes. But still, somewhat of this rigour is wanted if we would find our way through the maze of metaphysical ideas prevalent at any given period of the world, if we would not be "manacled and hoodwinked" by them, as I shall try to show in the sequel that Mr. Arnold frequently is. Metaphysic, Aristotle tells us, is the strictest—ἀκριβεστάτη—of all the sciences, and the habit which shall give us this power of accuracy is σοφία, the habit which we praise when we say of Pheidias that he was λιθουργὸς σοφός, a *finished* sculptor.[2] It is the *Fertigkeit*, the complete mastery of means, which gives the sureness and freedom of handling characteristic of the true artist. That Mr. Arnold has not this sureness and freedom in the handling of ideas of the social consciousness, and that these ideas consequently play fast and loose with him, and, while keeping him in a state of irritable watchfulness, lead him treacherously into all sorts of quagmires, I shall show in a subsequent paper.

CHAPTER III.

A PLEA FOR METAPHYSIC.

An attentive reader of my first paper on this subject will at least have drawn from it one conclusion. He will have understood that metaphysical ideas, when regarded from the point of view of development, become something quite different from what they are usually held to be. He will have seen that the idea of evolution has indeed transformed the whole aspect of this science, as it has transformed, or is transforming, all the other depart-

---

[1] "God and the Bible," Preface, p. viii.   [2] Arist., "Eth.," vi. 7.

ments of human knowledge. We saw, too, that this side of evolution is itself the latest of our metaphysical ideas, and that its genesis may be traced back continuously through a long pedigree of increasingly simpler forms of synthesis, up to the primordial synthesis of "Being," or the mere correlation of subject and object, which arises in the dawn of moral and rational experience, when man, hitherto an unconscious part of the Universe, is first aware of detachment from it, and of its standing over against him, and of himself standing over against it. "Oh, Dieu! est-il bien vrai que j'existe?" It is instructive to look back upon what metaphysic was before it thus transformed itself in the light of its latest synthesis. Here is Auguste Comte's description of it:—

In the theological stage, the human mind, seeking the essential nature of beings, the first and final causes (the origin and purpose) of all effects—in short, absolute knowledge—supposes all phenomena to be produced by the immediate action of supernatural beings.

In the metaphysical stage, which is only a modification of the first, the mind supposes, instead of supernatural beings, abstract forces, veritable entities (that is, personified abstractions), inherent in all beings, and capable of producing all phenomena. What is called the explanation of phenomena is, in this stage, a mere reference of each to its proper entity."[1]

It is clearly this old metaphysic, untransformed by the principle of evolution, that Mr. Arnold also clearly has in his mind when, in the second chapter of "God and the Bible," he treats metaphysicians to the following smart little fusillade:—

Continuo auditæ voces vagitus et ingens.

At the mention of that name *metaphysics*, essence, existence, substance, finite and infinite, cause and succession, something and nothing, begin to weave their eternal dance before us! with the confused murmur of their combinations

[1] "The Positive Philosophy," freely translated and condensed by Harriet Martineau (Trübner, 1875), vol. i. p. 2.

filling all the region governed by *her*, who, far more indisputably than her late-born rival, political economy, has earned the title of the dismal science.[1]

What I complain of in these words is not that they are too strong, but that they are not half strong enough. Let me recommend to Mr. Arnold's attention the terms in which another great religious reformer, Luther, speaks of the philosophical synthesis of the epoch in his time just about to expire. The Schoolmen are, for Luther, "locusts, caterpillars, frogs, lice." And of Aristotle, the father of Scholasticism, says Luther, as recently quoted by Mr. J. W. Draper :[2]—

Truly a devil, a horrid calumniator, a wicked sycophant, a prince of darkness, a real Apollyon, a beast, a most horrid impostor on mankind, one in whom there is scarcely any philosophy, a public and professed liar, a goat, a complete epicure, this twice execrable Aristotle.

Looked at critically, these two forms of words, Mr. Arnold's and Luther's, are only "a deeply moved way of saying" the synthesis of the immediate past has become insufficient for the present expansion of experience. This ardour of denunciation in fact occupies in the minds of religious reformers the place which we have seen that *humour* occupies in a philosopher like Plato; it is an imaginative way of detaching oneself from ideas by which one feels oneself to be dominated. Luther, as we know, was dominated, notably in his doctrine of consubstantiation, by the ideas of the "twice execrable Aristotle;" and we shall find in the sequel, I think, that Mr. Arnold is himself also, like St. Anthony in the desert, dominated by a whole swarm of detached and insubordinate metaphysical entities, buzzing about his head, and keeping him a stranger to "that serenity which," he tells us, "comes from having made order among ideas." Any one who has travelled in a hot country knows what it is

---

[1] "God and the Bible," p. 58.
[2] "The Conflict between Religion and Science" (King, 1875), p. 215.

to rise in the night and search diligently for the booming mosquito which has invaded our curtained bed : and then, when all is done, and the gauze closely drawn again, what it is to find that our pains have but prevented his escape, and that the obnoxious insect is shut in with us instead of being shut out, and is booming above, and settling on us as before. This is, I fear, to some extent the diagnosis of Mr. Arnold's symptoms with respect to metaphysical ideas, and is the real cause of his pathetic complaints. But there is another point of view from which his denunciation of metaphysic may be regarded. In " Culture and Anarchy," as we have seen, he was remonstrating with the Philistine Liberal, and in " St. Paul and Protestantism" with the religious Philistine, and is driven by the exigences of his argument to fall back upon the standpoint of modern metaphysic, of the *Zeit-Geist* and the " better self"—*i.e.*, upon the historical evolution of the collective consciousness. But now in " Literature and Dogma," and in " God and the Bible," he has taken in hand to reason with the irreligious and anxious-to-be-scientific Philistine ; and by sympathizing with him in his fixed ideas, by descending to his level, and by using his own language, to convince him, if it may be, that there is after all something in religion worthy of at least a portion of his attention. " Lo ! I have a controversy with the nations," Mr. Arnold seems to say : " behold, I will plead with all flesh."

It is doubtless well to reason with the Philistines, whether they be religious or irreligious, to try to bring home to them the importance of culture ; it is well to show them that religion is an indestructible and necessary element of true culture ; but it does not do to take them too much into our confidence, lest we become unwarily partakers of their crimes. And when he depreciates philosophy, to please and flatter the middle-class mind, Mr. Arnold should beware lest he be carried too far away from the main stream and vital movement of the best that is thought and known in the world; for he should remember that his new friends, the Philistines who despise philosophy, contemn letters also.

But it is not only his conscious detachment from the synthesis of the immediate past, nor his policy of fraternizing for the moment, and for the purpose of converting him, with the irreligious Philistine, that leads Mr. Arnold to give up the standing-point of the social consciousness, of the *Zeit-Geist*, and of the best self as organized and embodied in the State, which he maintained so fruitfully in " Culture and Anarchy" and in " St. Paul and Protestantism." His inability to maintain himself there is partly also the nemesis of his want of method, his desultoriness :—

Descartes, says Mr. Arnold in " God and the Bible," [1] had a famous philosophical method. . . . . Quite in a contrary fashion we sometimes flatter ourselves with the hope that we may be of use by the very absence of all scientific pretension, by our very want of " a philosophy based on principles interdependent, subordinate, and coherent ;" because we are thus obliged to treat great questions in such a simple way that any one can follow us, &c.

Mr. Arnold here forgets what he said in " St. Paul and Protestantism" [2] about the scientific sense " which seeks exact knowledge ;" that " it never asserted its claims so strongly" as now, and that " the propensity of religion to neglect those claims, and the peril and loss to it from neglecting them, never were so manifest ;" and that whatever hinders the filtering of philosophy and criticism into religious doctrine " hinders truth and the natural progress of things." It would seem, then, that if the conversion of the irreligious Philistine is to be accomplished only by a sacrifice of " coherent" and scientific thinking, of method in short, only by a treatment of great questions in a way so simple " that any one can follow us," it is to be bought at a great price. But let

[1] "God and the Bible," p. 37.   [2] "St. Paul and Protestantism," pp. 71, 72.

us see what Lord Bacon says about the importance of method, and the consequences of neglecting it. Bacon had no more love for metaphysicians than Mr. Arnold manifests in what we may call *his second manner*, his manner in "Literature and Dogma." But he is far too wise to say that truth is to be found by renouncing method. On the contrary he says:—

The intellect left to itself, unless governed and assisted, acts irregularly, and is quite incompetent to overcome the obscurity of things; " (cum) intellectus sibi permissus . . . . nisi regatur et juvetur, res inæqualis (sit) est, et omnino inhabilis ad superandam rerum obscuritatem."[1]

And then he goes on to tell us of the different kinds of illusions, or "idola," as after Plato he calls them, which besiege and gain entrance into the mind, unless it be forearmed against them by method; "ita ut veritati aditus difficilis pateat" ("so that it becomes difficult for truth to enter.")

First, there are illusions common to the human race at large, "having their foundation in the very constitution of man." These are called "the idols of the tribe:" the tendency which we all have, by reason of our natural indolence, to believe in first impressions, to think things much simpler than they really are, to look at great questions "ex analogiâ hominis" and not "ex analogiâ universi"—as we should say, to regard things from the point of view of the individual instead of from the point of view of the *Zeit-Geist*. We saw in the last chapter how baseless but how common is the opinion that society, the State, has the same moral duties as the individual citizen. This, however, is only a particular case of the tribal "idol:" the general character of this illusion is thus given by Bacon—" The spirit of man being of an equal and uniform substance doth usually suppose and feign in nature a greater equality and uniformity than is in

[1] "Novum Organum," xxi.

truth."[1] Instead of talking of the mind as an equal and uniform substance, we should say in modern language, that *the process of thinking, unless regulated, has a tendency, like all other processes in nature, to move along the line of least resistance.* When Mr. Arnold, for instance, makes his fundamental assumption on which "Literature and Dogma" is based, by saying, "The object of religion is conduct, ... and conduct is really the simplest thing in the world,"[2] he is feigning in conduct and religion "a greater equality and uniformity than is in truth." Conduct is a very difficult thing, and by no means simple, not only in the matter of doing but of knowing what ought to be done; and it becomes more difficult and less simple as society increases in complexity; it is again by no means clear or admitted that religion is concerned solely with conduct; that depends upon what religion you are speaking of, and upon the stage of culture at which you are supposing the worshipper to have arrived. In all religions there are other elements mixed, such, for example, as an interested curiosity about man's origin and destiny, or, it may be, *d*isinterested curiosity about the origin and destiny of the world. When we consider that it is out of the *nidus* of religion that all the sciences have sprung, we shall understand how important a part this disinterested or partly disinterested curiosity has played in religion. Then again, there is the enthusiasm for beauty which we remember was so large an element in the religion of the ancient Greeks; and there are many other factors in religion, such as consolation, quite independent of conduct; not to mention fear and lust and cruelty and magic, which form such large ingredients in the religions of primitive and barbarous peoples. To say, therefore, that religion is solely concerned with conduct, and that conduct is the simplest thing in the world, is to speak with desultoriness, to move along the

---

[1] See "Novum Organum," lii., and Stebbing's note.
[2] "Literature and Dogma," p. 14.

lines of least resistance. It is as much an "idol of the tribe," a fiction of simplicity where simplicity is not, as the assertion of a friend of the late Mr. John Austin, that he found as little difficulty in conceiving of the Trinity in Unity as in thinking of three men in one cart: to which Mr. Austin, a man of strict and logical mind, is said to have replied, "The idea you have to frame is not the idea of three men in one cart, but of one man in three carts." Not assuredly by this short and easy road along the line of least resistance, but only by means of the metaphysical synthesis, the difficult mental process which holds in solution conflicting streams of thinking, can we adequately grasp the greater aspects of life which are of most importance to our lives, conduct, religion and the idea of God.

Take, again, Mr. Arnold's second fundamental proposition in "Literature and Dogma," that "happiness follows conduct,"[1] or that "conduct brings happiness."[2] Mr. Arnold is so sure of this that he says (p. 27) that it is "undeniably" so, and in p. 45 that "we know" it is so, and that "of course" it is so. But the connection of pleasure with conduct is not so simple as all this; nor is it a matter of course at all, either that pleasure always follows conduct, or that it does *not* follow other things quite different from and even opposed to conduct. What does Mr. Arnold's own Bishop Wilson say, as quoted in "St. Paul and Protestantism."[3] but now apparently forgotten? If you can be good with pleasure,[4] God

---

[1] "Literature and Dogma," p. 27.   [2] P. 45.
[3] "St. Paul and Protestantism," p. 166.
[4] It may be remarked in passing, that Mr. Arnold nowhere defines happiness or distinguishes it from pleasure. Thus in "St. Paul and Protestanism," p. 119, he says: "Our pleasure from a spring day we do not make; *our pleasure even from an approving conscience we do not make*. And yet we feel that both the one pleasure and the other can, and often do, work with us in a wonderful way for our good. So we get the thought of an impulsion outside ourselves which is at once awful and beneficent." It is evident that the thought in this passage is the same as that which runs through "Literature and Dogma," *we did not provide that happiness should follow conduct* ("Literature and Dogma," p. 27). This is not the

does not envy you your joy; but such is our corruption that every man cannot be so. Not to speak of the saying of St. Paul, also adduced by Mr. Arnold in his earlier and more careful book: "He who would cease from sin, must suffer in the flesh."[1] But even admitting that it is in the majority of cases pleasant to do right, it is, such is the complexity of our nature, pleasant, very pleasant, also to do wrong. The gratification of all our desires is attended with momentary pleasure. What fruit is so agreeable to the taste as forbidden fruit? Indeed, a thing in itself indifferent may become an object of desire, and its attainment thenceforth pleasant, simply by being forbidden, as we may remember was the case with our first parents in the garden of Eden. If the consciousness, again, of duties performed is pleasant, the consciousness of duties unperformed is also pleasant.[2] Things quite indifferent, again, from the moral point of view, may, in certain temperaments, be attended with considerable pleasure. An American lady once confessed to Mr. Emerson that the consciousness of being well dressed imparted to her an inward tranquillity which religion was powerless to bestow. It is unnecessary to multiply instances to show how complex are the conditions of pleasure, and how obscure is its connection with right conduct. Some persons have conceived that all pleasure is but a particular state of the nervous system, and certain it is that some apparently high sorts of pleasure can be produced by purely physical means, opium for

place to enter upon a discussion of the difference between pleasure and happiness; but I think Mr. Arnold, after seeing these two passages in juxtaposition, will scarcely consider that I am doing him an injustice if wherever he uses the words "happiness," "joy," "satisfaction," I simply translate "pleasure."

[1] "St. Paul and Protestantism," p. 166.

[2] The late Dean Mansel used to tell a story of a colonel in the Life Guards who had been at the pains to invent a peculiar gratification of this sort for himself. His servant had to wake him every morning at five o'clock with the reminder that the parade was at six, in order that he might enjoy the satisfaction of saying, "D——n the parade!" and of then turning over and going to sleep again.

instance. One of the most erudite students of philosophy in this country once enounced his opinion as follows: "Many a man," said he, "has been reduced to the lowest depths of despondency by an obstruction in the major viscera, and has subsequently been restored to a sense of the Divine favour by a mild course of aperient medicine." As to the connection of pleasure with right conduct, perhaps, bearing in mind the various experiences with regard to pleasure here adduced, we might hazard a conjecture, that so long as a community is progressive, right conduct, being a series of actions along the lines within which the community is moving, will be for the most part pleasant; and that when the community begins to decline towards stagnation or dissolution, right conduct will encounter rebuffs both within and without, and become unpleasant; and contrariwise, bad conduct—that is action which moves within the lines of declension in a community, will begin largely to be pleasant. So that, inasmuch as in every community there are processes of growth going on by the side of and intermingled with processes of decay, we can never count upon virtue being pleasant or vice disagreeable, but must expect each to be sometimes the one and sometimes the other; whilst it is certain that if we make happiness the aim of our endeavours, we are sure to miss it. We see then how difficult and complex this whole question of the connection of pleasure or happiness with conduct is: so that when Mr. Arnold says, "of course" and "undeniably," "we all know," that to righteousness belongs happiness, he is "feigning" in human nature "a greater equality and uniformity than is in truth."

But, in the second place, Bacon says that there are "the idols of the cave," the illusions peculiar to each individual, arising from character, education, circumstances, preferences in study, and the like: and that these things lead a man into "specum sive cavernam quandam individuam," a den or cavern of his own. Let us examine Mr. Arnold's third fundamental proposition enunciated in "Literature and Dogma." It is— "When we are asked," he says,[1] "what is the objection to religion? let us reply, *Conduct.*" "And when we are asked further, What is conduct? let us answer, *Three-fourths of life.*" As a definition of conduct this is of course only quantitative or arithmetical, and as such is no answer at all to the question, "*What* is conduct?" of It is like saying: "When we are asked what is the object of human anatomy? let us reply, *Man's body.* And when we are asked further, what is the body? let us answer, *From nine to eighteen stone.*" But Mr. Arnold has told us on the previous page more explicitly *what* conduct is. After quoting an essay by M. Littré, he says—

All the impulses which can be conceived as derivable from the instinct of self-preservation in us and the reproductive instinct, these terms being applied in their ordinary sense, are matter of *conduct*. It is evident this includes, to say no more, every impulse relating to temper, every impulse relating to sensuality; and we all know how much that is. How we deal with these impulses is the matter of conduct—how we obey, regulate, or restrain them—that and nothing else.

And he adds—

It is evident, if conduct deals with these, how important a thing conduct is, and how simple a thing.[2]

Impulses relating to temper, impulses relating to sensuality—three-fourths of our life are to be occupied with the management of these! "Three-fourths"—this is not a rhetorical way of saying how large, how important a thing conduct is; but it is the expression of an exact proportion, such as we might have in a recipe—

As the discipline of *conduct* is three-fourths of life, for our æsthetic and intellectual disciplines, real as these are, there is but one-fourth of life left; and if we let art and science

[1] "Literature and Dogma," p. 18. [2] Ibid. p. 17.

le this one-fourth fairly between them, they will have just divide it eighth of life each.¹

And still more explicitly further on—

Conduct, plain matter as it is, is six-eighths of life, while art and science are only two-eighths.²

One would have said that the proportion which conduct should bear to the rest of life is not a constant proportion, but one depending upon temperament, character, circumstances, occupation, and the like. One can at least see that, in a man of genius like Goethe, questions about the regulation of the impulses towards self-preservation and towards reproduction, occupy a very small proportion indeed of his time and attention—scarcely any indeed. That is permitted to Goethe which is not permitted to me: for where would the modern world have been if Goethe had made conduct three-fourths of *his* life, and art and science one-eighth each? But, genius apart, one would suppose that the proportion which conduct should bear to the rest of life would at least vary directly with the strength of the impulses which it is occupied in regulating, with the *physique* in short; with the action of particular sets of circumstances, in strengthening or controlling them, and the like; and that these factors would vary indefinitely with different individuals, and in each individual with different periods of his existence. So that a universal proportion for conduct to bear to the rest of life it is not possible to fix. Regard for a moment the ancient Israelites, who had neither art nor science, and who, Mr. Arnold tells us, thought that conduct was not only three-fourths of life, but the whole³ of it. Were their lives better regulated, after all, than say the lives of the ancient Romans, or of the modern Germans, for this exclusive attention? We seem to gather from the Bible that the Jews were a stiff-

---

¹ "Literature and Dogma," p. 210.   ² Ibid. p. 354.
             ³ Ibid. p. 235.

necked and stupid people, always going wrong in some way or other in matters of conduct, and falling into every trap and temptation that their own impulses or the examples of the neighbouring nations set for them. So little does disproportionate attention to the regulation of the desires gain its end.

But what does Mr. Arnold himself say in "Culture and Anarchy," in his earlier manner as we have called it, about this predominance of the care for conduct? He is speaking of the Puritan character, the modern representative of what he calls Hebraism, the exclusive or predominant care for right practice, and is contrasting it with Hellenism, the passion for sweetness and light, for culture and intelligence, for art and science:—

> The true and smooth order of humanity's development is not reached in either way (either by Hebraism or by Hellenism). And therefore, while we willingly admit with the Christian apostle that the world by wisdom—that is, by the isolated preponderance of its intellectual impulses—knew not God, or the true order of things, it is yet necessary, also, to set up a sort of converse to this proposition, and to say likewise (what is equally true) that the world by Puritanism knew not God. *And it is on this converse of the Apostle's proposition that it is particularly needful to insist in our own country just at present.*[1]

For, as he explains in the same chapter—

> We have fostered our Hebraizing instincts, our preference of earnestness of doing to delicacy and flexibility of thinking, too exclusively, and have been landed by them in a mechanical and unfruitful routine.[2]

A man who is so landed, Mr. Arnold insists,[3] "is a victim of Hebraism, of the tendency to cultivate strictness of conscience rather than spontaneity of consciousness. And what he wants is a larger conception of

---

[1] "Culture and Anarchy," p. 153.   [2] Ibid. p. 174.
[3] Ibid. p. 157.

human nature, showing him the number of other points at which his nature must come to its best, besides the points which he himself knows and thinks of."

Hebraism and Hellenism—between these two points of influence moves our world ; . . . . and *it ought to be, though it never is, evenly and happily balanced between them.*[1]

Here, then, we see Mr. Arnold still on the high road ; he is moving in the element of the "better self" and the *Zeit-Geist ;* and has not yet entered into the "cage of Puritanism" and "turned the key" upon himself there, as in "Literature and Dogma." He is not yet in the "cave ;" what sends him thither ? "Vel propter naturam propriam et singularem ; vel propter educationem et conversationem cum aliis," are some of Bacon's reasons. Let us try the last, "propter conversationem cum aliis."

Mr. Arnold is in these later works of his addressing what he calls the Philistines—*i.e.*, the great middle class which rules our destinies in this country, in France, and in the United States of America. Now it must be confessed that although the Philistine is a man of inflexible morality in certain departments, and of eminent respectability in all, although he has all sorts of prejudices, it may be, and hard and fast lines about conduct, yet conduct itself is not exactly his *forte*, any more than it was Goethe's. "Sincere, gross of perception, prosaic," as Mr. Arnold rightly calls him, the Philistine has his three-fourths of life immersed in what is called "business," and business, with its famous guiding principle of "caveat emptor," is not regarded by him as falling within the scope of those rigorous principles and that inflexible morality of which he is fond of speaking. We have only to read the daily newspapers to be convinced of this, so that it is easy to see how a man like Mr. Arnold, who, by nature, education, and circumstances, has been impelled and habituated to that transparent uprightness

---

[1] "Culture and Anarchy," p. 129.

which we admire in his literary works, should receive somewhat of a shock when he finds himself confronting the Philistines and recommending to them conduct, and, as conduct touched with emotion, religion. This I think will be found to be the reason why in "Literature and Dogma" he sets free such a torrent of enthusiasm for conduct as to seem to magnify its importance out of all proportion to the other affairs of life, and certainly at the expense of that harmonious development of all those other points, "at which," he tells us elsewhere, "man's nature must come to its best." However this may be, to say that conduct is for every one three-fourths of life, is certainly an illusion, and just such an illusion as would come for the moment to a highly honourable and generous nature when pleading for conduct with those whose *forte* conduct is not, and who lose by not making it a stronger point than at present they do.

"Propter lectionem librorum et auctoritates eorum quos quisque colit et miratur," so Bacon goes on with his diagnosis of the idols of the cave. May we venture to say that Bishop Butler, Bishop Wilson, Pascal, Fénelon, St. Augustine, Mr. Arnold's favourite authors, from whom he seems to have derived the idea of writing about religion and conduct, though good and excellent men, are not the *great* thinkers of the world on these intricate questions, do not represent "the main stream and vital movement" of mankind's intelligence on these subjects; and that reading them too exclusively, dwelling on them, is like giving oneself in literature to the study of Kotzebue rather than Goethe, or of Crabbe and Waller to the neglect of Shakespeare? "The Germans," says Will Ladislaw, in "Middlemarch," when speaking of Mr. Casaubon's "Key to all Mythologies," "have taken the lead in historical inquiries, and they laugh at results which are got by groping about in woods with a pocket-compass, while they have made good roads." The "Key to all Mythologies" was, it will be remembered, the fruit of very much the same sort of studies as those which have recently found favour with Mr. Arnold.

But we must hasten on to the third kind of illusions which, Bacon says, infest the mind when it neglects the use of method. These are the "idols of the market-place," *idola fori*, the illusions of language. These illusions he considers the most troublesome, "omnium molestissima sunt;"[1] they insinuate themselves into the mind "ex fœdere verborum et nominum," from the association of words and names. Men believe that their reason governs words: "sed fit etiam ut verba vim suam super intellectum retorqueant et reflectant," but it also happens that words react upon the mind and govern it. These illusions of language are of two kinds: either they are the names of things which have no existence in fact; or they are the names of things which are real, but of which our idea is confused and ill-defined, and formed from a hasty and inadequate survey of the facts. The application of words, he explains, is often the work of the popular apprehension, and the lines by which they divide things are for the most part lines which the popular intellect can follow; and then "verba gignunt verba," words beget words, and in this way we come under the dominion of the "idols" of language. Let us see if Mr. Matthew Arnold has entirely escaped this dominion of words over his reasoning.

Already in "St. Paul and Protestantism"[2] we find him, in his polemic against the Dissenters, founding an argument upon the use, and upon the wrong use, of a word.

People, however, there were in abundance, he writes, who differed on points both of discipline and of dogma from the rule which obtained in the Church, and who separated from her on account of that difference. These were the heretics; *separatists*, as the name implies, *for the sake of opinions*.

---

[1] "Novum Organum," lix.   [2] Pp. 44, 45.

And *the very name, therefore, implies that they were wrong in separating, and that the body which held together was right.*

Now here, in the first place, Mr. Arnold is evidently thinking, not of "heretics," but of "schismatics." Heresy means a particular study or school of thought (αἵρεσις Ἑλληνική means the study of Greek history); it does not mean separation.

A heretic is not a separatist, unless he is expelled, from the main body, but simply, like Mr. Arnold himself, the adherent of a particular school of opinion. A schismatic, on the other hand, is the name given by the main body to one who of his own act and culpably separates from it. The verbal argument begins, therefore, with a mistake in the meaning of the word; but it does not hold any more if we substitute the right word; *i.e.*, it is not an admission of the wrongness of separation, unless it can be shown that the term expressive of blame is the term applied *by the separatists to themselves*, which it clearly was not, but to the separatists by the main body. So that no argument whatever can be founded on the use of the word, either way.

Similarly, when Mr. Arnold is pointing out that the moral law is "a prime element and clue in man's constitution,"[1] he says, the etymology of the word righteousness (= right, straight, way, road, a certain line, a necessary orbit) bears witness to its being so; but here he himself seems to be aware that *verba gignunt verba*, for he says that he will leave this kind of argument to Mr. Ruskin, and that "for these fanciful helps there is no need." Still on "these fanciful helps" he does come more and more to rely as he proceeds, and words more and more come to react upon his reasoning and to govern it. In "Literature and Dogma" his argument about the "Eternal Power not ourselves which makes for righteousness," is a fabric mainly, if not entirely, verbal;

[1] "St. Paul and Protestantism," p. 107.

it is constructed *ex fœdere verborum et nominum*. Let me try to make good this criticism.

The unconscious artifice—it is of course unconscious, not intentional—on which the whole edifice is built up is this: first, a word is taken which imports so little, and seems to lie so close to ordinary experience, and is besides so easy of comprehension, that it is readily admitted as representing a reality. Then a word a little stronger, and with a little more meaning in it, is joined with the first, as a kind of rhetorical improvement of it; and it is so little stronger that its addition is readily admitted. Then the original and very simple word is discarded; and with the stronger one standing alone, a third is next associated, which is a little stronger still, and has a little more, but scarcely appreciably more meaning; and this third word is then admitted as a synonym and rhetorical improvement on the second, and so on; until at last we find ourselves landed in an entirely new region, and have the illusion of being carried thither by a continuous stream of reasoning, whereas we really have been landed thither on the stepping-stones of words. Like Fame, in Virgil, Mr. Arnold's conception of the "Eternal:"—

> Mobilitate viget, viresque acquirit eundo;
> Parva metu primo; mox sese attollit in auras,
> Ingrediturque solo, et caput inter nubila condit.

Let us first take quite a simple instance of this method of progression by means of words: speaking of the primitive religious ideas of Israel, Mr. Arnold says:[1]—

In Israel's earliest history and earliest literature, under the name of Eloah, Elohim, The Mighty, there *may have lain and matured*, there *did lie and mature*, ideas of God more as a moral power, more as a power connected above everything with conduct and righteousness, than were entertained by other races; not only can we judge by the result that *this must have been so*, but we can see that *it was so*.

"May have," "did," "must," "was;" how little a thing it is to admit the first, how quite a different thing to

---

[1] "Literature and Dogma," p. 31.

admit the last and the last but one! Yet the progression has been inappreciable almost, we are carried along so easily by the words, it is so easy to think that the words are reasons, or that reasons fill the intervals between them.

What did they (the ancient Israelites) mean by the eternal? the eternal *what?* (asks Mr. Arnold). The eternal *cause?* Alas, these poor people were not Archbishops of York. They meant the eternal *righteous,* who loveth *righteousness.* They had dwelt upon the thought of conduct and right and wrong, till the *not-ourselves* which is in us and around us became to them adorable eminently and altogether as *a power which makes for righteousness;* which makes for it unchangeably and eternally, and is therefore called *The Eternal.*[1]

"There is not a particle of metaphysics," he says, rather uneasily perhaps, "in all this." Yet Mr. Arnold himself seems to suspect that even in this beginning there may have crept in elements which are not experimental. Eternal *cause* is metaphysical and must be at once rejected. But how about *eternal* or *unchangeable,* without adding cause? is that exactly experimental? Then the *not-ourselves,* is that not perilously like the *not-me* of metaphysic? Well, *righteous, righteousness, conduct,* and the thought of them, and the emotions clustering around them—these at least are experimental. Some such misgiving as this seems to pass through Mr. Arnold's mind, for on the next page but two,[2] the starting-point is very much reduced in scale. "The monotheistic idea of Israel," we there read, "is simply *seriousness;*" and again, further on,[3] "God is here really, at bottom, a deeply-moved way of saying *conduct* or *righteousness.*" Here then, at least, we get a point close to experience from which to set out in our survey of the experiences of Israel: we have no "not-ourselves," no "eternal," but simply *conduct and the emotional regard of conduct.*

But now, how to proceed? What does this

[1] "Literature and Dogma," p. 32.   [2] P. 35.   [3] P 47.

emotional regard of conduct prove? How do we, how did Israel, take the first step? Let us see what Mr. Arnold says of the limits of possible experience in an analogous case:—

When we see a watch or a honeycomb we say, It works harmoniously and well, and a man or a bee made it. But a yet more numerous class of works we know, which neither man nor the lower animals have made for their own purposes. When we see the ear, or see the bud, do we say, It works harmoniously and well, and a man or one of the lower animals made it? No; but we say, It works harmoniously and well, and an infinite and eternal substance, an all-thinking and all-powerful being, the creator of all things, made it. Why? Because it works harmoniously and well. *But its working harmoniously and well does not prove all this : it only proves that it works harmoniously and well.*[1]

What then does the experience of Israel, that the thought of righteousness kindled his emotions, *prove*? Does it prove the existence of a not-ourselves which makes for righteousness? Does it prove that there is a "tendency which is *not ourselves*, but which appears in our consciousness, by which things fulfil the real law of their being?"[2] Does it even prove that there is "a law of things which is found in conscience, and which is an indication, irrespective of our arbitrary wish and fancy, of what we ought to do?" I apprehend not. The fact that the ancient Israelite was deeply moved when he thought of righteousness only proves that he was deeply moved when he thought of righteousness. We may put the experience how we like. We may say the thought of righteousness moved him deeply, and made him blossom out into sublime and very imaginative religious poetry, or we may say that he was of such a character as to be deeply moved by the thought of righteousness ; or we may say that the thought of righteousness is a thought

[1] "God and the Bible," pp. 102, 103. See the whole passage.
[2] "Literature and Dogma," p. 43.

of such a kind as deeply to move a man like the ancient Israelite; but all these are only different ways of dressing up the original experience with which we set out, they are not inferences from it, they are not additional experiences. Aristotle describes the same phenomenon. Different things, he says, produce the emotion of pleasure in people of different characters: "a horse does in a man fond of horses, a spectacle in a man fond of spectacles; and in the same way just things are pleasant to the lover of justice, and generally virtuous things to the lover of virtue."[1] But the only inference Aristotle allows himself to make is an inference as to character. A man who likes good deeds likes them because he is good: "he would not be good if he did not rejoice in them"—οὐδ' ἐστὶν ἀγαθὸς ὁ μὴ χαίρων ταῖς καλαῖς πράξεσιν—and this is the only inference, if inference it be, that *can* be made. We can infer a man's character from the things which he likes doing. So from the consciousness of being deeply moved at the thought of righteousness it is impossible to infer that there is *anything* beyond us, whether it be eternal or not, or make for righteousness or not. The ancient Israelite made no such inference, and we can make none. Israel got its original idea of God, as all other nations did, mainly from the apparition of nature outside of man, not from the emotions about righteousness within him. This is proved, as I believe all Biblical critics are agreed, by the fact that the original God of the Israelites is conceived as allowing and approving things which are distinctly wrong: things as immoral in their way as the things that Homer's gods do are in theirs. It is only gradually that the *Naturgott*, with which all religions begin, becomes moralized: and he becomes moralized just in so far as the community begins to take the place of nature as the immediate environment of man, and as the community, and with it the individual conscience, grows towards its golden age, its perfection. Mr. Arnold

[1] "Eth. Nic." i. 8.

himself seems to have been partly aware of this once; for in "St. Paul and Protestantism,"[1] he says, "The righteousness of the earlier Jews of the Old Testament . . . . consisted mainly in smiting the Lord's enemies and their own under the fifth rib." So that when he says:[2]—

The idea of God, as it is given in the Bible, rests . . . . on a moral perception of a rule of conduct not of our own making, into which we are born, and which exists whether we will or no; of awe at its grandeur and necessity, and of gratitude at its beneficence. This is the great original revelation made to Israel, this is his "Eternal;"—

we cannot but feel that he is perhaps expanding rhetorically the experience of deep emotion which Israel felt in its best days for righteousness, rather than re-stating in an inaccurate form the historical fact which in "St. Paul and Protestantism" he had stated correctly. But how the original experience groans and creaks under this added weight! How little it is capable of such expansion we see from Mr. Arnold's own account of it, when defending it under the pressure of adverse criticism. What, after all, is the "eternal not-ourselves?" "It is no metaphysical conception," he tells us, in "God and the Bible."[3] Let us see.

The word "eternal" has three different meanings, and in all these three meanings it is used by Mr. Arnold. Two of these are philosophical, the third colloquial. First, "eternal" means that which is *exempt from duration*,[4] withdrawn from sequence and succession: it is in this sense that the Bible speaks of God as to whom "a thousand years are as one day." In this sense it is used once of "the Eternal that loveth righteousness" by Mr.

---

[1] Preface, xvii.; cf. p. 57.
[2] "Literature and Dogma," p. 122.   [3] P. 92.
[4] We can realize this meaning by remembering one of those moments when we have been engrossed by some occupation, or, better, when we have been under the influence of some overpowering emotion, and have lost count of the succession of external circumstances, and of the lapse of time.

Arnold.[1] Secondly, "eternal" is used of the *whole of duration*, regarded as an endless series of successive events—*i.e.*, it means *everlasting*, the sense of eternal against which the late Mr. Frederick Denison Maurice spent his life in fighting. This is also a very common sense of the word eternal in the Bible, and we find it used by Mr. Arnold when, in explanation of eternal, he says, "The righteous is an *everlasting* foundation,"[2] and that the eternal is the "unchangeable,"[3] or the "permanent,"[4] or the "*enduring*."[5] The two philosophical meanings of "eternal" are really two fragments or factors of the metaphysical sense of the word. The two streams of thinking, of *that which is exempt from duration*, and of *that which endures from the beginning to the end of duration*, find their proper place and meaning when held together by means of what we have already described as the metaphysical synthesis. And it is in this complex sense, which includes and fuses the two senses of "eternal" in the Bible, that we apply strictly and scientifically the word "eternal" to God. But there is a third use of the word eternal which is colloquial—one might even say that is now a vulgarism: as when we say, "So-and-so is *eternally* taking snuff," meaning that he *habitually* does so. This use of the word was more common a few generations ago than it is now: thus, in Miss Burney's "Evelina" we read that Captain Mirvan and Madame Duval are *eternally* quarrelling. Mr. Arnold has restored this somewhat old-fashioned use of the word, as when he says,[6] "This argument of popular theology rests on its *eternal hypothesis* of a magnified and non-natural man," &c., meaning the hypothesis which popular theology habitually frames; and as when he says of the German critics of the canon of the Gospels,[7] "They are *eternally* reading its literature, reading the theories of their col-

---

[1] "Literature and Dogma," p. 350.
[2] Ibid. p. 123. [3] Ibid. p. 32. [4] Ibid. p. 48.
[5] Ibid p. 61. [6] Ibid. p. 176. [7] "God and the Bible," p. 179.

leagues about it." Now one would not have prophesied beforehand, on a view of Mr. Arnold's earlier works on religion, that he would first have used the word "eternal" in the two Biblical and philosophical meanings of "beyond time and sequence" and of "everlasting," all through an elaborate work like "Literature and Dogma," to give sublimity to the idea of righteousness; to give it outwardness as a kind of cosmical operation going on whether we like it or not, whether we obey it or not; to bring this idea of righteousness within the sphere of religious emotion; to *accomplish* (in a word) *the apotheosis* of righteousness; and then at length, when pressed by criticism, as he rests from his labours, with the objection, "You say that you go only on experience, that you bring forward nothing which is not verifiable by experience; now this idea of the eternal is a metaphysical conception not given by experience,"—would reply, "I never meant to take eternal in either of the first two senses, but only in the third or colloquial sense." I say, we could not have anticipated that he would answer so. And yet this is what in his reply to his critics in "God and the Bible" he does:—

Yes indeed, *eternal*, as that which never had a beginning and can never have an end, is, like the final substance or subject wherein all qualities inhere, a metaphysical conception to which experience has nothing to say. But eternal, *æviternus*, the age or life-long, as men applied it to the Eternal that makes for righteousness, was no metaphysical conception. From all they could themselves make out, and from all that their fathers had told them, they believed that righteousness was salvation, and that it would go on being salvation from one generation of men to another.[1]

Now let us look at this passage a little closely, and let us translate it into terms of experience. The original experience was, we remember, that of profound emotion at the idea of righteousness. What part of this expe-

[1] "God and the Bible," p. 92.

rience is covered by the word *eternal*, or what additional element was there in the experience which had not been brought out before, but which we now emphasize by the use of that word? This: combined with the *emotion* at the idea of righteousness, we now learn that there was an *habitual* and *traditional belief* in the consciousness of the ancient Israelite that other people before he was alive had felt, and that other people after he was dead would feel, the same profound emotion as he did at the idea of righteousness.

This, then, is the solid bit of experience, an *emotion* at the thought of righteousness, *combined with a belief* that other people would feel, and had felt, the same, around which Mr. Arnold has woven his envelope of words. Yet if the irreligious and anxious-to-be-scientific Philistine, whose *forte* conduct is not, can be made to feel this emotion and nourish this belief, a great point will doubtless be gained. But in the meantime is it not unfortunate that Mr. Arnold does not give him any aid in setting himself to try to excite and to nourish them? Yet no; at this point Mr. Arnold gives the Philistine the cold shoulder—" If you don't feel them already," he says in effect, " it's no good talking to you."

Every one has some affinity for them, although one man has more and another less. But if any man is so entirely without affinity for them, so subjugated by the conviction that facts are clean against them, as to be unable to entertain the idea of their being in human nature and in experience, for him " Literature and Dogma " was not written.[1]

Again, it would have been something, at least, if Mr. Arnold had been able to tell the Philistine, as an encouragement, that the ancient Israelite's traditional belief that his posterity would go on feeling the emotion for righteousness as he felt it, that the emotion was so firmly grounded in his constitution by habit that he could not conceive this habit not being propagated in his

[1] "God and the Bible," p. 157.

children, and so becoming what Mr. Arnold calls
"eternal"—it would have been something if he could
have told the Philistine that this expectation was not
destined to be disappointed by the event. But Mr.
Arnold's characteristic honesty will not allow him to do
this. The expectation of the ancient Israelite *was*, after
all, disappointed: in the decline of the Jewish community, "righteousness had lost, in great measure, the
mighty impulse which emotion gives, and in losing this,
had lost also the mighty sanction which happiness gives."[1]
So that, after all, the use of the Bible to the irreligious
and anxious-to-be-scientific Philistine, should he be
tempted to re-open it, will be not so much to show him
"that righteousness is salvation verifiably," but to incul-
cate "the faith that this is so"—*i.e., the faith that it is
verifiable!*[2] The little solid bit of experience, round
which Mr. Arnold has woven his envelope of Biblical
words, seems thus to crumble on being touched, and to
come after all to little or nothing. But let us now
examine for a moment the structure of this envelope in
which it is enshrined. As often happens, the relic, when
we come to get a near view of it, is inconsiderable, but
the case in which it is kept is beautiful and gorgeous. In
this instance the shrine is composed of nothing less than
the names, or synonyms of the names, which are given
in the Bible to Jehovah; viz., "unchangeable" ("Literature
and Dogma," p. 32), "enduring" (p. 61), "almighty"
(p. 124), "infinite" (p. 265), "extending infinitely
beyond consciousness" (p. 322), "ruling" (p. 323),
"loving righteousness" (p. 349), and the "author" of it
(p. 331); "perpetually intervening" ("God and the Bible,"
p. 93), giving a "divine sanction" to conduct (p. 137),
"the centre and source of those ideas of moral order and
of conduct which are in human nature" ("God and the
Bible," p. 142). These and many more are attributes
of, and used as synonyms of, "the Eternal" in the two

---

[1] "Literature and Dogma," p. 85.   [2] "God and the Bible," p. 156.

Biblical senses of Him who is everlasting, and of Him in whose sight " a thousand years are but as yesterday when it is past;"[1] but they are, it needs no proof to show, not in any way synonyms of the "Eternal" in the third or colloquial sense, in which alone Mr. Arnold says that he applies it to the Israelite's *habitual* regard of the thought of righteousness with emotion, and to his expectation— disappointed as we have seen by the event—that this habit would continue in his children. If we say, as Mr. Arnold says, that " God" means *seriousness*, and " Eternal" means habitual, then we shall have to translate the text " Hear, O Israel: the Eternal our God is one Eternal," into " Hear, O Israel: the habitual our seriousness is one habitual;" and this even the Chevalier Bunsen, who did so much to give a modern and Aryan rendering to Semitic terminology, would have perceived to be absurd.

There is, we must observe, no juncture of an experimental or inferential kind between the piece of experience which Mr. Arnold brings forward and the magnificent edifice which he throws around it. The juncture is verbal, and is to be found in the ambiguity of the word "eternal." The God of the Bible and of modern religion is eternal: the fact of experience adduced by Mr. Arnold is also eternal: *therefore* the God of the Bible and of modern religion is the same as the fact of experience. Yes, but " eternal" as applied to God means one thing; and "eternal" as applied to the fact of experience means a totally different thing. And thus it happens, as Bacon says, that while " men believe that their reason governs words,' words also react upon the reason and govern it."

There remains the *not-ourselves* which plays such an important part in " Literature and Dogma," but which in no wise, as we saw, could be made to grow out of the ancient Israelite's emotional regard for righteousness. The thing that strikes us about "the not-ourselves" is that it is a conception purely negative; it is not the

[1] Ps. xc. 4.

affirmation of anything beyond ourselves, but merely the negation of ourselves. Now there is no more common confusion in logic than a confusion of the distinction between contradictories and contraries. The distinction is this: in the case of contradictories one term stands for *something*, and the other term stands for *nothing* at all. In the case of contraries both terms stand for *something*. "Rich" and "poor" are contraries, and both, as we know, exist; but "ourselves" and "not-ourselves" are contradictories, and the latter term stands for nothing at all. Let me, in illustration, quote a passage from one of Mr. Goldwin Smith's writings in controversy with the late Dean Mansel.[1] He says:—

When we are told that "the conviction that an Infinite Being exists seems forced upon us by the manifest incompleteness of our finite knowledge," we fall back into the fallacy of the positive-negative *Infinite*. *Infinite* is not the *complement* of *Finite*, but its negation. At this rate the philosopher might, by the simple instrumentality of a negative prefix, become the creator of intellectual entities without end. By prefixing a negative particle to *Horse*, he might create the complementary entity *Not-Horse*; and then we should have *Not-Horse* filling the universe, crushing human reason into the dust, and exalting the humility of its enemies to the skies.

And he adds elsewhere:[2]—

If I am not mistaken, we might as well allow the frown of a negative particle, as the frown of the "Infinite," to cast its shadow over our souls.

But here we are getting out of the region of mere language and its illusions—the *idola fori* as Bacon calls them—and into that of the illusions of logic and philosophy. These Bacon calls the idols of the theatre, (*idola theatri*.) He says:—

At idola theatri innata non sunt, nec occulto insinuata in intellectum: sed ex fabulis theoriarum, et perversis legibus demonstrationum plane indita et recepta.[3]

---

[1] "Rational Religion" (Whittaker & Co., 1861), pp. 131,132.
[2] Ibid. p. 121.   [3] Novum Organum, lxi.

The "idols of the theatre" are not inborn in man, but consciously adopted either from baseless theories or from wrong canons of reasoning. The wrong canons of reasoning we can understand without difficulty, as Mr. Arnold has already provided two instances of it: in the foundation of a would-be experimental theosophy on the ambiguity of the word eternal, and in the confusion of contradictories with contraries. So that we have been obliged to anticipate among idols of the market-place much that also belongs to our present section; so closely intertwined are the illusions of language with those of thought. Mr. Arnold's construction of the "eternal not-ourselves that makes for righteousness" will also come under the class of illusions called *fabulæ theoriarum*.

Bacon gives instances of these *fabulæ theoriarum*, which might be illustrated from Mr. Arnold's works; but what he is especially thinking of under this title would seem to be an illegitimate use of the philosophical conceptions of the past. Now, what is this illegitimate use *for us* in the nineteenth century, living nearly a hundred years after the appearance of Kant's "Critique of Pure Reason?" What makes conceptions which were once true, which once carried conviction to all the superior minds of an epoch, "fables" to us? Why should such ideas as "essence, existence, substance, finite and infinite, cause and effect, something and nothing," seem to keep round Mr. Arnold a kind of Witches' Sabbath and Walpurgis night in the air, whenever he thinks of metaphysic? This inquiry will bring us back to the point from which we started at the beginning of this chapter, and thus give a kind of unity to what we have hitherto been saying.

In our last chapter we saw that a metaphysical idea, or synthesis, is the structural form or outline which the *total* experience of an epoch assumes and within which it continues to grow up, until the particular synthesis becomes insufficient for it, and is then discarded for and absorbed in a larger and more complex synthesis.' The metaphysical or formal element in experience is nothing by itself apart from or prior to experience; any more than the shape of an oak, into which an acorn grows, exists apart from the oak or before the oak has arrived at maturity.[1]

But now suppose the *Zeit-Geist*, or common consciousness of an epoch, to have grown out of its old form into a new one, what happens? Two things happen. The old structure is absorbed and built into the new structure; but the old form also remains as such—*i.e.*, unabsorbed, in the memory of mankind and in the literature of the age which is just closing, and it dominates still, it may be, the minds of the elder generation of men, whose thought have ceased to move with the times. Only it becomes

---

[1] The form ultimately assumed may indeed be regarded as a kind of programme which is destined to be carried out by the growing organism; as when M. Renan says, "Il faut admettre dans l'univers ce qui se remarque dans la plante et l'animal, une force intime, qui porte le germe à remplir un cadre tracé d'avance" ("Fragments Philosophiques," pp. 177, 178); or as when George Eliot says in speaking of the fashion of different streams of thinking: "Has there not been a meeting among the pathways as of the operations in one soul, where *an idea being born and breathing draws the elements towards it, and is fed and grows?*" ("Daniel Deronda," vol. iv. p. 249.) This apparent distinction of the form from the contents, and priority to them, arises, I cannot but think, from an unconscious comparison of things in nature to things made by man. A man has a *cadre tracé d'avance* in his mind or on paper of what he is going to make before he makes it; and hence we go on to suppose the same in nature. However this may be, we have become habituated through so many generations to think in this way, that now we cannot well avoid it. The important thing is not to allow ourselves to suppose that by this kind of priority, which we cannot help giving to the form over the contents, we mean priority *in time;* we can avoid this by calling this kind of priority, as some writers have long ago done, priority *naturâ*, as distinguished from priority *tempore*. I should prefer to call it *apriority*,* as getting rid altogether of the idea of time, and preventing us from making the sort of mistake that Plato made.

---

* Arguments *à priori* will then mean arguments derived from a consideration of the structure of experience; whilst arguments *à posteriori* will mean arguments derived from the consideration of its contents.

every day more and more empty of experience; the new experience will not fit into it; until at last, when men's minds have moved still farther away from it in subsequent generations, it becomes entirely emptied of contents, a mere formula or "stock notion," as Mr. Arnold very well says, and as such it survives to confuse and irritate mankind. Nobody knows where it came from, and yet it cannot be got rid of. It has become one of the "*fabulæ theoriarum;*" and metaphysic is supposed by many to provide a kind of asylum in which these attenuated creatures drag out a miserable existence. For it is no good trying to put them out of their misery; "like immaterial and aëry beings they elude the sword which smites them, and part but to reunite."[1] It is no good turning your back upon them, as Mr. Arnold does, and saying, "I don't know anything about them, and I don't care: on this subject I am dead to the prick of shame." For the poor shall not perish out of the land; the metaphysical ideas are there; we cannot escape them, any more than we can escape the consequences of our forefathers' vices. Our minds are filled with the débris of preceding minds,[2] as our bodies are filled with the rebellious desires which are the "survival" of our animality. And as with the rebellious desires, so with the effete metaphysical ideas; they dominate us each in its turn, all the more for our not knowing about them, and we are, all the more for not caring, their unconscious slaves. Now the man who follows his bodily desires one after the other, and is absorbed in each as each comes uppermost, we are accustomed to call the *natural* man, as distinguished from the moral or civilized man, to whom his place in the community has given a central principle and aim in life, so that he can methodize his desires in

---

[1] Wallace's "Logic of Hegel," Prolegomena, lvi.

[2] "Their thoughts the withered husks of all things dead
Holding no force of germs instinct with life."
  ("College Breakfast Party," by George Eliot.)

relation to the common good and his own. Such a methodizing of the unruly impulses within us we praise under the name of morality, as distinguished from asceticism, which turns its back upon the desires, and tries to get rid of them; or, if it attempts their systematization, gains its principle for doing so from an imaginary environment, instead of from the real environment of the community.

It is the same with the (in their way) not less rebellious and importunate "stock notions" which fill the air into which we are born, and get imbedded in the tissue of our minds. The *natural* man is the slave of each as it presses its claim; he is tossed from one to the other during his youth, and is fortunate in mature age if he has succeeded in making terms of permanent surrender with only a select number of them, and excluding the rest. This is the ordinary mental condition of the Philistine after middle life, when he tells you, "I have made up my mind on all-important topics, and don't wish to have it unsettled again." The "stock notions" to which he has been attracted by temperament or circumstances have honeycombed themselves together into a kind of rookery within his thought, and seem to him to be the supporting framework of the mind itself. Now here comes in metaphysic to liberate us from the tyranny of fixed ideas, as morality liberates us from feeling "the weight of chance desires;" and it liberates us in the same way. It gives us a central principle by which we may dispose of this detritus of extinct processes of thought, by showing us our place and part in the *Zeit-Geist*, in the movement of the collective consciousness, of which the hereditary and detached ideas are extinct forms. It tells us that none of the ideas are absolutely true, as we suppose, nor again any of them absolutely untrue: as morality tells us that none of the bodily desires are absolutely and in themselves either good or bad. The first are only true or untrue, as the latter are only good or bad, *relatively* to a given stage of advancement in us. The "fixed ideas" which we cherish or by which we feel ourselves burdened have no existence, and no value, apart from the past experience of which they were the modes. It is their detachment from the onward movement of experience, by experience having ceased to flow through and fertilize them, and moreover from their names being handed down in language, that makes them simulate an independent existence and value which they have not.

But there is another semblance which metaphysical ideas put on when detached from their *nidus* in the collective consciousness, and regarded, as we are all apt to regard them, in isolation. This is their semblance of *outwardness*. They are supposed to be not merely thoughts or modes of thought in us, but, as Auguste Comte says, "abstract forces, veritable entities, inherent in all beings," or, as Plato fabled, having their abode in some remote and appropriate place, perhaps in heaven.[1] Now, how does this *outwardness* come about? Whence do we get the supposition that behind and beyond our experience there is a region of things, abstract but real, which we do not and cannot experience? This tendency in metaphysical ideas to become the *mirage*, or double, of experience, has been named in past times their transcendental character, their capacity for "transcending" or climbing over the wall of experience to the other side of it.[2] And it arises in this way: (1) The ideas have become detached from living experience; they have been shed like the shell of a cretacean that was too tight. (2) They are preserved in language, and a name always carries with it the illusion of representing a reality, whether it does or no. (3) They represent an experience which preceded the experience in which we are now living, and

---

[1] For ἐπέκεινα τῆς οὐσίας, see Plato, "Republic," p. 509.

[2] Lewes's word "metempirical" accentuates the abnormal condition of the metaphysical ideas—*i.e.*, their detached condition.

so, although now empty forms, seem to have a priority in time to experience as we know it. (4) They retain, like empty wine-bottles, the savour, so to speak, of the reality which they once contained. All these causes serve to give them an outwardness in regard to experience as it is; but there is also another cause of apparent outwardness as strong as all these put together, which is more difficult to understand. This cause is to be sought in the peculiar relation which the individual, as such, bears to the community of which he forms a part. By the individual *as such*, I mean the individual conscious of his independent existence, his desires, his separate experience, &c., but not yet conscious, or not yet *so distinctly* conscious, of his existence as part of the community. To the individual, therefore, beyond the brightly-lighted chamber of his own thoughts, there looms a world of twilight filled with strange echoes which he cannot interpret; beyond the familiar valley there lies the seat of government, and here lie London and Paris and Washington, of which he has heard, but of which he knows nothing, and yet from these seem to arrive influences operative in his own life. From this outer and dim world have come to him language and religion and law and the arts, and such changes as have grown over these and over the lineaments of his own narrow experience. From it too may come to him, he knows, some day, the claim of some common good for the surrender of all that he has and of his own life; a claim which he will obey. But at present he has followed the pathways leading to this larger and surrounding world, only up to the point where they cross his own horizon. Such metaphors as these may explain, perhaps, better than the technical language of philosophy, the relation between the individual consciousness and that of the community. The relation is one of contrast and of solidarity combined; and it is this relation which gives to the extinct modes of collective experience which we have called metaphysical ideas,—in addition to the outwardness which we saw that they got from language, and from the other causes before enumerated—the same illusory character of "veritable entities," of "abstract forces," which the other products of the collective consciousness, language, religion, law and morality have.

To stay, then, "the eternal dance" of "essence, existence, substance," and the other metaphysical ideas which keep Mr. Arnold in a state of irritable watchfulness, and which are much more numerous than those he has been at the trouble to specify, there are two remedies which the science of metaphysic, frankly embraced and attended to, supplies.[1] First, it heightens our usually low consciousness of solidarity with the social medium or "better self;" and secondly, it relegates to their place in the historical development of this social medium those ideas which, in their isolation and detachment from it, have from time immemorial hoodwinked and imposed upon mankind. Mr. Arnold has and applies the first of these remedies; he uses it fruitfully in "Culture and Anarchy" when he applies the "better self" as a cure for social anarchy; and in "St. Paul and Protestantism" when he applies the *Zeit-Geist* as a cure for the narrowness of Puritan dissent; but he has not and cannot apply the second remedy, because in "Literature and Dogma" and in "God and the Bible" he renounces the use of method in handling ideas, and so he cannot relegate these importunate entities to their historical place in the development of the social medium. The science of metaphysic is essentially a method: not an artificial method like the method by which a man makes a clock, but a natural method like the method by which a living organism grows and makes itself. Metaphysic may thus be called the morphology of collective experience; and its method is the process going on within collective experience itself

[1] Renan compares the "conscience de tout" with that of the polypus and the oyster.

and transforming it. To appeal to experience, then, as Mr. Arnold does, is to appeal *to* metaphysic, the science of the formation and transformation of experience; not, as Mr. Arnold supposes, an appeal *from* metaphysic to something more real and solid. And it is bad—*i.e.*, unmethodized—metaphysic latent in his mental constitution, it is the illegitimate use of the ideas of the past, it is metaphysic with its ideas detached, promiscuous, flying and buzzing around him, which makes Mr. Arnold shy at metaphysic altogether, which sends him on his embassy to experience, and, as Bacon says, "arripere ex experientia varia et vulgaria, eaque nec certo comperta, nec diligenter examinata et pensitata." It is metaphysic itself which is here playing fast and loose with him, and driving him into the dim, dismal quagmires over which hover the illusions of language, the illusions of the *intellectus sibi permissus*, the idols of the theatre and of the den.

But it is time that we considered briefly, according to our programme, Mr. Arnold's criticisms on Descartes' philosophical ideas, which form the staple of his positive and direct attack upon metaphysic in the second chapter of "God and the Bible." These criticisms relate to two points in Descartes' philosophy—(1) the proposition *cogito ergo sum*, and (2) the proposition that "ideas which represent substances to us . . . . contain more objective reality—that is to say, they partake by representation *in more degrees of being* or perfection—than those which represent to us modes or accidents only."[1]

Of the first, the *cogito ergo sum*, Mr. Arnold says he understands the meaning of the first word, but not of the last. "Now what to think is we all know . . . . a thing, says Descartes, which thinks is a thing which doubts, which understands, which conceives, which affirms, which desires, which wishes, which declines, which imagines also, and which feels." But Descartes does not explain

[1] "God and the Bible," pp. 64, foll.

his terms, *I am, I exist,* "because to him they carry an even more clear and well-defined sense than the term, *I think*. But to us they do not." Mr. Arnold then looks into Dr. Curtius's "Outlines of Greek Etymology," and gives us his philological variations on the text, "I grow," "I feel that I am alive," &c., which made everybody in England smile. Now here one might point out, *in limine*, that if *to think* is satisfactorily explained by an enumeration of its modes, "to doubt, to understand, to conceive," &c., it is difficult to see why *to be* should not also be satisfactorily explained in like manner; *to be*—*i.e.*, "to stand, to appear, to be handled, to be a stone, a man, a tree. We all exist; we affirm it of each other every day of our lives, and of things around us." And so on, by enumerating the different modes of being.

It is not necessary for me to go further, as I had originally intended, into Mr. Arnold's criticism of this dictum of Descartes, for one of the most exact and accomplished of our English philosophers, Mr. Shadworth Hodgson, has shown in a recent number of the quarterly journal called *Mind*[1] that Mr. Arnold has misconceived the meaning of *cogito ergo sum* through not knowing a passage in the "Meditationes de prima Philosophia," in which Descartes explains it. It means "I think"—that is to say, "I am;" "my existence means my consciousness;" "I am" means "I think;" so that all the structure built upon the foundation of "I grow," "I feel myself to be alive," is superfluous, and falls to the ground.

Now let us take Mr. Arnold's second criticism—viz., of the statement that *some ideas have more objective reality than others*. He gets to this second proposition of Descartes in his search for the meaning of *to be* in the first.

We find that with Descartes to possess more perfection means to possess, not what men commonly call by that name, but to possess more being. And this seems to be merely

[1] No. iv pp. 568, foll.

going round in a circle, and we have to confess ourselves fairly puzzled and beaten.[1]

Now here, too, as in the former case, what is wanted is not any extraordinary philosophical acumen, but merely accurate knowledge of fact. The fact is this—*Being* in the second proposition belongs to an entirely different order of ideas to *Being* in the first proposition, and therefore in no way helps to an elucidation of the latter. In the *cogito ergo sum*, " I am—*i.e.*, I think" is the last point reached in a process of doubt, of which it is impossible to doubt—*i.e.*, it is an idea arrived at, conditioned by a process of reasoning in Descartes himself. In the second proposition, on the contrary, that "more perfection" means "more being," Descartes is simply Platonizing; he is putting forth with assurance an idea, and a false idea, which he, along with every other person educated in the scholastic controversy about " Universals" had in that age imbibed, and which Descartes had not consciously abandoned. It was false—*i.e.*, it was obsolete and meaningless—and Descartes' own *cogito ergo sum*, by giving philosophy a new starting-point, rendered it, if nothing else did, obsolete. But put it back into its proper place in Plato's ideal theory, and it at once has a meaning.

But it is most natural for a man to appeal with assurance to hereditary ideas which are unsound, but which he has never consciously abandoned; just as Mr. Arnold himself in this very chapter talks with assurance of *objects which strike our senses*, a mode of thought unsound and misleading, and having its only place in a crude realism which has long been obsolete.

But the reader may ask, How did Plato get this notion of *degrees of Being?* This is a long and difficult problem, scarcely appropriate for discussion here, and open, moreover, to much dispute; perhaps, however, the following remarks may throw a little light upon it.

[1] "God and the Bible," p. 71.

Plato, then, conceived the world as a pyramid, the base of which is formed by groups of recurring sensations similar (in each group) to one another. Immediately above this base-line is a shorter row consisting of *particular objects of perception*, corresponding each to one of the groups of exactly similar sensations in the base, chairs, tables, trees, &c., as we know and use them in actual life. Above this second line is a still shorter row, consisting of the *classes* to which the chairs, tables, trees, &c., respectively belong, their common properties being attended to and their individual peculiarities neglected, "chair," "table," "tree," &c. Above this row of classes is a fourth and still shorter row of wider classes, to each of which several of the narrower classes on the third row belong—*e.g.*, "chair," "table," "tree," would all come under the class "vegetable substance;" and similarly there would be other groups of classes, such as "mineral substance," "animal substance;" then the different classes of substance would come under the larger class of substance; and so on, until, by throwing off differences at each stage, a single highest class, "Being," is reached, forming the apex of the pyramid. Now Plato seems to have remarked that the lowest row but one consisted of items which, as being permanent objects of perception—this chair, this table, this tree, &c.—are more real, that is, more definite and more permanent, as well as more outward, less dependent on my subjective state than the similar sensations which recur to me and then vanish, whenever I look at each of these objects and then look away again; thus the *chair itself* is there whether I am looking at it or not. Remarking this greater reality in the object of perception than in the series of evanescent sensations, Plato inferred—and here he went wrong, for it was an unwarrantable inference—that because the objects of perception in the second row were more real than the group of sensations, *therefore the class of ideas which form the items in the third row are more real than the objects of perception;* and the wider and more abstract class of ideas in the fourth row, more real than those in the third; until he came to Being, the highest, widest and most abstract class-idea of all, which was, he thought, by a parity of reasoning, the richest and fullest of all, instead of the emptiest.

Having reached the top of his pyramid, and coming down the scale again, it is very easy to see how natural it was for Plato to say that the rows of more abstract class-ideas, as being nearer to the top, *partook more of Being* than the rows lower down, and that the lowest row of classes partook more of Being than the row of objects of perception, until the minimum of reality was reached in sensation.

This dictum about partaking of more degrees of Being thus becomes easy of comprehension so soon as we see how it arose; how it is part of a system of thought; and how natural it was in Plato, handling the artifice of classification for the first time, and anxious to give it importance and show its cogency, to make just the false step that he did make. This illusion of a "world turned upside down" (*eine verkehrte Welt*), in which the most abstract ideas have the most reality, dominated the Middle Ages; it is the foundation of Scholasticism; but so soon as we can put our finger on the point where the error began, it all falls through, and Scholasticism with it; so that we need have no uneasiness about the monumental fragment of it which Descartes—"mathématicien sans pareil, physicien moins heureux, moraliste et psychologue de second ordre"[1]—Descartes, educated in the Scholastic Philosophy and not yet free from its illusions—built into his philosophical system. At the same time we may remark that Plato's ideal theory has many points of resemblance to Mr. Arnold's construction of the "Eternal not-ourselves that makes for righteousness." Like the "Eternal," it is a hollow structure built of words; and yet both the one and the other is founded on a basis of

[1] Renan, "Fragments Philosophiques," p. 321.

experience. Plato is faithful to experience when he says you must rise out of the chaos of sensation into the cosmos of perception, and you shall have greater reality; Mr. Arnold is faithful to experience when he says you must rise out of the chaos of the animal desires into the cosmos of the moral life of righteousness, and you shall have joy; Plato then makes a false but very natural inference, and takes his flight into the air; Mr. Arnold also makes his verbal confusion of the meanings of the word eternal, and takes his flight into the air too; we lose sight of them both at the same point, and from henceforth we hear the flapping of their wings, but cannot follow them.

In conclusion it remains to ask whether there is any thing in experience corresponding to Mr. Arnold's new religious construction, "the eternal not-ourselves that makes for righteousness;" or, in other words, *what is it that really and experimentally makes for, or promotes, righteousness in the world as we know it? is it a not-ourselves, is it outside of ourselves? is it eternal in any exact and scientific sense of the word?* The first of these is a question upon which Mr. Arnold scarcely touches. He promises to do two things: to show first what was the experience of the ancient Israelite, upon which he based his religion; and to show, in the second place, what is the experience which we have in common with the ancient Israelite, whereon we can base ours. The first of these promises he performs, and we have already examined his performance of it; but the second he never performs at all, and when in "God and the Bible," after "the God of miracles" has been dismissed, and the "God of metaphysics" has been exploded, he comes to the "God of experience," instead of telling us what are the experiences of our life of to-day upon which we may base our religion and our idea of God, he gives us little more than a recapitulation of the Biblical passages by which he endeavoured before, and as we think failed, to show that the "God of the Bible" was an inference from the profound emotion with which the ancient Israelite regarded the thought of righteousness. Such a foundation could by no means be made to carry such a superstructure.

But now, as to our own experience, of which Mr. Arnold, instead of considering it fully by itself, makes a problem ancillary, or, as we may say, parasitical, to the problem of Jewish experience—what are the data? Do we experience a force outside of us always drawing us towards good, and never towards evil? Are the righteous always happy, and the wicked never prosperous?[1] It is said that Diagoras of Melos, when he saw the offerings of the sailors in the temple of Poseidon, remarked, "We count those who were saved: no one counts those who were drowned, who yet made their vows like the rest." So we count the good who prosper, and the wicked who are miserable; no one counts the wicked who are so insensate as to be happy, or the good who are so sensitive as to be miserable. To Schopenhauer, on the other hand, the sight of man's unhappiness, irrespective of his actions, was so overpowering that he drew from it the conclusion that the Supreme Will was malevolent. We must at any rate not blink this side of experience, if we would be just in our estimate. It seems doubtful if we know yet what the secret of happiness is: it would appear to be very much more an affair of the nervous system, of the temperament than of conduct. It attends us unsought; and if we seek it, it flies from us. If we pursue righteousness of set purpose to obtain happiness, we miss happiness, and our righteousness becomes immoral, because it ceases to be disinterested. If this were not so, if to righteousness were really annexed happiness, happiness and the pursuit of it would be that which more than anything else "makes for righteousness." But this is not the case. What is it then which bears us, like a stream

[1] "Le soleil a vu sans se voiler les plus criantes iniquités, il a souri aux plus grands crimes."—RENAN: "Fragm. Phil.," pp. 13, 41, &c.

upon its bosom, when we are acting in a certain way, and which buffets and baffles us, and gives us an intolerable sense of isolation, if we act in the opposite way? It is the social medium, the community of which we are organic parts: not only the opinion of our immediate circle, nor the arm of the law, nor the pen of the scribe, nor the preaching of the Churches, but a certain stress and direction in the march of events themselves, which impel us to do the things which shall be of the greatest and widest benefit, whether we find them agreeable or not.[1] I often think, when a criminal is punished for an offence against the law, that about one-third of the penalty he suffers is his due, and that the rest ought to be set down to the account of the community, whose imperfections in past generations and in this have made him what he is. So with laudable actions, we get praise for them as if they were our own several estate, and yet but for that larger collective life of which our own is the outcome, we should not have been capable of them. In every action of the individual, how much is due to character, and how much to the circumstances of his position, will vary with each case: but certain it is that as societies become more complex and firmly knit together, the part played by character becomes increasingly less. And then what is character itself but a crystallization of social conditions round a single point? Yet man is free in his action, each in his measure, in so far as character reacts upon the social environment. That which "makes for righteousness in the world" is the ascent of a society towards its zenith; that which makes for unrighteousness is the decline of a society towards stagnation or dissolution. In the former case all or most of the social conditions go to the nourishment and fertilization of character; and it blossoms naturally, like the trees in spring. In the

---

[1] Theodore Parker gave about three parts out of a hundred of the result of any life to freedom, the rest to necessity (*The Unitarian Review*, Boston, Oct. 1878, p. 424).

latter case, character has to subsist for the most part upon its native stamina, *i.e.*, upon the transmission through individuals of hereditary qualities. In a declining community righteousness is what the anthropologists call "a survival;" such was the righteousness of a man like Marcus Aurelius; it drew its sustenance not from the present but from the past. But yet the world progresses upon the whole? It does, and this is the reason—because in the intercourse of nations the principles of conduct which have characterized one society in its highest development may be taken as the starting-point of an infant community. Such were Roman institutions and Jewish religion to the German barbarians of the third century. Such were English institutions and Puritanism to the American commonwealth, so that the decay of the old communities counts for little in the history of the world, although it counts for much in the life of the individual citizen. Stoicism and asceticism are the forms which righteousness takes in a period of social decline; and these before long, like plants transferred to a vacuum, living organisms placed under a receiver, begin *in vacuo* to lose their freshness, and decay too. Then the study and pursuit of the old righteousness, especially under the influence of a nascent society around them, begin to organize themselves anew in social *nuclei* apart from the main community, in brotherhoods and orders of religious. These orders then begin to simulate the changes which come over the great society outside them, at the same time that they become its teachers. "Asceticism," as I have said elsewhere, "itself the negation of all institutions, becomes itself an institution." Anachoretic in a time of anarchy, it comes in contact with feudalism, and becomes itself the owner of serfs and of land; in a lettered age it becomes lettered; in an age of chivalry chivalrous; in the dawn of physical science and of popular ideas it becomes scientific and democratic; and then, lastly, becomes corrupt and drops off, like an aged parasite, from the main trunk of social life, as it expands towards its full stature.

This then, I would submit, is the history of what Mr. Arnold calls "righteousness" in the world; and this is the *total* fact of experience with which we have to deal. But upon this, as before upon the partial experience of the ancient Israelite, *no religious tenet whatever can be founded*. The only thing that we know of by experience, as making for or promoting righteousness, is the healthy and normal growth of a human society; but this growth is no more a metaphysical abstraction outside of the individual, than his conscience or his actions are outside of him; and it is no more "eternal" in any recognized or intelligible sense of the word, than human society itself. That human society is not eternal *ex parte ante* we know, because we have record of a time when man did not exist upon the surface of the globe; it is not eternal *ex parte post* because we have every reason to suppose that conditions incompatible with the existence of organic life will again supervene. In the meantime, and between these two limits, we have as a fact of actual experience, communities of men, each the embodiment of a collective consciousness, of a common experience; so that we may hope some day to give organic expression to the collective mind and conscience of mankind; to organize not a *Zeit-Geist* merely, the spirit of a particular community, or group of communities, or of a particular time, but a *Welt-Geist*, a world-spirit, in which all that is partial shall be done away, and the race shall be as conscious of the unity of its total life as a man is now. Such an idea, however, can only find its true expression in what we have called the metaphysical synthesis. And after all it may never be realized: the chances seem against its realization. "Both the world and society tend of themselves by a sort of law of inertia towards equilibrium which will be their death."[1] "An irremediable deca-

[1] "Dial. Philos.," 53.

dence of the human species is possible."[1] "The exhaustion of coal and the generalization of the principles of egoism," *i.e.*, the erection of selfishness into a principle, may cause the decline of man, long before the cooling of the sun shall drive him from the temperate to the torrid zones, and from the outer limits of the torrid zone to the equator. Society, character, religion, and the arts and sciences will, in that event, die before they have come to their perfection.[2]

Is there then no God in heaven? Must we cry with Novalis, "Children, ye have no father"? By no means; M. Renan says, "Un monde sans Dieu est horrible." I say so too. But the "eternal not-ourselves which makes for righteousness" is not what we mean by God: it is simply the disembodied ghost of the *Zeit-Geist* or "better self" on which Mr. Arnold enlarged so well in his earlier books; so far as it is more than an edifice of words built on the quicksands of an ambiguity, it is *the mirage or metaphysical double* of the community. It is a metaphysical idea, or rather it is the moiety of a metaphysical idea. It is not the whole, it is not the synthesis, the *Begriff;* it is one of the factors of the synthesis, without its complementary factor. The synthesis embraces the tendencies which promote righteousness, combined and interwoven with the tendencies which hinder it. In any given community this is the total fact of experience, if you will face it, and this is the fact as metaphysic interprets it. But an abstraction of the understanding, crowned with a negative particle, and robed with the Eternal Name,—"the eternal not-ourselves which makes for righteousness," does it not impose upon us with the illusory definiteness of an empty formula from which the contents of the actual religious consciousness have been sedulously excluded? is it more substantial than the enunciation of Mr. Dombey's elegant and languid mother-

---

[1] "Dial. Phil." p. 64.
[2] "Elle mourra avant d'avoir atteint la sagesse," *ibid.* p. 67.

in-law:—"There is no What's-his-name but Thingummy; and What-you-may-call-it is his prophet?"[1]

To sum up. We have seen Mr. Arnold driven to take the true metaphysical point of view by the exigences of his polemic against the Liberal Philistine in "Culture and Anarchy," and again by the exigences of his polemic against the religious Philistine in "St. Paul and Protestantism;" we have then seen his decline and fall from this point of view in "Literature and Dogma" and in "God and the Bible," conditioned by the exigences of his efforts to persuade the irreligious and desirous-to-be-scientific Philistine to reopen his Bible and to appreciate the importance of conduct. We have seen that he tries to "get round" the irreligious Philistine by saying, "Come now, we will give up all metaphysics, and we will go only upon the ground of experience." We have seen that by thus descending to the Philistine's level, he does not really get out of the metaphysical region, but only out of the region of good metaphysic into the region of bad metaphysic, of idols and illusions such as the Philistine knows and rejoices in; and that he thereby leaves the main high road along which travels the large experience of mankind, and of which metaphysic is the formal science, and shuts himself up in the small parcel of experience, with which the Philistine nourishes and flatters himself. And the fundamental assumption which lies at the root of all this bad metaphysic, and this frustrated appeal to experience, is to be sought in a latent tendency in Mr. Arnold himself, which appears as early as in his first book.[2] It is the assumption that "thought and speculation is an individual matter," it is the tendency to "philosophize alone," instead of moving in the broad pathways along

---

[1] "Dombey and Son," ch. xxvii. The passage should have been quoted entire: "The idea! my dearest Edith, there is such an obvious destiny in it, that really one might almost be induced to cross one's arm upon one's frock, and say, like those wicked Turks, 'There is,'" &c.

[2] "Culture and Anarchy," pp. 185, 186.

which knowledge is actually advancing. This assumption is at once the basis of the private judgment on which the religious Philistine relies, and of the popular empiricism upon which the irreligious Philistine builds. It is the same assumption as that of the individual as something given on the one side, and of experience as something given on the other: and this assumption is itself metaphysical, only it is bad metaphysic, it is a petrified fragment of a metaphysical synthesis, instead of the living whole of a synthesis of the *Zeit-Geist*. May we not say of metaphysic in the words of the poet—

> "They reckon ill who leave me out,
> *When me they fly I am the wings;*
> I am the doubter and the doubt,
> And I the hymn the Brahmin sings."

Having spoken so severely of Mr. Arnold's later works in their scientific aspect, I desire to record my enjoyment of them and gratitude for them in every other. What can be more delightful than the passage in "Literature and Dogma" about the "Muse of Righteousness"?[1] The account, too, of St. Paul's doctrine in "St. Paul and Protestantism;" and of the early witnesses and of the "method" and "secret" of Jesus in "Literature and Dogma;" and again of the Bible Canon and of the Fourth Gospel in "God and the Bible," seem to me, in spite of what the learned critics have said about their inaccuracy, to be quite admirable in their way. They surely contain with sufficient accuracy all that a man of general cultivation, as distinguished from a professional student, need know about these subjects. And then the purity and freshness of the thoughts which hide from us the angular and unlovely lineaments of the Puritan metaphysic—how charming they are! I always experience the same sensation in reading these books of Mr. Arnold as I have when reading Mr. Ruskin's later works; it is the sensation

---

[1] P. 23.

as of a breeze bringing health from sweet and sunny fields, and blowing for a moment across the exhausted atmosphere of a German lecture-room. But then to enjoy this refreshment one must turn away from the thing said to the means and manner of saying it; and one must listen to these, not as to an exposition of fact, but as one listens to a nocturne of Chopin, or to the sound of wholesome rain dropping on a dry place.

AMERICAN EFFORTS

AFTER

INTERNATIONAL COPYRIGHT.

AMERICAN EFFORTS AFTER INTERNATIONAL COPYRIGHT.

The questions of principle involved in International Copyright, and in the American practice of reprinting English books freely in the absence of a Copyright Convention with this country, have been so completely handled a year ago by Mr. Edward Dicey in this Review,[1] that I do not propose to enter upon that part of the subject. I would only add to his exposition one or two illustrative points which are generally unknown or forgotten in this country. The first is this: that the practice of freely reprinting books in the absence of international copyright has been and is still common in Europe. The Irish publishers, and notably Swift's Dublin publisher, Faulkner, were accustomed to reprint Lord Chesterfield's Letters, Richardson's novels, and a host of other English books, without paying for them. And at the time of the Union it was put forward as a grievance by the Dublin publishers, that this large and lucrative branch of trade was taken away from them. Similarly, the Belgians, before the Convention of 1861, pirated French books by wholesale; the Dutch to this day systematically pirate German music; the Germans, as systematically, the Russian novels of Turguenief and Pushkin; until recently the German States reprinted each others' books; not to mention the large number of American books which have been pirated by ourselves. But universal practice is of course no justification; and the second point to which I would draw attention is that the

[1] *Fortnightly Review*, January, 1876.

general principle upon which the Americans defend both their opposition to a convention with Great Britain, and also their practice of reprinting freely in the absence of one—viz., that they consider themselves bound to consult exclusively the benefit of their own people—is a principle which has been repeatedly laid down in cases of disputed copyright by the judges in our English courts and in the House of Lords;[1] whilst it has been stated by Pütter, one of the greatest legal authorities of the last century in Germany, that no principle of right is violated by the mere reprinting of foreign works, provided the reprints be not smuggled into the country of the original work, as was formerly done in the German States in respect of one another, and by the Belgians and Dutch in respect of France. The third point to which I would direct Mr. Dicey's attention is this. He does not seem to be aware that a practice has grown up, during the last fifteen or twenty years, with the best firms in the United States, of paying liberally for the English books which they reprint, although under no compulsion in law or equity to do so. The largest reprinting firm, that of Messrs. Harper and Brothers in New York, has paid not less than £50,000 during the last twenty years to English authors. The exact sums that they have paid for some score or more of the most famous English books I have myself, at their invitation, copied down from their ledgers.

But it is time to turn to what are my especial aims in the present paper. They are twofold. I desire in the first place to bring into one view the different directions which opinion has taken of late years in the United States on the subject of copyright, and in the second to give a connected account of the various efforts which have been made by American authors and publishers to bring about a convention with England. In the course of this history I shall lay before the reader a

[1] See the cases in Short's "Law Relating to the Works of Literature." London: Cox. 1871.

number of documents bearing upon the subject, some of which exist only in manuscript in the Library of Congress at Washington, and many are unknown to the majority of Americans themselves.

It is generally supposed in this country that, on the subject of international copyright, American opinion is homogeneous. This is far from being the case. There are half-a-dozen more or less divergent groups of opinion among different classes of persons concerned in the question, and in different parts of the country. There are, first, the authors of New England and a small number of publishers, of whom I may take the firm of Messrs. J. R. Osgood & Co., of Boston (formerly Ticknor & Fields), as the type, who are in favour of international copyright pure and simple, without restrictions or conditions of any kind. The highest class of newspapers, not only in New England, but throughout the country, whether Free Traders or Protectionists, whether Democrats or Republicans, are accustomed to advocate, with more or less of qualification, the same liberal measures. At the other end of the scale of opinion stands the Pennsylvanian School, which opposes international copyright of all kinds and with whatever qualification. Of this school Philadelphia is the head, and the aged and much-respected economist, Mr. Henry C. Carey, is the thinking brain. To this school one firm in New York of the first importance, Messrs. Harper and Brothers, of Franklin Square, may be said, with reservations, to belong; and it does not want friends amongst the manufacturers and farmers of the Middle and Western States, and amongst the trades which are ancillary to the publishing trade, such as type-founders, paper-makers and binders, throughout the Union.

Between these two extremes there are three or four smaller groups in favour of international copyright under conditions, but differing as to what are the best conditions. We may call these groups of intermediate opinion collectively the New York School, as the practical measures in which they have been embodied have issued for the most part from the leading publishing firms of New York.

To begin with the extreme opponents and with Mr. Carey, a name reverenced in Pennsylvania and celebrated throughout the Union both by friends and foes, not less than is that of the late Mr. Mill in England. In this country his works are scarcely known, but in Germany they are translated and held in honour; whilst in Russia, whose area and some of whose other conditions are somewhat like those of the United States, they are, or were within the last few years, in use as a text book.[1] Mr. Carey's views on copyright have at present the advantage of being the only ones based upon a coherent economical theory. The fundamental idea of Mr. Carey's social science is that of the decentralization of industry. A community, he holds, should aim at producing all the commodities it needs, so as to be independent of its neighbours. This he regards as the condition of political independence. Secondly, in an extensive country like America the production of the necessary commodities should be, as far as possible, equally spread over the whole area, so as to bring the producer and consumer into immediate relations, and eliminate "the middleman." This internal decentralization produces diversity of employments, stimulates the circulation and interchange of social elements, and is the condition of sound and progressive popular education. Now international copyright, supposing it established, would either place the monopoly of the American market for English books in the hands of the great English firms, thus making America dependent on her neighbour, or else it would place it in the hands of five or six of the most important firms in the three chief Atlantic cities—New York,

[1] The reader will find a short but intelligible account of Mr. Carey's views in the *Academy* of January 27, 1877.

Boston, and Philadelphia—thus conflicting with the principle of internal decentralization. Further, he thinks that the introduction of cheap reprints of English books does not compete unfavourably with the more expensive editions of native authors, but prepares a market for them; and this opinion is held by many practical men. As to the payment of English authors, he says he does not agree with those who protest against international copyright on the score that such payment would increase the price of these reprints.

If nothing better than this can be said (he exclaims)[1] we may as well at once plead guilty to the charge of piracy and commence a new and more honest course of action. Evil may not be done that good may come of it, nor may we steal an author's brains that our people may be cheaply taught. .... We stand in need of no such morality as this. We can afford to pay for what we want; but even were it otherwise, our motto here and everywhere should be the old French one, *Fais ce que doy, advienne que pourra*.

But copyright, he thinks, is a wasteful way of collecting what is due to the author, inasmuch as nine-tenths of what is collected would go to the parties standing between the author and the reader—*i.e.*, to the "middlemen." As Mr. Carey was in earlier life himself a publisher, this statement may be worth consideration. On the other hand, if we must have some sort of copyright, he adds finally, let it be in the form of a royalty, fixed by law and paid to the author by every publisher who reprints his book; and let all, on this condition, be at liberty to reprint, in the same way as all managers of theatres are at liberty, on payment of a royalty to the author of a play, to act his piece.[2]

Solidaire wholly or in part, and for practical purposes wholly *solidaire* with Mr. Carey, are three other important

---

[1] "Letters on International Copyright" (2nd Edition. New York: Hurd and Houghton), p. 21.

[2] Ibid., p. 77.

interests which we must now specify. The first of these is the powerful New York publishing house of Harper and Brothers before mentioned, who hold that an international copyright is objectionable because it would increase the price of books, and thus tend to bring down and narrow the popular intelligence. And it must be remembered that, so far as any influence upon Congress is concerned, the little finger of Mr. Harper is thicker than the loins of all the literary and scientific men in the United States put together.

The second large interest which works more or less with Mr. Carey and his friends is that of the considerable *booksellers* of the Middle and Western States, who are not publishers to any appreciable extent, but would be glad to have their pickings, like the rest, out of the English, and, for the matter of that, out of the native market too, and who would oppose international copyright, and may so be classed along with the other constituents of Mr. Carey's phalanx. At present the bulk of the English reprints are monopolized by five or six leading firms in Boston, New York and Philadelphia. They get everything worth having, partly because they have exceptional opportunities of knowing at the earliest moment what is to be had, and have long established communications with England; partly because they control the channels of distribution through the whole area of the Union, whilst the Western bookseller only commands the limited area of perhaps half-a-dozen States in his immediate neighbourhood; and lastly, but not least, because they alone are strong enough to quash competition. After many mutual invasions and reprisals, these leading firms of the East have established what is called a "courtesy copyright" between themselves—nominally, I am aware, extended to all publishers being American citizens, and not representatives of London houses—but practically confined to those who are able to retaliate when the "trade courtesy" is violated. This "courtesy copyright" is a tacit understanding that when one great house advertises the fact that it has made arrangements with the English author or publisher for the reproduction of his book, the other great houses are not to reprint that particular book. This system of "courtesy copyright," which has been gradually growing up of late years, should be spoken of with respect, for it represents an improvement in commercial morality, as well as of loyalty towards each other, and of good feeling towards England; and so far as the English author and publisher are concerned, it is an increasingly efficient substitute in the majority of cases for the benefits which they would derive from copyright. But this is not the view taken of the coalition by the booksellers who are left out in the cold, and who have scarcely a chance of getting hold of an English book before it has been snapped up in one of the Atlantic cities. These booksellers have little opportunity of coming across the English author and getting his latest book; their names are unknown in England, their solvency and sea-worthiness, and the extent of their means and appliances for making a book succeed, and the area of their habitual operations, can only be understood by those who have visited America. Some of them nourish the greatest jealousy of the half-dozen fortunate firms, and would regard any form of international copyright which has been proposed as securing for good the monopoly of the Eastern against the Middle and the Western cities. Their grievances would find local expression in the newspapers, and the Congress-man, who comes up to Washington with his mind, as is generally the case, a perfect blank on the merits of copyright, cannot afford to overlook the expression of opinion in the local newspaper, to which perhaps he owes his seat. Only on very stringent terms, framed expressly to break down the Eastern monopoly, would the bookseller who is ambitious to become a publisher consent to international copyright. Here is a sample proposition as it frames itself in the mind of such a bookseller. "We will only," one said to me, "consent to the protection of English books in this country, provided you can establish some system which will give us the same chance of getting them to publish as the New York houses have. This might be done by a public agent at Washington, who should be charged to receive all English manuscripts which were for sale to American publishers. He should advertise their titles and invite tenders for them; and of these tenders he should then be compelled to accept the highest, from whatever part of the country it came, provided it was the tender of a firm of known respectability and solvency." Whatever may be thought of the economical eccentricity of this proposal, there is very little doubt that the great firms of the East would be able to bring sufficient pressure to bear upon Congress to prevent any such measures being taken for the undermining of their monopoly.

We must add lastly to the account of the forces and interests with which the advocate of international copyright has to reckon in the United States, the growing conviction among the farmers and the manufacturing classes in the Western States of the inutility and injurious effects of the system of patents. Copyright, whether domestic or international, is, after all, nothing but a kind of patent, and the recognition of their identity in principle was shown in a characteristic manner by the American Act of 1846, since superseded, which prescribed that books to be copyrighted in the several States of the Union should be deposited with the district clerks in order to be sent to the Patent Office at Washington.[1]

The growing disfavour with which patents are regarded has found expression not only in the United States but also in Europe. Switzerland has abolished the system altogether, and its abolition in Holland was discussed in the Legislature of that country in 1869. But the

[1] *American Library Journal*, vol. i., Nos. 2 and 3, p. 89. Paper of Mr. A. R. Spofford, the Librarian of Congress, on Copyright.

weightiest European exponent of the case against patents is Prince Bismarck, in a message which he sent to the North German Federal Parliament, December 10, 1868.[1] As the arguments against patents are identical with those against copyright, it may be worth while to summarize the statement of them given by the German Chancellor:—

After taking the opinion of the Chambers of Commerce and the Mercantile Corporations, the Prussian Government, on the occasion of the German Federal Assembly Session of 31st of December, 1863, gave utterance to the doubt whether, under present circumstances patents for inventions may be considered either necessary or useful to industry. Since then the Royal Prussian Government has taken the question once more into serious consideration and feels bound to answer it in the negative on the strength of the following arguments.

The arguments then given may be succinctly stated as follows:—(*a*) Patents are not warranted by a natural claim on the part of the inventor, nor (*b*) are they consequent upon general economical principles. (*c*) They involve an attack upon the inalienable right which every man has of applying each and every lawful advantage to the exercise of his profession. (*d*) The development of communication enables an inventor, without the aid of a patent, to make sure of a temporary profit in advance of competitors in proportion to the service rendered to the public. (*e*) It is the opinion of experienced officers charged with the examination of claims for patents, that it is practically impossible to master the matters submitted, or to uphold anything like a strict criterion of originality. (*f*) Patents are for the most part taken out with a view to swindling speculation;[2] and complaints are made of the abuses and impediments which they bring upon industry. (*h*) Patents have not proved an actual benefit either to the proprietor

---

[1] See his arguments in "Abolition of Patents, Recent Discussions," &c. (Longmans, 1869), p. 185.

[2] In Prussia, 87 per cent of the requests for patents have been non-suited during the last ten years.

or to the public, and the profits have gone just as often into the pockets of strangers as into those of the inventor; a satisfactory reform in the mode of granting them seems to be impossible. The evils are inherent in the very constitution of the privilege. (*i*) The great inventions of the past were made without this stimulus, and the absence of patent-right in Switzerland has not been found at all prejudicial to the public at large. Lastly, it has not been found that where patents have been abolished inventors have turned themselves to countries still willing to protect them.

I have preferred to state the arguments against patent monopoly as they are set down by the great European statesman, partly because they are here expressed with greater clearness, order, and conciseness than can be found, so far as I know, in any Transatlantic writer, and partly because I wish the reader to appreciate the fact that the movement in opposition to patents, involving as it does precisely the same principles as the movement in opposition to copyright, is not a peculiarity of the Americans, in which we in Europe have no part. Indeed it is easy to see that every argument adduced by Prince Bismarck hangs together with the economical theories just expounded of Mr. Carey and his followers. For it should be noted that Mr. Carey's argument against monopoly carries with it not only the condemnation of international copyright, but of domestic copyright also. And he warns his countrymen, in a characteristic passage, to let international copyright alone, lest they be overtaken by the demand for a discussion of the grounds upon which their own domestic copyright is based. However this may be, it seems out of the question to hope for anything but opposition to an International Convention with England from the Western farmers and manufacturers, who at present have not had their attention directed to copyright, but who are already showing signs of dissatisfaction with the kindred institution of patents.

These are the various parties, interests, and directions of opinion which the advocate of international copyright finds ranged against him in the Middle States and the "great West," the two sections of the American Commonwealth which are every day more and more determining the character and policy of the whole. On such a subject as copyright the South is silent; since the war, it neither buys nor produces books. Which way it would be likely to go, if the discussion ever got beyond the Library Committee of the two Houses of Congress into Congress itself, I know of no data for predicting. New England we have already seen to be (roughly speaking) in favour of international copyright in the same unconditional sense as international copyright is understood in Europe. Its literary men (and there are but few literary men out of New England) believe as a body in the inherent and inalienable rights of the author, just as Mr. Charles Reade might do.

We come lastly to New York, standing midway, both in opinion and geographically, between the extreme opponents of international copyright to the south and west of it, and the extreme advocates of the same to the north and east of it. Its leading publishers unite in themselves the brilliant business qualities characteristic of the one area, with the culture and academical training of the other. From New York, then, have issued the only practical and practicable proposals that have been made for a reconciliation of these conflicting interests. Before giving an account of these proposals, and of the varied discussions to which they have given rise, I will lay before the reader a short account of the inconveniences which American publishers say they experience in the absence of a Copyright Convention with England, which one of them has put into my hands.

The present system of payment for "advance sheets" of English books, which is becoming almost universally the custom with the best houses, gives the American publisher no legal protection against competition, but purchases for him, in fact, nothing tangible, except a week or two's start in point of time over others in the trade. Payments similar in amount, or not much greater, under an international copyright, would give the publisher the required protection, and thus enable him to issue his reprints more leisurely and in better and more uniform shape; would enable him, in fact, to give his customer more for his money. Under the present system the lack of uniform editions of many of the best reprints is a serious annoyance to the book-buyer, and, in that it serves to diminish sales, causes material loss to the publisher. The books of Mr. George Macdonald are an example. They were very generally scrambled for, and the different volumes were published by four or five houses in very different styles. In the case of most of the books the author received payments for "advance sheets." They had a good initial sale in the United States as new books, but have failed to find a steady permanent sale, chiefly because it is the interest of no one house to push and advertise the set as a whole, and each publisher hesitates to advertise the volumes which he brings out because part of the advantage of such advertising would accrue to other firms. If these works could have been copyrighted in America, they would, in the natural course of things, have all been placed with one house, and the customer could then have obtained a decent uniform edition of the whole at a moderate price; the series would have been permanently catalogued and advertised, and the ultimate profits much greater both for publisher and author. Under a copyright for English books a great many desirable reprinting enterprises would be undertaken by American publishers which at present they dare not touch at all, or which, if they touch, they are obliged to carry out in a hasty, superficial, and unsatisfactory manner. Any enterprise requiring a long investment of capital is attended with special risks when subject to unscrupulous competition. The issue of a numerous set of books, for instance, may be begun with proper care and in good style, and money may be invested in the preparation of the first few volumes, and in advertising the series. But if the undertaking promises well, there is nothing to prevent an unscrupulous neighbour from printing the volumes as rapidly as the original undertaker, and perhaps, by printing them with less care, selling them at a lower price, and obtaining the advantage of the advertising and of the literary judgment of the original undertaker. This risk prevents a great many desirable things from being done, or causes them to be done improperly, and in this way it is an injury to the buyer of books as well as to the publisher.

It remains to see what practical efforts have been made on the part of the Americans to remove these inconveniences by the establishment of a limited measure of international copyright; and this will be the best form in which to consider the intermediate groups of opinion which we have characterized collectively as the New York school.

In 1838, immediately after the passing of the first International Copyright Act (Vict .1 and 2, c. 59) of the present reign, Lord Palmerston invited the American Government to co-operate in establishing a Copyright Convention between the two countries. In the previous year the late Mr. Henry Clay, as chairman of a Select Committee, had reported to the Senate of the United States very strongly in favour of such a Convention, upon the ground that the author's right of property in his work was similar to that of the inventor in his patent. The discussion of Mr. Clay's Report was crowded out at the end of a Session; and Lord Palmerston's proposal met, so far as I can learn, with no response. It is stated in an official return that at this period no less than six hundred American books had been reprinted in England.[1] A memorial was then

[1] House Document, No. 76, 30th Congress, 1st Session: quoted in Mr. Baldwin's Report (1868).

presented to Congress to the effect that international copyright would "derange and oppress the American book trade, by suddenly giving the benefit of copyright to foreign books already published."[1] This retrospective action was, I need scarcely say, not contemplated in Mr. Clay's report.

In 1843, ninety-seven firms and persons representing the book trade petitioned Congress in favour of international copyright, on the ground that its absence was "alike injurious to the business of publishing and to the best and truest interests of the people at large."[2] A memorial was presented in the same year against it, setting forth amongst other things, that it would prevent the adaptation of English books to American wants;[3] and Mr. Baldwin remarks that the mutilation and reconstruction of American books to suit English wants was also common to a "shameless" extent.

In 1853, the question of a Copyright Treaty with England was again mooted, based upon the principles set forth in the following letter from five of the New York publishing firms to Mr. Everett, at that time Secretary of State :—

"New York, *Feb.* 15*th*, 1853.
"To the Hon. Edward Everett, Secretary of State.

"Dear Sir,—As it is in contemplation to present, for the ratification of the Senate, a treaty for an international copyright between England and the United States, we deem it proper to state some points of practical necessity in passing such a treaty. In order that a British author shall require American protection it should be insisted upon that the titles of the foreign work should be entered at the United States District Court or the Department of State before its publication in England, and if within thirty days of its publication in England the work is not printed in this country, then any one in this country shall have the right of reprinting it as at present. In order to show the publisher's right of protection

---

[1] House Document, No. 416, 25th Congress, 2nd Session : quoted *ibid.*
[2] Baldwin's Report, p. 4.
[3] Senate Document, No 323, 22nd Congress, 2nd Session, *ibid.*

under this treaty, he must show his right to the book from the author in writing. In case the copyright is secured as above, it shall be provided that the type shall be set up and the book printed and bound in this country. The necessity of this provision is obvious; for if an English publisher or author may print and bind a book in England and at the same time secure a copyright without being required to print and bind his book here, then more than one-half of the mechanics and women employed in the type-founderies, printing-offices, paper-mills, book-binderies and the various collateral branches, will be thrown out of employment and great distress must follow. The people of this country are accustomed to cheap books, and great care should be had to guard against placing the power in the hands of the English publishers to force us to buy only English copies, which, from their expensive style, must be much higher in price even without the duty. This provision is right, for it protects the people from high foreign prices, and gives the author all he can desire if he will only conform to its provisions. On this plan the English author is placed upon the same footing as the American. His rights are fully protected and the largest profit accrues to him from the American sale of his books, while a suitable and just protection is also given to American mechanical industry in the manufacturing department of book-making. With great respect, we are your obedient servants,"

D. APPLETON & CO.
G. P. PUTNAM & CO.
ROBERT CARTER & BROS.
CHARLES SCRIBNER.
STAMFORD & SWORDS.

In view of this treaty, the Hon. James Cooper, a Pennsylvania Senator, asked Mr. Carey, the economist, for "information calculated to enable him to act understandingly in reference to the International Copyright Treaty now awaiting the action of the Senate;" and in the autumn of the same year Mr. Carey published his six letters on International Copyright, the fundamental positions of which I have already endeavoured to expound. Mr. Carey adduced also two other considerations, the first of which he has often reiterated to me in conversation. This is, that the facts and ideas in a book, as distinguished from the language in which they are clothed, are the common property of society. In these it is impossible to have copyright ; and the embodiment and presentment of them in words is as often as not merely mechanical bookmaking, unworthy of protection, whether national or international. Somewhat similar views have been enunciated in this country by Mr. D. Robertson Blaine, in the discussion on Lord Westbury's Bill (1836) " to extend the protection of copyright in prints and engravings to Ireland ;" and by M. Michel Chevalier in a speech before the Société d'Economie Politique, June 5, 1869.[1] Mr. Carey's other objection was to a point of form. A question affecting the population so widely, he held, must not be disposed of in a treaty to be negotiated by the Senate, but must come before the more popular branch of the legislature, otherwise it would be repudiated by the people within a year.[2] After this the question seems to have been shelved, or, as Mr. Carey phrases it, " evaded," for fourteen years.

In 1867, it was reopened in the October number of the *Atlantic Monthly*, by an article urging the same points as Mr. Clay had brought forward thirty years before. This was answered by the republication of Mr. Carey's letters of 1853 : but Congress, at the beginning of the following year, instructed the Committee on the Library " to inquire into the subject of International Copyright, &c., and to report by bill or otherwise." This committee consists of three members from each House, and is charged with the direction of the Library of Congress, an institution embracing the functions of the British Museum and of

---

[1] See " Recent Discussions on the Abolition of Patents, &c.," pp. 324 and 168.

[2] This was put still more explicitly in his subsequent pamphlet, " The International Copyright Question considered." Philadelphia : H. C. Baird. 1872. P. 4.

Stationers' Hall. The three members from the Senate were Mr. Morgan (New York), Mr. Fessenden (Maine), since deceased, and Mr. Howe (Wisconsin); those from the House of Representatives were Mr. Pruyn (New York), Mr. Spalding (Ohio), and Mr. Baldwin (Massachusetts), chairman. In Mr. Baldwin's Report,[1] to which I have already had occasion to refer, it is stated that "your committee feel that no country has greater need of International Copyright than ours;" and the following considerations are brought forward in support of a measure: (1) A sense of justice to the author's right of property in his work should be sufficient to secure the establishment of International Copyright laws. (2) Such laws would contribute powerfully and successfully to develop our own literature and make it national, instead of its being, as at present "it has to a large extent remained, provincial to that of Great Britain." (3) International Copyright would very much improve the business of manufacturing, publishing, and selling books in the United States, by giving it stability and certainty. (4) It would greatly promote the interests of American book-buyers. Copyright is the price paid by the publisher for security in the market; and with this security he could afford to sell cheaper, and to print and bind better. As a writer in the *North American Review* says, "Copyright would procure not a less, but a greater multiplication and cheapness of copies." The principal inconveniences alleged against International Copyright are then discussed, the most important objection, "that this policy would give British manufacturers of books entire monopoly of the American market," being thus answered: "It is enough to reply that the measure we propose would make such British monopoly of our market impossible; for American

---

[1] Fortieth Congress, 2nd session. Report No. 16, House of Representatives. I have to thank Mr. A. R. Spofford, the courteous Librarian of Congress, for placing this and other official documents, both printed and MS., at my disposal.

editions of foreign books, to have the proposed benefit of Copyright, must be wholly manufactured here." Mr. Baldwin, from the Committee of the Library, at the same time reported a Bill to the House[1] giving effect to this proviso, and adding the further one that the reprints, as a condition of their protection, shall be "issued for sale by a publisher or publishers who are citizens of the United States." The benefit of Copyright would appear also by sec. 4 to be expressly limited to "the author, and the heirs, assigns, or other legal representatives of the author." The Report was ordered to be printed and recommitted; and the Bill, introduced February 21st, 1868, was read twice, ordered to be printed and also recommitted to the Committee on the Library.

It was not until the close of the year 1871 that the subject was again mooted in the American Legislature. In the autumn, Mr. William H. Appleton, one of the partners in the New York publishing house of D. Appleton & Co., wrote to the *Times* (Oct. 20) explaining and defending the qualified copyright advocated in the publishers' letter to Mr. Everett, and in Mr. Baldwin's Bill. He also explained, in opposition to the statements made in a number of recent letters to the *Times*, soundly rating the Americans for unscrupulous "piracy," &c., that the best American houses had for some years adopted the policy of establishing direct relations with English authors, and, in default of the legal compulsion of copyright, paying them voluntarily and regularly the same royalty on the reprints of their books as they would have received if they had been American citizens. Replies to Mr. Appleton from Mr. F. R. Daldy (Bell & Daldy), and Mr. M. H. Hodder (Hodder and Stoughton), were published in the *Times* of Oct. 24, the latter admitting that the advantages to be gained by a Copyright Convention "are, no doubt, on the side of England," but adding, from

[1] H. R. 779.

his own experience as a recent visitor, that "America was never, perhaps, more ready than now to agree to what is just and right." Mr. Appleton then returned to America and expounded his views anew in a couple of letters to the *New York Times*, in the latter of which he answers the objection that his "idea of copyright can only be reached when Congress legislates that no Englishman shall hereafter be naturalized, and that no American shall have an interest as a partner in any English publishing house." He protests that he meant nothing of this illiberal nature; and that he does not believe the English publishers will endeavour, as a class, to circumvent the Americans by this manœuvre. On the 6th of December Mr. Cox introduced a Bill into the House of Representatives substantially identical with Mr. Baldwin's measure; which was also read twice, ordered to be printed and referred to the Library Committee. This second committee contained one member, Senator Howe, of Wisconsin, from the previous committee of 1868, Senator L. M. Morrill, of Maine (chairman), and Senator Sherman, of Ohio; and from the House of Representatives, Mr. Peters (Maine), Mr. Wheeler (New York), and Mr. Campbell (Ohio).

At the beginning of January, 1872, Mr. Henry C. Carey again appeared on the scene with a pamphlet, "The International Copyright Question considered" (Philadelphia: H. Carey Baird), in which he reiterated the arguments of his previous letters and criticized unfavourably the chief points of Mr. Baldwin's Report; whilst the new Library Committee of Congress called upon the publishers and others interested in the book trade to aid in framing a Bill. The result of this call was a meeting of publishers in the Mercantile Library, New York, on the 23rd of January. To this meeting 101 publishers from the three principal Atlantic cities were invited, 50 from New York, 27 from Boston, and 24 from Philadelphia. Nineteen firms only were

represented, 17 from New York and 2 from Boston:
Mr. Lippincott, of Philadelphia, was accidentally prevented from being present,[1] but expressed his adhesion
to the principle of copyright with the condition of remanufacture. At this and the subsequent meeting on
February 7, a memorial was presented by Mr. William
Appleton from British authors, in which the condition of
re-manufacture is accepted, with the remark that " it is
clear that the Americans have strong reasons for refusing
to permit the British publisher to share in the copyright
which they are willing to grant to the British author."
The memorial is signed by Mr. Herbert Spencer, Sir John
Lubbock, Professor Huxley, Mr. John Stuart Mill,
Mr. Thomas Carlyle, Sir James Paget, Mr. Darwin, Dr.
Hooker, Professor Tyndall, Mr. John Morley, Mr. Ruskin,
Mr. William Black, Mr. G. H. Lewes, Mr. Thomas
Hughes, Mr. Froude, Rev. James Martineau, Miss Harriet
Martineau, Mr. Shirley Brooks, Mr. Tom Hood, Mr.
Edmund Yates, Mr. Henry Labouchere, Mr. Edward
Dicey, and many others, fifty in all. A report was then
drafted containing the text of an International Copyright
Bill under the condition of re-manufacture in the United
States, and stating, amongst other considerations, that
copyright would not increase the price of books to any
greater extent with English than with the works of
American authors. For this the following nine firms
of publishers voted—viz., D. Appleton & Co., Robert
Carter & Bros., Sheldon & Co., A. D. F. Randolph & Co.,
J. B. Ford & Co., D. W. C. Lent & Co., W. H. Bidwell,
Dodd & Mead (all from New York), and Lee & Shepherd
(Boston). The late Mr. G. P. Putnam did not remain to
vote; but his son, Mr. Haven Putnam, informs me that
he was in favour of the Report. Three publishers from
New York, and Mr. J. R. Osgood, of Boston, declined to
vote. The remaining five firms dissented—viz., Charles

[1] See letter in *New York Evening Post*.

Scribner & Co., Holt & Williams, Hurd & Houghton, James Miller, and E. P. Dutton & Co., all from New York; and Mr. Edward Seymour, one of the managing partners in the firm of Scribner, drew up a minority report stating the following objections to the proposed Bill:—

1. It is in no sense an International Copyright Law, but simply an act to protect American publishers, regardless of the rights of American authors. It has so narrow a basis, therefore, that it can never receive the endorsement of the public.

2. Even if it were possible for American publishers to secure the "protection" proposed in compelling the manufacture of foreign copyrighted books in the United States, *such "protection" would be wholly exclusive, since the copyright which the English publisher could hold indirectly through an American partner, would secure him the absolute control of this market, whether the book was made here or in England.*

3. For the reasons above stated, the Act is objectionable in prohibiting the importation of stereos and electros (stereotype and electrotype plates), in failing to provide for the copyrighting of cyclopædias, &c., and in giving the American publisher power to exclude revised editions of works of which he may own the copyright.

It may be remarked on these two reports that, of the signers of the former, not more than two firms are of first-rate importance, and that the firm to whose influence the minority report is due are not only publishers, but the largest *importers* of English books in the United States.

During the same week the executive committee of the Copyright Association, consisting chiefly of authors, adopted the following draft of a Bill made by their secretary, Mr. Charles Astor Bristed, entitled "An Act to secure authors the right of property in their books." It has the merits of shortness and simplicity.

After the enacting clause it proceeds:—

1. All rights of property secured to citizens of the United States of America, by existing copyright laws of the United States, are hereby secured to the citizens and subjects of every country, the Government of which secures reciprocal rights to citizens of the United States.

2. This Act to take effect two years after its passage.[1]

Meanwhile the opponents of copyright in Philadelphia began to stir. On the 27th of January a meeting of printers, publishers, booksellers, paper-makers, &c., was held under the presidency of Mr. Henry Carey Baird, a relative, I believe, of Mr. Carey. Mr. W. Lippincott was one of the secretaries. After the proceedings of the New York meeting had been read, the following memorial, presented by Mr. B. H. Moore to be forwarded to Congress, was adopted:—

We oppose an International Copyright for the following reasons:—

1. That thought unless expressed is the property of the thinker; when given to the world is, as light, free to all.

2. As property it can only demand the protection of the municipal law of the country to which the thinker is subject.

3. The author of any country, by becoming a citizen of this and assuming the burdens and performing the duties thereof, can have the same protection that an American author has.

4. The trading of privileges to foreign authors, for privileges to be granted to Americans, is not just, because the interest of others than they are sacrificed thereby.

5. Because the good of the whole people, and the safety of our republican institutions, demand that books shall not be made too costly for the multitude by giving the power to foreign authors to fix their prices here, as well as abroad.

6. We oppose the Bill as proposed in New York, because it would enable the foreign author and his assignee in this country, by an absolute monopoly in the production, to fix the price of his book, without fear of competition.

7. Because the great capitalists on the Atlantic seaboard would naturally and almost necessarily represent foreign authors, from their world-wide reputation, the security of

[1] See *Weekly Trade Circular*, New York, February 1, 1872.

authors in dealing with them, and their greater facilities in distribution of books, thus centralizing the publication of them in few hands.

8. Finally, because the reprints of really valuable works on science, which are now published at prices so low in this country that the day labourer can afford to purchase them, would be raised by an International Copyright, or any proposed modification thereof, beyond his means; and he would be obliged to confine his purchases mainly to cheap literature, not improving to his mind, frequently immoral in its tendency, and inculcating not rarely principles dangerous to the peace of society."[1]

On the 29th of January Mr. Morrill, the chairman of the Library Committee of Congress, called a meeting " for the hearing of all parties interested." The New York publishers' meeting was represented by Mr. W. H. Appleton, Mr. Sheldon, Mr. Van Nostrand, and Professor Youmans. The Copyright Association was represented by Mr. C. Astor Bristed, its secretary, and Mr. E. L. Andrews, of the New York bar, who also drafted the subsequent form of the Bill proposed on behalf of the New York publishers and the authors. This gentleman drew up a " brief," in which he founded the plea for International Copyright upon a passage in the Constitution of the United States, to the effect that Congress shall have powers " to promote the progress of science and the useful arts, by securing for limited times to authors and inventors the exclusive right to their respective writings and discoveries." Mr. Andrews contended with much ingenuity that, *American* authors not being specified in this clause of the Constitution, the word *authors* must mean *all* authors, irrespective of nationality.[2] Now it is impossible to protect foreign authors except by way of International Copyright; it follows, then, he argued, that

[1] From the *Printer's Circular*.
[2] It is curious that Lord Westbury, in the case of Boosey *v.* Jeffreys, committed himself in the House of Lords to a similar interpretation of the English Copyright Act. See Shortt on " The Law relating to Literature" (London: Cox), p. 32.

the Constitution does not leave it optional with Congress to pass or not to pass a law giving copyright to foreign authors, but "in this respect is mandatory in its character." This singular argument, there is little doubt, did a great deal of harm to the cause which Mr. Andrews espoused, and it has had the further detrimental effect of creating a false impression in the public mind. In the ultimate report of the Library Committee it was, of course, set aside on the reasonable ground that it could not be supposed that the framers of the American Constitution had in view any class of persons except citizens of the United States. But from this statement of the report that such an argument for International Copyright could not be construed out of the words of the Constitution, an impression has got abroad amongst Americans who have never had the actual documents before them, that the committee declared *International Copyright to be unconstitutional*; so that this unfortunate and far-fetched argument has, perhaps, done more to shelve the question than even the opposition of the Philadelphia publishers.

The deputations then proceeded to lay the following documents before the committee: (*a*) the report of the New York publishers' meeting—not a strong production, by the way; (*b*) the minority report of Mr. Edward Seymour and his friends; (*c*) the memorial of the British authors; and (*d*) the memorial of the Philadelphia publishers. This last was presented by Mr. Willis Hazard, of Philadelphia, accompanied by three workmen connected with the manufacture of books. Messrs. Harper and Brothers, of New York, were represented by counsel (Mr. Hubbard, of Boston), and also laid before the committee the following letter:[1]—

The question now before the Joint Committee of Congress upon the Library, however it may be confused or complicated

[1] This document exists in the Library of Congress, in the handwriting of Mr. Spofford, the librarian.

by the conflicting claims and interests of various classes, has always appeared to us under a very simple light.

In considering the propriety of International Copyright legislation we deem it entirely inappropriate to urge upon you the claims of authors, publishers, booksellers, printers, binders, press-makers, or any other body of tradesmen, to be especially and exclusively recognized in such legislation. The interests of the people at large are to be regarded, and those interests alone.

It seems to us that the whole question before your honourable committee really is whether the intelligence of the whole people, or, as the Constitution calls it, " the promotion of science and the useful arts," will be advanced by granting a copyright to foreign authors.

There are men who believe, for plausible reasons, that a protected monopoly of publishing the books of such British authors as now arrange with us for the issue of their works would be of immense value to a large publishing house like ours, and that we should therefore gain much by the adoption of one of those Bills now before your committee. But while a law enabling us to obtain several prices for our books would secure to us enormous profits for a time, it would certainly within a generation diminish our business, as publishers for the people, by narrowing the popular intelligence.

Publishers who aim at a permanent business, which shall continue to prosper under successive generations, will desire above all else that general diffusion of knowledge, and consequent general demand for literature, which can only result from the circulation of books cheap enough to be within the reach of all. This consideration, it seems to us, must govern the consideration of the question before your committee. Whatever of useful work in the world has been done by the publishers as well as the authors of this country, has been done by contributing to the progress and diffusion of knowledge and culture. It has been our aim and boast to furnish in an acceptable form the best reading for the people at low prices; and we point with natural satisfaction to our own lists, out of which a good and handsome library of standard and recent English works can be selected, at a price less than one-fifth of that which the same or similar books would cost in British editions or under an International Copyright Law. But the reduction of the price of a good book to one-fifth means, on the average, an increase of its circulation about twenty-fold; and it is our conviction that, had an international copyright existed for the last quarter of a century, the works of Macaulay, Tennyson, Bulwer, Dickens, Thackeray, Lecky, Darwin, Wallace, Kingsley, Robertson, Reade, Collins, George Eliot, Mrs. Gaskell, Miss Mulock, and the like, would to-day be known by less than one-twentieth in number of the citizens of the United States who are now familiar with them.

In view of the great results which have grown out of the freedom of literary exchange which we now enjoy, of the general education of our people, of the extent and efficiency of our common schools, the number and circulation of village and country libraries, and the liberalizing, broadening, elevating influence upon the national mind of the choicest thoughts of another great and cultivated people now so freely opened to it, it is our belief that the adoption of any serious restriction upon this freedom would be a very hazardous experiment, and possibly an irrevocable calamity to the nation.

We have the honour to be, very respectfully,
Your obedient servants,
HARPER & BROTHERS.

These were substantially all the materials at this time laid before the Library Committee of Congress. Speeches were made on the 12th February by Mr. Andrews and Mr. Bristed, on behalf of the Copyright Association, in favour of unqualified International Copyright; and a written statement was read by Mr. W. H. Appleton, on behalf of the New York publishers' meeting, in favour of copyright, subject to the condition of re-manufacture; whilst Mr. Hazard stated the arguments of the Philadelphia remonstrants. Professor Youmans followed, urging the claims of British authors upon the singular ground that they were very badly paid in their own country and desired American sympathy—falling into a smart passage of arms with the previous speaker. On the following day Mr. Hubbard "took the floor," and, after reading Messrs. Harper's letter, stated that "he came to represent no interest but one, and that one the highest—the interest of the people." His speech appears to have excited considerable amusement, and in the course of it he admitted that his argument carried with it the repeal of the existing law of domestic copyright. The committee requested him to commit his views to paper.¹ On the 17th February Mr. H. Carey Baird sent a fly-sheet to the committee, entitled "Copyright, National and International," in which he brought forward the additional consideration against International Copyright, that, if it were established, the American authors and publishers would be subject to perpetual litigation with the English proprietors of copyright, favoured by the comparative cheapness of the American courts of law, whilst they would be prevented by the dearness of the British courts from maintaining their own copyrights against infringement in England.

The undersigned has been informed, and he believes, that it is no uncommon thing for American inventors to find, on application for patents in England, under existing laws, that their machines and processes have already been patented by other parties. These specifications and drawings have been obtained from the Patent Office here by agents whose business it is, and forwarded to England in time to prevent the real owners from obtaining the benefit thereof.

This letter came before the last meeting, a private one of the committee on the 19th February, at which also a final draft of what was now called the "Authors' and Publishers' Bill," based upon a compromise between the Copyright Association and the publishers, was presented. The only alteration in the amended Bill consists in the omission—after specification of the condition that the "foreign author shall enter into a contract with an American publisher, a citizen of the United States, to manufacture the book in all its parts"—of the words "so that it shall be wholly the product of the mechanical

---

¹ See two *ex parte* reports of the proceedings, from opposite sides, in the *Weekly Trade Circular*, March 7 and 14.

industry of the United States."[1] I presume, though I have no direct authority for stating, that the omission of this more stringent clause was intended to admit to copyright foreign books, not set up in type in the United States, but printed, as is very often the case at present, from stereotype plates sent from England. This is a considerable saving of expense as well as time, but it sacrifices the printing interest in America to the extent of the price of the setting up of the type.

Along with this, Mr. Appleton, Mr. Sheldon, and Mr. Van Nostrand, as the Publishers' Committee, addressed a final statement to the Library Committee, wherein they stated their objections to a rival scheme of copyright which had sprung up during the discussion, and which was known, from one of its apparently simultaneous propounders, as the Elderkin Bill.

Mr. John P. Morton, a publisher in Louisville, Kentucky, wrote, during the session of the Library Committee,[2] to the Hon. S. S. Cox, as one of the oldest publishers and booksellers in the United States, that he was not satisfied with the Bill put forth by the New York publishers' meeting of February 7th, and that he had requested the Hon. J. B. Beck to present for the consideration of the Library Committee a Bill containing the following provisions:—

A foreign author may copyright his book in the United States on condition:—(*a*) That before his work is published or for sale in America the title-page thereof must be recorded in the office of the Librarian of Congress; (*b*) *The work to be free to be printed and published by all responsible publishers;*

[1] A printed copy of the amended Bill is to be found in the library of Congress, endorsed in the handwriting of Mr. W. H. Appleton: "Authors' Copyright Bill as amended by the Publishers. All rights of property secured to citizens of the United States are hereby secured to citizens and subjects of every other country, whenever the foreign author makes arrangements directly with the American publisher and the work is manufactured in the United States."

[2] Letter in MS. in the Congress library, dated February 16, 1872.

the copyright (royalty to be paid by publishers) not to exceed ten per cent. on the selling price ; (*c*) the author shall have an agent prepared to make contracts, notice of which shall be given through the public press ; (*d*) if the author shall fail to comply with the above requirements, the book, map, chart, or design may be republished the same as might have been done before the passage of this Act ; (*e*) *nothing in this Act is to prevent the importation or sale of the foreign edition of said work.*

In this letter Mr. Morton says that he wishes to add to his Bill, on further consideration, "that the copyright (royalty) should be ten per cent. on the selling price *in sheets* or paper binding, leaving the (American) publisher free from any tax for the labour that may be put on the work in the way of binding. There is no reason or justice in allowing a foreign author a percentage on such labour and skill." At the end of his letter Mr. Morton adds—

Whether Congress ought to pass an International Copyright Law or not is another question. But if they should do so, they should look to the interests of the millions of readers, and not to the *protection* (I believe that is the word) of the few publishers.

A similar proposal "to pay authors a fair per cent. (say five per cent.) on the retail price, leaving the privilege of reprinting open to all," was made on Febuary 7th, by a correspondent in the *New York Evening Post*. The principle involved had been stated with approval in 1853 by Mr. Carey, in his "Letters on International Copyright,"[1] as removing "much of the difficulty relating to copyright."

This idea, which was laid by Mr. Elderkin before the Library Committee, was taken up by one of its members, Senator Sherman, and embodied in what was hereafter known as "The Sherman Bill,"[2] which he introduced into

---

[1] Page 77. See p. 251.
[2] S. 688, 42nd Congress, 2nd Session.

the Senate on the 21st of February. The second section is as follows:—

Sec. 2. That any person within the United States may publish, in such form or numbers as he may deem best, any book or work copyrighted under this Act, subject to the payment to the author, or to his legal representatives or assignees, during the term of such copyright, of five per centum of the gross cost of the publication of such work; and the said author, or his legal representatives or assignees may publish such work in the United States, or contract with any publisher in the United States for the publication of such work in the United States, and demand, sue for, and recover the stipulated price for such copyright; and, in the absence of any specific contract for such publication, such author, or his legal representatives or assignees, may demand, sue for, and recover, as liquidated damages, in any court of competent jurisdiction, the said sum of five per centum on the gross cost of the publication of such work; and, to secure or recover the same, have the benefit of process in law or equity, as in other cases of joint interest in the proceeds of publication.

In their "final statement," Mr. W. H. Appleton and his two colleagues on the Publishers' Committee, take two objections to the principle of the Sherman Bill. (1) In many cases the books would (and in all cases could) be published by irresponsible parties, and the foreign author would be unable to collect anything. (2) The irresponsible publishers would reap the fruits of the advertising of the responsible one; and the latter, therefore, would be prevented from expending the necessary capital for making the book known.

The Library Committee reserved their report; meantime "The Sherman Bill" was read twice in the Senate, referred back to the Committee on the Library, and ordered to be printed.

Discussion continued in the public newspapers, and especially in the trade organs in England as well as in America, during the ensuing spring, but without adding any suggestion of importance. The single exception, perhaps, is to be found in an article, and the draft of a bill, published in the London *Bookseller* for April, 1872, and attributed by the Americans to Mr. Whittaker. After calling attention to the difference of conditions in the book market, not only in the United States but in Canada, where British subjects prefer to purchase the cheap American reprints to buying the expensive English editions of English authors, the writer very sensibly pleads for the disuse of all irritating and offensive expressions towards American publishers :—

Let it be conceded that the natural rights of authors extend no further than the boundaries of their own countries, and within these boundaries only so long as their own laws permit. This concession made, the ground will be cleared for further negotiation; there will be no charges of pilfering, stealing, or piracy, nor will there then be any ugly or offensive terms used. There is no need for them. The New York or Philadelphia publisher is as free from blame in reprinting Macaulay's "History of England," as Mr. Murray is in reprinting the works of Alexander Pope. Neither of the works named is protected by law, and if it be wrong for Mr. Harper to reprint Macaulay, it must be equally wrong for Mr. Murray to reprint Pope. Both works are property, both are unprotected by law, and both have been reprinted without any payment being made by the publishers to the authors or their representatives; and therefore, all that may be said of one transaction may be said of the other.

And he then suggests the following draft of a Bill, identical in its principle with the Elderkin and Sherman Bills :—

1. All original works composed by citizens of either nation shall be considered copyright in the other's country, for the term of the author's lifetime, or for twenty-eight years, whichever may be the longer term.

2. Any person desirous of reprinting books so copyrighted may do so on the following conditions, viz. :—

Before printing an American (or English) work he shall give notice to the proper authority, saying how many copies he proposes to print and the price at which such work will be sold in cloth, and pay down ten per cent. upon such selling price; he shall then be furnished with an order for the printer named to print that number of copies. As soon as the printer has done his work, he shall certify that he has printed so many and no more, and an authorization shall then be given to publish the edition: which authorization shall be printed upon the back of the title."

This proposal, I may add, is in substance no new one, even in this country. It was set forth as early as 1837, in an article in the *Mechanics' Magazine* (vol. xxvii.) by the late Mr. Thomas Watts, keeper of the printed books in the British Museum, and was advocated more recently by Mr. R. A. Macfie, M.P. for Leith, in the *Leith Herald*.[1] A similar scheme was also mentioned by M. Renouard in his "Traité des Droits d'Auteurs" (Paris, 1838); and in Italy, after the expiration of forty years' exclusive copyright, the law prescribes the payment of an analogous royalty. In England it is found practicable to collect for the author of a play royalties from all the provincial theatres for every night on which it is acted. On the other hand, Hon. J. Rose, the Canadian Minister of Finance, reported that it was found impracticable to collect at the custom-houses the duties levied for the benefit of the author on the introduction of American reprints into the Dominion.[2]

In the middle of the following short session of Congress, February 7, 1873, Senator Morrill produced his Report as

[1] See extracts of both these articles in "Recent Discussions on the Abolition of Patents," pp. 296-300.

[2] See an article in the *Athenæum*, July 17, 1869, reprinted in "Recent Discussions on the Abolition of Patents," p. 310. An *ad valorem* duty, ranging from 15 to 20 per cent., was levied on behalf of the English author, on the importation of his works into nineteen of the English colonies, of which a list will be found *op. cit.* p. 326. But whether the collection of these duties has been successful there seems to be no evidence. A letter from Mr. C. H. Purday, of Great Marlborough Street, the brother of the defendant in a celebrated copyright case, Boosey *v.* Purday, advocating the same solution of the International Copyright difficulty, will be found, pp. 314-15 of the same work.

chairman of the Library Committee, and with this terminated for the time the American efforts for International Copyright. The concluding paragraph of the Report sums up the opinion of the committee as follows :—

In view of the whole case, your committee are satisfied that no form of International Copyright can fairly be urged upon Congress upon reasons of general equity or of constitutional law ; that the adoption of any plan for the purpose which has been laid before us would be of very doubtful advantage to American authors as a class, and would be not only an unquestionable and permanent injury to the manufacturing interests concerned in producing books, but a hindrance to the diffusion of knowledge among the people and to the cause of universal education ; that no plan for the protection of foreign authors has yet been devised which can unite the support of all or nearly all who profess to be favourable to the general object in view; and that, in the opinion of your committee, any project for an International Copyright will be found upon mature deliberation to be inexpedient.[1]

With regard to the condition of re-manufacture, whether involving the setting up of the type afresh, or merely the printing from imported stereotypes, I think that Mr. William Appleton[2] would now be prepared to make a still further concession. In the autumn of 1875 I had a conversation with him in New York, and asked him if he was prepared, in any proposal of International Copyright, to accept the *status quo* in respect of re-manufacture. At present the reprinting publishers occasionally have their reprints entirely manufactured in England ; sometimes wholly in America ; sometimes again the re-manufacture is partly done in England, partly in America. In any case, the American publisher follows his own convenience in this matter, and is not bound by any hard and fast line, as he would be under the proposed Bill of the "authors

[1] Senate Report, No. 409, 42nd Congress, 3rd Session.
[2] It may be well to mention that the writer of this Paper has no connection by way of relationship or otherwise with any member of the New York firm.

and publishers." Upon the supposition that the publisher shall be an American citizen, holding directly from the English author as his assignee, I asked if Mr. Appleton was prepared to waive the clause in his Bill about re-manufacture, and to this I understood him to assent.

ATHEISM AND DOUBT.

(THEOLOGICAL ESSAYS.)

ON ATHEISM.

ATHEISM is the denial of the existence of God. Ἄθεος ὁ μὴ νομίζων εἶναι Θεόν (Clem. *Strom.* 504). In discussing this subject we shall investigate—I. The Name; II. The Thing; III. Its Causes; IV. Its Arguments; V. The Verdict of the Bible upon it; and VI. The Books, Tracts, &c., written in favour of and against it.

I. *The Name* has been applied variously and widely: to Mezentius (Virg. *Aen.* 7) and the Cyclops (Hom. *Od.* 9), in Beyerlinck's *Magnum Theatrum*, &c.; by the Athenians to Diagoras of Melos, and thence to all the Melians, whence "Melius" is applied in the sense of ἄθεος to Socrates (Aristoph. *Nubes*, 831), see Suidas, *s. v.*; to Anaxagoras, Aspasia, &c.; to Euemerus of Messena (Lactantius and Eusebius, *Prep. Evan.* lib. 2); to Theodorus and Bion (v. Cic. *de Nat. Deor.* i. 1); to the Christians by the pagans (Julian *ap.* Sozomen. v. 15, *cf.* Athenagoras, *Legatio*, and Clem. *Strom.* 7, who adds, καὶ ὁμολογοῦμεν τῶν τοιούτων Θεῶν ἄθεοι εἶναι); to the pagans by the Christians (Clem. *Protrept.* p. 11; Beza *ad Ephes.* ii. 12); to the heretics by the orthodox; to Eunomius by St. Jerome (*Ep. ad. Pammach.*); to Arius by Athanasius, &c.; to Anastasius the Emperor by Zosimus and Paulus Diaconus; by Catholics to Protestants (Possevinus, *Bibliot.* viii.; Claudius de Sainctes, *Tract. Pecul.*; Chiconius *c. Cavillum*; Campanella, *Atheismus Triumph.*; Mersenne, *Comm. in Genes.*); by the Jesuits to the Machiavellians (see Voet, *de Ath.* p. 116; Lessius, *de Provid.* Dedic. p. 1); by Perkins to Turks, Jews, and Papists (*Works*, ii. 526); to Vorst the Calvinist, to Socinians, to Arminians, by their respective opponents (Voet, p. 120); to the Mahometans (*ib.* p. 122); by Calvin to the Pope and Cardinals (*Inst.* iv. 7, 27); to Erasmus by the Jesuits; to Charron by Mersenne; to Aristotle by Tycho Brahe; to Descartes, for rejecting Aristotle; to Taurellus by the Heidelberg Divines (A.D. 1610); to a usurer by Luther (Voet, *l. c.* pp. 121–4); to the "mystical" physicians, and to the deniers of magic (*ib.* 125–9); to Vanini, Fludd, Montaigne, J. Bruno, Cardan, Machiavelli, Charpentier, Basso, Charron, Campanella, by Mersenne (*L'Impiété des Déistes*, &c.); to the Socinians in Poland, Geneva, and elsewhere, by the same; to the Sceptics, Epicureans, Cabbalists, "Hermetico-Lullistae," "Hermetico-Paracelsistae," &c. (Voet, p. 131); to the "Enthusiastae," "Spirituales," &c. (*ib.*); to the Anabaptists (Voet, 118); to Ranters (Somers, *Tracts*, 6, 24); to the followers of Rabelais (Voet, *l. c.*); by Seckendorf to Puffendorf (1685); by the Spanish theologians to the French, Venetians, &c. who favoured the House of Austria; by the author of the *Vindiciae Gallicae* to the Spanish theologians (Voet, p. 116); to the French Deists by Voet, H. Stephanus, and Mersenne (Voet, p. 117; Mersenne, *Questions rares et curieuses théologiques*, &c., 1630); to the Japanese, Chinese, Indians, Tatars, the ancient Prussians, the aborigines of New Spain and other American peoples, the Souldani of South Africa, the tribes of the middle of Africa, and other barbarians, &c. (Hoffmann, *Lex. Univ.* s. v., Lessius, *de Prov.* &c.); and lastly by Maréchal to almost every eminent person who has ever lived (*Dict. des Athées*, passim).

II. *The Thing* is the denial, either by words, in theory, or in practice, of the existence of a spiritual cause of the universe, whether that cause be conceived as one or many; and, as a consequence of this, the supposition that visible Nature is the ultimate fact with which the human mind has to deal. Historically we may distinguish two kinds of Atheism—Atheism as a prevailing sentiment, which is the result of moral, political, and other causes, and Atheism as a philosophical theory, which is the conclusion of a reasoned deduction from certain premises. Speaking roughly, the Atheism previous to the middle of the eighteenth century was mainly of the former type; that prevailing since that time of the latter. The first, as Bacon, writing at the end of the sixteenth century, said, "is rather on the lip than the heart of man," which is shown by "nothing more than this, that Atheists will ever be talking of that their opinion, as if they fainted in it within themselves, and would be glad to be strengthened by the consent of others; nay, more, you shall have Atheists strive to get disciples as it fareth with other sects; and which is most of all, you shall have of them that will suffer for Atheism and not recant; *whereas if they did truly think* that there were no such thing as God, why should they trouble themselves?" (*Essays*, xvi.) It was, in fact, a fashion of feeling, speaking, and unfortunately also of living—a state of anarchy in the breast of the individual which was the natural reflex of the anarchy—religious, moral, ecclesiastical, political, intellectual—in society at large. The contemporary writers in defence of the Being of God, of whom, especially towards the latter end of the seventeenth century, there was a prodigious number, appear therefore to have made a mistake in meeting the Atheism of their time by the direct assault of counter-argument. For, although Atheism pervaded society, it did not appear in books. Until the year 1750, when the great French *Encyclopédie* was published, there is scarcely an Atheistic book or tract to be found (see Buckle's *Civilization*, i. cap. 14). It became necessary, therefore, both to imagine the individual antagonist, invent the arguments that he would be likely to use, and then refute them. Thus the shots went safely over the heads of the enemy; no one was convinced; and, as the same man played both his own and his adversary's hand, there was no winner. The real and only "refutation" was that which history slowly brought about in the settlement of society and of opinion, the amelioration of the general estate of man, and the consequent elevation of European morals. The Atheism of this period was, in short, not so much an argument to be rebutted as a disease to be cured. "We must not think," says Perkins, "that this wicked thought is onely in some notorious and hainous sinners, but it is the corrupt mind and imagination of every man that cometh of Adam naturally, not one excepted save Christ alone" (*Man's Naturall Imagination, Wks.* ii. 525). The natural man, *as such*, has no knowledge of God; and in a period of protracted social disturbance, when the spiritual support of established opinions and institutions gives way, all but the noblest and strongest have a tendency to relapse more or less into a state of Nature. It is of this kind of Atheism that Milton speaks—

> Unless there be who think not God at all;
> If any be, they walk obscure;
> For of such doctrine never was there school,
> But the heart of the fool,
> And no man therein doctor but himself.
>
> *Sams. Agon.* 293.

III. *The Causes of Atheism.*—(*a*) Almost all the contemporary writers agree in the connection of Atheism with a widespread libertinism of life (so Meric Casaubon, Glanvil, "Dorotheus Sicurus," Reimmann, Spizelius, Grassius, Meier, Rajesanyi, Jenkin Thomasius, Bishop Dawes, Lessius, Mersenne, Gisbert Voet, &c.), which Bacon thus explains: "They that deny a god destroy a man's nobility; for certainly man is of kin to the beast by his body" (*l.c.*). It appears, however, to have been rather the cause of Atheism than its effect: for the speculative Atheism of the later French school, of which the following passage may be taken as characteristic, seems to have been in great measure free from it:—

> Des coupables plaisirs sectateurs insensés,
> Des folles passions esclaves abusés,
> Gardez-vous de penser que ma muse novice
> Daigne vous élargir la carrière du vice ;
> Je n'écris pas pour vous : ma morale à vos yeux,
> O mortels abrutis, paraîtrait exaltée ;
> Pour votre châtiment je vous laisse à vos dieux,
> L'homme vertueux seul a le droit d'être Athée.
>
> Sylvian Maréchal.

Connected with libertine Atheism was also the profane and sceptical wit, which is included by writers of the time under the word "drollery" (*cf.* Glanvil's *Whip for the Droll, Fuller to the Atheist*), and which gave rise to the terms "Lucianicus," "Rablaesianus" (follower of Rabelais), as synonymous with Atheist (Voet) ; the pride, security, and luxury of life (Bacon, Dor. Sicurus) ; the weakening of the family tie, and neglect of parents (Jenk. Thomasius), and unnatural conduct (*cf.* Massinger's *Maid of Honour*, Act III. sc. 3), where the king who refuses to ransom his natural brother is said—

> To break
> The adamant chains of nature and religion,
> *To bind up atheism*, as a defence
> To his dark counsels.

The term "Epicurean," which occurs in the general sense of a bad man, has several shades of meaning in connection with Atheism. In a satirical address supposed to be presented to William III. on his accession, the signers call themselves "the Atheists or the sect of the Epicureans" (*v. infr.*), and go on to speak of "all religion as a cheat." But the name seems originally to indicate, along with "Stoic," "Peripatetic," "Atomist," merely a modern adherent of the later schools of Greek Philosophy, thence an opponent of the Scholastic Aristotelianism, and not unfrequently of the religious belief which it had been used to defend (so Voet). The licentious and pagan ideal of life which came in with the

Revival of Letters found a theory ready made for itself in the philosophy of Epicurus, and hence the term "Epicurean" became synonymous with a man of pleasure who was prepared to defend his practice, and hence with the libertine Atheist: τέλος ἐστὶ τοῦ μὴ νομίζειν θέους τὸ μὴ φοβεῖσθαι.

It was against this tendency to shelter libertine Atheism under the name of Epicurus, that Gassendi wrote his great work in three folio volumes (A.D. 1649), to show first, that Epicurus was not an Atheist, and secondly, not an evil-liver. The book was thus written, not so much in the interests of Atheism as of Deism; but, by promoting Deism, it indirectly promoted Atheism, whilst by rendering the pursuit of pleasure respectable, it indirectly fostered its licentious indulgence. For the inference is easy from the Deist's denial that God has any care for man to the Atheist's denial that man need have any care for God, or for the moral life—

Je n'ai pas plus besoin de Dieu que lui de moi.

Thus, as before, the root of Atheistic sentiment is the want of a proper conception of the dignity and spiritual aim of human life.

(b) What was commonly called "Enthusiasm"—i.e., the religion of excited emotion—is an opposite but co-ordinate effect of a disordered state of society and opinion with libertinism, and, like it, closely connected with Atheism. Voet does not scruple to speak of the "Enthusiastae," "Spirituales," "Phantastico-Contemplativi et Sublimantes" of his time as Atheists or tending to Atheism. And for this Henry More gives as a reason that this "temper disposes a man to listen to the magisterial dictates of an overbearing fancy rather than to the calm and cautious insinuations of free reason." By this he apparently means that in his feelings man is purely passive and "over-borne," whereas in his reason he is "free"—i.e., active. The belief in God of the "Enthusiast" depends upon physical causes, and "by change of diet, feculent old age, or some present damps of melancholy," may disappear. The "Enthusiast" thus plays into the hands of the Atheist, even if he do not himself ultimately become one; and while, on the one hand, the pretence of the latter to wit and natural reason makes the former secure that reason is no guide to God, the latter, on the other hand, concludes religion to be merely fancy and "a troublesome fit of over-curious melancholy." (*Comments on Glanvil's "Whip for the Droll*," &c., p. 27, folio; see also *Enthusiasmus Triumphatus*.)

(c) *The State of Theology and the Religious World* is another cause of Atheism insisted on by the seventeenth century writers. Thus Reinmann complains of clerical scandals; Casaubon of the use of fallacies in support of religious truth (*e.g.*, Achilles and the tortoise); "Dorotheus Sicurus" of the disuse of reasons and learning in religious controversy, and of the quarrels about ceremonies; Voet of the "new method of the Jesuits Arnald and Verron, who, by throwing discredit upon the validity of the natural reason in Divine things, aid the growth of scepticism," so that "non ab hereticis .... sed a Papistis arma Atheis certatim suppeditari" (*De Ath.* p. 119; *De Ratione Humana in reb. fidei*). With this we may compare the dictum of the Père Mersenne, the friend of Descartes, that none of the proofs of the Being of God are satisfactory to the reason (*Letter to Florianus Crusius*). On the other hand, Voet admits with the Romanist theologians that the spirit of private judgment, and the change from one sect to another, was productive of Atheism (*De Atheismo; cf.* Cornelius a Lapide, *ad Ep. Jud.* ii., *ad* 2 *Tim.* iii. 9 : "Lutheranismum et Calvinismum abire in Atheismum;" Glanvil, *A Whip*, &c., p. 22, and More in his *Notes*). So also Dor. Sicurus speaks of the factions and divisions of religion, the fierce disputes, wars, and devastations of the Reformation period, the difficulty of choosing the true religion, and the weariness and dissatisfaction of changing. Voet further mentions the reaction against the excessive ceremonial of the Mediæval Church as leading to the abandonment of all outward expression of the religious life, and generally of the "praesentium et antiquorum fastidium," as alike leading many to Atheism. To which Spizelius adds general religious confusion, simulation, and (the result of all) what he calls "Gallio-ism," the neglect of and aversion from theological questions.

(*d*) *The Secularization of Politics* and growth of the utilitarian view of religion as an instrument of police in the hands of the magistrate. It is this notion as calculated to throw discredit upon *all* kinds of religion, and therefore as tending not only to antichristian, but to antitheistic habits of thought, against which the defensive writers are contending when they condemn the "Politici" (*i.e.*, the followers of Machiavelli and Hobbes), who are neutral, "ad cujusque religionis susceptionem .... modo aiunt, modo negant." (So Lessius and Voet, the last of whom remarks pertinently "Omnis religio nulla religio.")

(*e*) *The Decline of Belief in Magic* was closely connected with the growth of Atheistic sentiment (Glanvil, *A Whip*, &c.). It is curious that, whilst the belief in occult science tended in the "mystical" physicists (Cardan, Vanini, &c.) to a kind of semi-Atheism by deifying matter, its decay—due partly to the revolution against the ecclesiastical miracles of the Middle Ages, but mainly to the growth of experimental science and the explanation of many phenomena hitherto deemed supernatural—should promote Atheism by leading to a suspicion that the whole region of the supernatural was capable of being explained away. The fact is, that Magic was regarded as a kind of outwork of religion, which it was necessary to defend, lest the citadel should be attacked. "One reason why God permits sorcery," says Meric Casaubon, "certainly is that men, generally so inclinable to Atheism, might certainly know, if not wilfully blind, that there is something besides flesh and blood, and what may be seen with the bodily eyes, *i.e.* ordinary nature, to be thought upon." " It is certainly a point of excellent use to convince incredulity," and " hence it is that they that deny or will not believe any supernatural operations by witches and magicians are generally observed to be Atheists, or well affected that way," or, at least, " it cannot be denied but that the opinion is very apt to promote Atheism, and therefore earnestly promoted and countenanced by them that are Atheists." For we may reason, he adds, with Origen, that a man who believes magic will probably believe miracles, by a kind of *à fortiori* argument from the power of the devil to that of God (*Credulity and Incredulity*, &c. p. 91, and the *Sequel*, p. 171). Similarly, Mersenne writes in defence at once of theology and alchymy, and Voet enumerates the existence of the " novi Saducaei," who refer magical operations and apparitions to natural causes, amongst the causes of Atheism (*v.* Glanvil, *Saducismus Triumphatus*).

(*f*) *The Growth of Experimental Science and of Mathematics*, though not perhaps in itself necessarily adverse to religious belief, operated for some time prejudicially to religion, and is set down by many as a cause of Atheism. To take the last first : the study of mathematical methods led men to try to apply them to all things in heaven and earth. They appeared to form a standard of certainty, which might serve to divide the truth from the false in common belief. Hence the attempt and failure to prove the existence of God by mathematical methods threw a haze of suspicion over the doctrine. Accordingly, we find Casaubon complaining that divinity should be tried by mathematics, and made subservient to them, and Mersenne giving up the Theistic argument as hopeless. It seems to have occurred to nobody that possibly mathematical demonstration, and not the Theistic argument, might be at fault, and that the latter might really have an *equal* without having a *similar* kind of certainty.

It was a misfortune that the rise of experimental science should have been connected with a revival of the old Atomism of Leucippus and Democritus, and its moral accompaniment, Epicureanism: ἀθεΐαν, ἀτόμους καὶ ἀφιλόσοφον ἡδονήν. It is against Atomism rather than against any conclusions of natural science, as such, that the great argument of Cudworth is directed (*Intellectual System*, pref. p. 41). So Casaubon, Rajcsanyi, J. Thomasius, Voet, Bacon. Apart from this, however, as tending to draw away attention from metaphysics, or to impart an unphilosophical character to them, and as calculated to concentrate study upon secondary and material causes, experimental science was "very apt to be abused or to degenerate into Atheism." "This is a great precipice," writes Casaubon, "and the contempt of all other learning an ill presage." And Spizelius (*De Atheismi Radice*, p. 39) to the same effect. The idea of the constancy of natural law which was beginning to dawn upon the world seemed to many, if admitted, a fatal blow to religious belief; as, in the existing state of speculation, the operation of Divine Providence by way of suspension and interruption seemed to be a clearer proof of the existence of Deity than the placid and orderly fulfilment of the Infinite Will through the operation of general laws.

(*g*) *The Gradual Increase of a Sceptical Spirit* in regard to all things seems partly attributable to the resuscitation of ancient Pyrrhonism, partly to the Cartesian theory of doubt as the first step in thought. On this subject see Buckle, *Hist. of Civiliz.*, i. cap. viii.

IV. *The Arguments of Atheism.*—As has been said, after the middle of the eighteenth century, Atheism becomes less a morbid habit of character and feeling pervading social life, and becomes much more distinctly a theory, and while gradually ceasing to be essentially libertine,* it becomes more distinctively literary. We shall endeavour to set before the reader three principal types of the Atheistic argument which have appeared at intervals of half a century since 1750.

---

* See, however, Carlyle's Description of the Society at D'Holbach's ("Diderot," p. 243.)

(*a*) D'Holbach's *Système de la Nature* (1770).—Starting from the assumption that nothing exists but matter, and the motion which is essentially inseparable from it, the theory goes on: there is no design or order in Nature, but only necessity. The cause of motion is the tendency of things to self-preservation, and at the same time to attract and repel other things. These three conditions of motion are called in Physics—Inertia, Attraction, and Repulsion; and in Morals—Self-love, Love, and Hate. Both Physics and Morals are the same, the only difference being that whilst in some cases the motion of molecules is on a sufficiently large scale to be visible, in others it is not. It is from drawing a qualitative, instead of merely a quantitative, distinction between the motion of the brain molecules and the other motions of the body or of the world, that man has come to regard himself as a union of two substances of different kinds, one of which, the soul, shows its unreal character by its only being capable of description by negative predicates. The soul is really only a name for a part of the body, the brain, the molecules of which are set in motion by the impact of external things, the result being what we call thought and will; the motion itself being called sensation in the one case, and passion in the other. Moral action is thus wholly a product of the passions, and these of the mixture of fluid and solid elements in the constitution. It followed naturally from this conception of himself as a compound of two substances, that man should extend the same view to the universe of which he is a part. This is the origin of the idea of God as distinguished from the world, an idea which explains nothing, consoles no one, terrifies all, and the unreality of which, as of the soul, is shown by its being a bundle of negative attributes. Theology is a mass of contradictions, banishing God to the utmost distance from man by virtue of His metaphysical attributes, and on the other hand drawing Him into the closest relations with man by virtue of His moral. True knowledge, the privilege of the few, substitutes force for Deity, and natural laws for His attributes and providence. At the same time it must not be supposed that the idea of God is a pardonable error, or one useful or necessary for the government of the rude and uncultivated. It is hurtful, and its use for any purpose is as unjustifiable as to administer poison to prevent a man from misusing his bodily powers. This noxious character arises from two illusions which it draws with it; freedom and a future life. The doctrine of freedom is merely an artifice to reconcile the conception of God as a moral Being with the existence of evil, and involves the absurdity that if a man can really introduce a new factor into the world, the world so modified is really a new world, and the free-agent a creator as really almighty as God Himself. The doctrine of the other world is pernicious, because it draws men away from attention to their vocation in this. Materialism, on the other hand, is at once logical and beneficent. It frees man from his fear of God, and from the pain of remorse, and of longing for what is unattainable; both of which vanish before the knowledge that all action is necessitated, and that it is the part of man to live happily in the present, and not sacrifice his enjoyment to a phantom.*

Such in substance is the doctrine of this remarkable book; a doctrine perfectly logical, and commanding assent at every point from any fair mind—*if* the premises be admitted. But if the keystone be taken out, the whole arch falls to pieces. That keystone is the unproved assumption that matter is an ultimate fact, and capable of being known as such.

(*b*) Maréchal's *Dictionnaire des Athées* (A.D. 1800) represents in many respects the opposite pole of Atheistic thought to the *Système de la Nature*. Like the latter, it is a consistent theory of life; but unlike it, it is wholly

---

* Carlyle's Miscellanies ("Diderot," p. 253, vol. iii.)

unargumentative and dogmatic. There seems no reason why Maréchal should have been an Atheist except that he was one. The instructive part of his work, however, consists in a Preface to his Dictionary, enumerating the different eminent persons who have been wholly or in part Atheists. The Catalogue is framed on the loosest and most arbitrary principles, and includes, along with Charron and Montaigne, St. Augustine, St. Chrysostom, St. Gregory, Pascal, Grotius, Fénélon, Bossuet, and our Lord Himself. The Preface lays down the following ideas:—
" Dieu n'a pas toujours été." He was unknown to the child of Nature, who in the age of gold recognised no higher being than the father of the family which constituted the entire sphere of his activity (p. 1). And the modern Atheist is one who, disengaging himself from social bonds which were contracted without his knowledge or consent, " remonte à travers la civilisation à cet ancien état de l'espèce humaine " (p. 3). He is not the Sybarite who gives himself out as an Epicurean when he is only a debauchee, nor a follower of Machiavelli, nor a renegade priest turned *savant*, nor the fanatical iconoclast who preaches the *cultus* of reason to the populace who cannot rise above instinct. Neither is he the hypocrite, nor the man of the world and follower of Atheistical fashion, nor the timorous philosopher who blushes at his own thoughts, nor the physician who denies God in order to have the gratification of constructing the world himself, nor, in fine, one who feels no want of God because he can be wise without one. *He is no elaborate reasoner against Theism*, but simply one who says, " the question as to whether there is a God in Heaven interests me as little as the inquiry whether there are animals in the moon" (p. 4). A modest and tranquil recluse, he dislikes to make a noise, or to parade his principles; he practises virtue in order to be at ease with himself. Jealous of his honour, and too proud to obey even a Deity, he takes no commands but from his own conscience (p. 38). He

does his duty as a citizen, though declining to enter into politics, but with an activity like that of Nature, of which he feels himself an indispensable part, he co-ordinates himself with Nature in performing those duties which are imposed upon him by his relations with other beings (p. 10). "His life is full like that of Nature," and in the quiet uprightness of family life he perceives the nothingness of social distinctions and of the gross pleasures of the herd, while he dismisses the abject terrors of the believer in God (pp. 11–13). Atheism is thus the most natural and simple thing in the world, and "*le plus parfait désintéressement* est la base de toutes les déterminations de l'Athée."

In this view of Atheism, the following characteristics are remarkable:—First, that it is the picture of an ideal character and not the exposition of a theory. Secondly, it takes for granted that a discussion upon the subject has gone before, and a conclusion in favour of Atheism has been arrived at, about which argument has ceased. Its object therefore is not so much to convince the understanding about the doctrine, as to enlist the sympathies on the side of the ideal practiser of it. Thirdly, this ideal *consciously* excludes any approach to the old libertine Atheism. And, lastly, it is intimately connected with retirement from social relations and duties into the seclusion of family life. In this last point it touches Rousseau on the one hand, and, while giving up all the more offensive and unphilosophical traits of popular Epicureanism, Epicurus on the other. It is therefore only on this last subsidiary point that the theory of Maréchal admits of a refutation. A mere assertion, unsupported by evidence or argument, unless in itself ostensibly probable, may legitimately be met by an equally naked denial; but an ideal of life which involves the negation of all the wider social economy of man, especially when such a view is not the vagary of the individual, but the characteristic of many of the highest minds of the age, is a fair subject of criticism.

In the first place, then, such an ideal as a life for all is a self-contradiction ; for if we suppose society disintegrated into an infinite series of separate families, it is obvious that, in order to continue in this patriarchal isolation, it will be necessary for the families to unite in some system of common agreement and protection, as a substitute for that shelter which they have hitherto enjoyed in the state. And such a system is simply society over again under another name. If, on the other hand, such a life is for the few and not for all, it ceases to be a human ideal, and becomes merely a counsel of perfection for a few rural philosophers. Secondly, we may argue that, even supposing it possible for the modern citizen to return into the primitive condition of family life, such life must as inevitably develop again into the state (unless the nature of man itself could be essentially changed) as it has necessarily developed into the state in the past. Hence, even supposing such an ideal attainable by all, it could never, under existing conditions, be a permanent form of life. But, thirdly, a little attention to the subject will discover that society and the state, besides being a mere shelter from violence, sum up in themselves all those laws and institutions which have arisen out of the relations of men one to another, and which therefore form a permanent embodiment of the activity of man on the unselfish or spiritual side of his nature. For a man to recede from society is, therefore, for him to attempt the attainment of a higher life by receding from his nobler or social, into his individual or ignoble, self. And this point it is important to make, because it at once reveals the origin and weakness of the Atheistic theory which is so closely connected with it. Whether Nature reveals upon the whole a predominance of good over evil or the reverse may be a matter of question, and therefore its testimony to the existence of a beneficent Creator may be matter of question also; but it cannot be denied that society and the state are a standing evidence to the triumph of good in the world. If Nature, then, in one of her aspects at least, reveals a Deity, society as a spiritual creation reveals Him much more; so that the Atheist of the Maréchal type is open to the same confutation as the libertine, though from a different point of view—viz., that his inability to discern the existence of God arises from his taking too low a view of man. He fails to see the Divine image in the conscience, because he turns his back upon that social order through which (in the first instance) that image is reflected upon the "heart" of the individual. Here, then, we have as before rather to account for Atheism by revealing its cause, than to answer its arguments. That cause in the case of Maréchal was the utter rottenness of existing political arrangements before the outbreak of the French Revolution, producing aversion from society altogether. It would follow that here, as before, the best refutation of Atheism is the growth of a sound state of the body politic.

(*e*) Radenhausen's *Isis* is important as a type of the more refined Atheism of the present generation. In a dialogue between a modern Atheistic *savant* and his father, the following ideas are developed:—"The Atheist and the Theist have the same facts of consciousness, feelings, &c. to interpret, which the one calls the knowledge of a Divine Being, whilst the other calls them by another name. They thus differ, as Copernicus and Tycho Brahe differed—merely in their mode of formulating the same phenomena" (p. 410). The belief in God originated in the course of thousands of years from the observation of Nature, and is the result of primitive science. The idea, once formed, was withdrawn by the priests from progress, and therefore has crystallized. These ideas about the universe as a whole, and man's relation to it, are necessary products of the human mind, and therefore imperishable. The form which these ideas assume is that of a series of projections by man of the image of himself, differing from one another as one nation from another. The *common* elements in these various beliefs arise—(1) from the general similarity of the outer world as it is known to man, which subjects him more or less uniformly to a series of influences that are stronger than he; and (2) from the general similarity of men in their capacities and defects, as possessed of limited powers of sensation, and as having a memory and an understanding capable of development. On the other hand, these influences on man differ in different regions, and these capacities are differently developed in different races and individuals (pp. 422–3). These differences give rise to local differences in the names and outward expression given to such natural influences, and to a gradual development in the corresponding ideas. The Fetish worshippers, the idolater, the Atheist and the Theist have thus all precisely the same material for thought—viz., the presence of forces and influences in the outward world, in the face of which man feels himself weak or powerless. The Fetish worshipper elevates everything unwonted or inexplicable into a personal agency and worships it. The idolater conceives the operation of these influences—the sirocco, the inundation, the clouds, the thunderstorm, the jungle-fire, the sand-storm, &c., under visible forms. Hence, among the Egyptians and the Semitic and Aryan races, the images of the gods bear, in their original shape, a strong resemblance to these powers in Nature, but show a tendency to become gradually humanized, until in Greece they attain the perfection of the human form. The fusion of races and religions then eliminates in the course of ages the local character of these impersonations, or rather produces gradually the mental image of one Supreme Power, whom the Theist worships, and to whom the local deities are subordinate. Thus the thirty-three gods of the Vedic hymns become the limbs of Brahma, and the devils and inferior spirits of the Parsees: so, too, the Bible asks, " Who is there among the gods or among the clouds that can be compared to Jehovah?" and declares, " Thou art exalted above all gods." In Christian countries, again, the saints are merely the ancient local deities of Europe under new names (p. 424). The character of this Supreme Personification was determined by the climate and natural conditions of the different localities. In torrid regions, characterized by extreme fruitfulness on the one hand, and wholesale or violent destruction of life on the other, the attributes of the one Deity are great goodness coupled with savage vengeance. In temperate climates, on the other hand, where the alternations are not so violent, and the conditions of life more regular, the Divine attributes are conceived as moderation, justice, certainty in rewarding and punishing, &c. The Atheist, then, has the same materials for thought as these three kinds of believers in the existence of God; he is far from holding man to be omnipotent, or from ignoring that the order of Nature is on such a scale that, compared with human motives and limitations, it may rightly be designated almighty, infinitely good, wise, omnipresent, &c.; he recognizes also that some one pervading force lies at the root of all these powers which bear upon man. What he denies is that these powers, whether one or many, are anything distinct from Nature (p. 426).

The remainder of the dialogue is taken up with criticisms of the Ontological, Cosmological, and Physico-theological (Design argument) proofs of the Being of God, the consideration of which belongs more conveniently to an article on Theism.

On the principal argument, it may be remarked (i.) that it is not so much a positive theory of Atheism, such as we have had in D'Holbach and Maréchal, as an attempt to explain away Theism: (ii.) that it can scarcely be said that we know enough at present of the growth of mythology and language, or of the genesis of ideas in the mind of primitive man, to enable any sound and duly cautious reasoner to be certain that the idea of God arose in the way described; (iii.) that even granting that it arose from a personification of the powers of Nature, the irresistible tendency in man to suppose a being or beings, spiritual like himself, as the creating and sustaining cause of the world, is left unexplained, and is quite capable of being explained as itself an evidence of the existence of a Supreme Spirit, to whom the finite spirit experiences the attraction of affinity. (iv.) Lastly, the argument is only valid against Deism, *i.e.*, against the belief in a Supreme Abstraction remote from a world in which he has never revealed himself; but proves nothing against the Christian doctrine of a God who has revealed Himself in Nature and to the human mind, and who is reconciling the world to Himself.

Besides these three types of speculative Atheism, we may mention, as influencing the modern mind, the theory of Auguste Comte, and that of a host of books on natural science (too numerous to mention, but of which Dr. Büchner's little work on *Force and Matter* may be taken as a type), which insinuate or profess Atheistic tenets.

As to the first type, which does not so much deny the Being of God, as decline the controversy, whether there be or be not such a Being, as inaccessible to the human mind, we may remark that this is an opinion shared by many Theists, as we have seen in the case of the Père Mersenne, some of the Jesuit writers, &c.

As to the second, it is important to observe that experimental science, as such, and without trespassing into the region of metaphysics, has no logical *locus standi* for denying the existence of Deity; for it deals confessedly with physical phenomena only and their laws, *i.e.*, generalizations from them; and it is not pretended by any Theist that Deity is either a phenomenon or the law of phenomena. Science, therefore, can only say with the astronomer, "I have swept the heavens with my telescope again and again, and can find no God;" it cannot decide whether or not there are other means of arriving at the knowledge of Him. When it attempts to do this, and speaks of matter and force, it has gone beyond the region of phenomena, with which alone it has to deal, into the sphere of metaphysics, and must stand or fall, not as experimental but as philosophical. Its denial of the possibility of metaphysics on the ground that nothing exists but force and matter, is therefore a contradiction in terms; and, as a matter of fact, the ground upon which such a denial is made in scientific treatises will almost always be found to be some modification of the theory of D'Holbach. *Theology, it cannot be too often repeated, has nothing to fear from the progress of the natural sciences, but everything to fear from the prevalence of bad metaphysics.*

V. *The Passages in Holy Scripture bearing on Atheism* contemplate two classes of persons who deny the existence of God: the "wicked" and the "fool." The "wicked" (Heb. *rasha*) is he who (Job xxi. 14) says unto God, "Depart from us, for we desire not the knowledge of thy ways. What is the Almighty that we should serve Him, or what profit should we have if we pray unto Him?" The same word is applied (Gen. xviii. 23) to the Sodomites; (Job ix. 24) to the violent wrong-doer, "who covereth the faces of the judges;" (*ib.* xv. 20) to the "oppressor" (cf. A. V. margin, and chap. xx. passim); (in Ps. vii. 9) to Cush the Benjamite, the persecutor of David; (*ib.* xi. 6) to "him that loveth violence;" and (Isa. xiv. 5, &c.) to the Gentiles as the oppressors of Israel. In a word, the "wicked" man is, like Plato's tyrant, the wrong-doer on a sufficiently large scale to override the laws and escape punishment.

The "fool" (Heb. *nabal*) on the other hand, who (Ps. xiv. 1 and liii. 1) "hath said in his heart that there is no God," is corrupt and filthy, eats up the people like bread, shames the counsel of the poor, &c., does not call upon God, and, as one of "the workers of iniquity, has no knowledge." The word occurs once (Prov. xvii.) in the sense of "stupid," but in Prov. vii. 22 the "fool goeth to the correction of the stocks," *i.e.*, comes under the hands of the law. In Jer. xvii. 11, he "getteth riches, but not by right." More often the word means "impious, wicked, abandoned;" thus Nabal the "churl" (1 Sam. xxv. esp. v. 25) is "such a son of Belial, that a man cannot speak to him." So (2 Sam. iii. 33), "Died Abner as a fool dieth? Thy hands were not bound, nor thy feet put into fetters." In Job ii. 10 the word is applied to Job's wife for urging him to "curse God and die."

This induction seems to show that the "fool" is like the "wicked" in being impure and unjust, and differs from him in being a petty wrong-doer, whose proper place is the stocks. (Compare Ps. xxxvi. 2; Eph. ii. 12; 1 Thess. iv. 5; 1 Cor. xv. 32–34; Job xxii. 12, 13; &c.)

From such passages no distinct verdict can be extracted as to the theoretical Atheist, if his speculative Atheism is dissociated from practical immorality. Nothing of course can be found in his favour: as the only denier of God there contemplated is the practical Atheist, whether great or small, whose character is the opposite of "just;" that is, the opposite of the man who is fair, law-loving, benign, liberal, temperate, truthful, wise, and generally blameless (*v.* Gesenius, s. v. *Tsadik*).

VI. *Literature of Atheism.*—It may be useful for purposes of further study of this subject to present in one chronological view the different books, pamphlets, &c. which have appeared during the last three centuries. The list does not pretend to be more than an instalment of the great number of treatises for and against this doctrine.

(*a*) *The Sixteenth Century.*—1536, Calvin, *Instit.* iv. 7, 27, speaks of the prevalence of secret Atheism in the Roman Court, mentioning especially Popes Julius II., Leo X., Clement VII., and Paul III. Not long after this we have the story of Cardinal Perron demonstrating the existence of God before the Emperor Henry III., and then offering to disprove it on the morrow. For this he was very properly ordered out of the room (Voet, *Diss. de Atheismo*, p. 118). Towards the end of the century appeared the Abbé Charron's book, *De la Sagesse*, which led to his being regarded as an Atheist by the Jesuits (v. *De la Sagesse*, i. 4, 366; see also Buckle, *Hist. of Civilization*, vol i. 475, follg.; Reimmann, *Hist. Atheismi*, s. v.). In 1595, *Arcana Atheismi revelata*, by Cuper, appeared at Rotterdam. This was an examination of the system of Spinoza, which was erroneously supposed by many to be, or to lead to, Atheism. Cuper, in spite of his criticisms of Spinoza, is supposed by More to have been a covert Atheist (see Hoffmann, *Lexicon Universale*, Leyden, 1698, s. v. *Atheus*, who classes also Boulainvilliers among the Crypto-Atheists). In 1597 appeared Bacon's Essay on Atheism (*Essays* xvi.), and in 1599, *Atheomastige*, by Guil. de Assonville (Antwerp).

(*b*) *First Half of the Seventeenth Century.*—1605. *A Confutation of Atheisme*, by John Dove, D.D. (Lond.). 1608, *Man's Naturall Imagination*, by Perkins, *Wks.*, ii. 446, 525; *Engl. Wks.*, iii. 175. 1615, *Amphitheatrum aeternae providentiae divino-magicum, christiano-physicum, nec non et astrologo-catholicum adv. rett. philosophos, atheos, epicureos, peripateticos et stoicos*, by Gisbert Voet (Lyons). 1617, *De Providentia Numinis et animi immortalitate*, libb. ii. *adv. Atheos et Politicos*, by Lessius, S. J. (Antw.). 1616, Vanini *de Admirandis naturae reginae deaeque mortalium arcanis*, otherwise called *The Dialogues of Nature* (Paris). In 1619, Vanini is said to have confessed at the stake that thirty Atheists had set out from Naples to propagate their views in all parts of Europe. And Mersenne, writing shortly afterwards, speaks of fifty thousand Atheists in Paris alone, who had learnt it from Vanini, and of the circulation of a number of books, partly in manuscript, partly printed, which he does not name, but which had the effect of insinuating Atheistic opinions. 1624, *L'Impiété des Déistes, des Athées et des Libertins;* and 1625, *La Vérité des Sciences contre les Sceptiques* (Paris), both by the Père Mersenne. In the latter (p. 15), he says he does not think any of the proofs of the Being of God satisfactory to the reason. 1631, *Atheismus Triumphatus seu reductio ad religionem per scientiam veritatis* (Rome), by Campanella, was accused of covert Atheism. 1639, *Disputatio de Atheismo*, by Gisbert Voet (*Disput. Select.* pt. i. pp. 114–226), one of the most learned and exhaustive treatises on the subject. 1643, *L'Athéisme convaincu* (Saumur), by Cappel, who says (p. 2), "Il se voit plus d'Athées et de prophanes qu'il ne semble y en avoir jamais eu, même entre les payens, ce qui paroit par le desbordement estrange et la corruption horrible des mœurs qui se voit aujourd'huy si commune mesmes entre les Chretiens."

(*e*) *Latter half of the Seventeenth Century.*—Gassendi, *Animadversiones in Diog. Laërt.*, lib. x. *qui est de vita, moribus, placitisque Epicuri*, 3 vols. fol. 1649. This book, which is a rehabilitation of Epicurus as one "who did not fear God and yet lived well," is said to have "made many Atheists," so much so that had Gassendi "had the advice of all the Atheists that ever were, had he advised with Hell itself, he could not have lighted upon a more destructive way to all religion" (Meric Casaubon, *Credulity and Incredulity in Things Natural, Civil, and Divine*, Lond. 1668, p. 224, and Additions). The book, though confessedly written only "exercitationis gratia," was received "with so ready assent and applause" by "so many professing Christians" as to be "an argument to" Casaubon, "with many others of the inclination of the age" (*ib.* 226).

Gisb. Voet, *Apparatus ad controversiam adv. Atheos, Evere. et Bibl. stud. Theol.*, Ultraj. 1651; Spizelius, *Scrutinium Atheismi historico-aetiologicum*, Aug. Vindel. 1663, and *Ep. ad Meibomium de Atheismi radice*, *ib.* 1666; Moore, *Divine Dialogues*, London, 1668; "*The Humble Address of the Atheists or Sect of the Epicureans*" to William III., dated Devil Tavern, presented by Judge Baldock, and "graciously received" (a squib), Nov. 5, 1668 (Bodl. *Pamphl.* 178); Meric Casaubon, *Op. supr. cit.* 1668; Reiserus, *de origine progressu et incremento Antitheismi,* Aug. Vindel. 1669; Malpighius (anatomist), *The Microscope's Evidence to the Existence of an Intelligent Author of Nature,* 1669: Howe's *Assize Sermon at Northampton, against Atheists, Independents, Presbyterians, and Anabaptists,* 1669; Sir Charles Wolseley, *The Unreasonableness of Atheism,* 1669; *Recantation* of Daniel Scargill, B.A., Fellow of Corpus Christi College, Cambridge, who confesses before the Vice-Chancellor "that he (formerly) gloried to be an Hobbist and an Atheist, . . . agreeably to which principles and positions I have lived in great licentiousness, swearing rashly, drinking intemperately, boasting myself insolently, corrupting others by my pernicious principles and example," July 25, 1669 (Somers, *Tracts,* vol. vii. 370); Glanvil, Λόγου Θρησκεία, 1670; also *On the Tendencies of the Philosophy of the Royal Society,* 1671; Jo. Müller (prof. at Wittenberg, and Lutheran writer against Jansenism), *Atheismus devictus,* Hamb. 4to, 1672; Glanvil, *Sin of Scoffing,* &c., Lond. 1676; Wagner, *Examen Elencticum Atheismi Speculativi,* Tübingen, 4to, 1677; Cudworth, *Intellectual System, a confutation of the reason and philosophy of Atheism, and a demonstration of the impossibility of it,* London, 1678, in which (c. 2) the arguments in favour of Atheism are so well stated, said Dryden, that the writer had failed to answer them in c. 5 (*Dedic. to Aeneid,* ii. 378). *The Libertine Overthrown, or a Mirror for Atheists* (undated), being the egregious vicious life and eminently and sincerely penitent death of John Earl of Rochester, who died 1680, "abstracted for the use of the meanest capacities" from Burnet and Parsons; Bp. Manningham, *Popery one great cause of Atheism,* Lond. 1681; Glanvil, *A Whip for the Droll* (*i.e.,* the scoffer), *Fidler to the Atheist, being Reflections on Drollery and Atheism,* a letter to H. More, with comments by More,

1682; Dr. Grew (botanist), *The Microscope's Evidence to an Intelligent Author*, &c.; Redi (entomologist), to the same effect; J. P. Grüneberg, *de Atheorum religione prudentum*, and *Disputationes de Scientiâ Dei*—all about this date; Jac. Abadie, *de Veritate religionis Christianae* (pt. i. c. 18, p. 129), Rotterdam, 1684; *Origine of Atheisme in the Popish and Protestant Churches*, shewn by Dorotheus Sicurus, made English, with a preface by E. B., Esq., 1684; *A Discourse upon the Reasonableness of Men's having a Religion or Worship of God*, by His Grace George d. of Buckingham (Somers, *Tracts*, ix. pp. 13–19), 1685. To this an answer appeared, only described in Somers, and a rejoinder by the Duke, in which he says he does not understand the answer, but offers to give the author £1000 if he will prove that he is the same George Duke of Buckingham that he was twenty years ago. (The point of the Duke's tract is that matter is not eternal.) *The Atheist unmasked by a person of honour*, Lond. 1685; Untereyk, *Der narrische Atheist*, Bremen, 1689; *The Second Spira*, by J. S., 1693. This was an account of the last sickness of an Atheist and reprobate, the member of a club, which "within the last seven years" (A.D. 1687–92) "met together constantly to lay down such rules and method as that they might be critically wicked in everything that they could, without the laws taking hold of them." "A deal of company" came to witness his despair during eight days' illness; and hear him "curse the day when he exchanged the Christian faith" for the Creed "of Spinoza and the Leviathan." It is said that the publisher sold thirty thousand copies of this tract in six weeks. (Lowndes' *Bibliographical Manual*.) By the same author, *A Conference betwixt a modern Atheist and his Friend*, London, 1693; Bentley, *Boyle Lectures against Atheism*, 1693; *An Anatomy of Atheisme, a poem by a person of quality* (Dawes, Bishop of Chester), 1693; Hoffmann, *de Atheo Convincendo*, an inaugural lecture delivered at Halle, *Wks.*, v. pp. 125–130, 1693; *Sermon* by the Archbishop of Canterbury (Tillotson) on *Atheism*, circ. 1694; Pritius, *Diss. de Atheismo in se foedo et humano generi noxio*, Leipsic, 1695; Jablonsky, *Stultitia et irrationabilitas Atheismi*, Magdeb. 1695; Edwards *Thoughts concerning the causes and occasions of Atheism*, 1695; Grassius, *An Atheismus necessario ducat ad corruptionem morum*, Rostock, 1697; Hoffmann, *Lexicon Univ.* s. v., Leyden, 1698; Lidgould (Fellow of Clare Coll., Cambr.), *Proclamation against Atheism*, 1699.

(d) *First Half of the Eighteenth Century.*—Abicht, *De damno Atheismi in republicâ*, Leips. 1703; Jenkin Thomasius, *Hist. Philosophica Atheismi*, Altdorf, 1703; Jo. Rajesanyi (S. J.), *Itinerarium Athei ad Veritatis viam* (A dialogue against the Machiavellians), Vienna, 1704; Jo. Fabricius *Consideratio Controversiarum*, pp. 1–23, 1704; Jo. Christ. Wolfius, *Dissertatio de Atheismi falso suspectis*, Wittenberg, 1710; H. More, *Enthusiasmus Triumphatus* (in which Enthusiasm is shown to be one of the causes of Atheism), also *Antidote to Atheism*, 1712; Philips, *Diss. Historica de Atheismo*, Lond. 1716; *The Third Spira*, memoirs of a young English gentleman at Paris (went through two editions), 1717; Buddeus, *Theses de Atheismo et Superstitione*, Jena, 1717; Biermann, *Impietas Atheistica sceptico-sceptica detecta*, Hanov. 1720; Jo. Jac. Syrbius, *Diss. de Origine Atheismi*, Jena, 1720 (v. Zedler and Jöcher); Reimmann, *Historia Atheismi et Atheorum falso et merito suspectorum*, Hildesheim, 1725; J. Alb. Fabricius, *Delectus argumentorum*, &c. p. 286, ib. *Philosophis et gentibus falso imputatus Atheismus*, p. 286, ib. *Scriptores adv. Atheos*, from which this bibliographical notice may be considerably extended, p. 340, 1725; Warburton's *Divine Legation*, bk. i. sec. 3–5, Lond. 1738.

(e) *Latter Half of the Eighteenth Century.*—In 1751 appeared the celebrated French *Encyclopédie*, "the first work in which Atheism was openly promulgated" (Buckle's *Civilization*, i. p. 786). "Dans un intervalle de douze années, de 1758–70, la littérature française fut souillée par un grand nombre d'ouvrages où l'Athéisme était ouvertement professé" (Lacretelle, 18ième Siècle, ap. Buckle, op. cit. i. 787). In 1764, Hume met at Baron d'Holbach's a party of the most celebrated men in Paris. Hume raised the question as to the existence of a bonâ fide Atheist, and was told that he was in company with seventeen such (Burton's *Life of Hume*, ii. p. 220, ap. Buckle). In 1764, Walpole writes of the educated Parisians, that "their avowed doctrine is Atheism" (*Letters*, v. 96, ed. 1840, ibid. Boulainvilliers, *Doutes sur la Religion*, Lond. 1767).

In 1770 appeared *Le Système de la Nature*, by Miraband, Baron d'Holbach (or, in part perhaps, La Mettrie). It was read very widely by "des savants, des ignorants, des femmes" (Voltaire, *Dict. Phil.* s. v. *Dieu*). "The views it contains are so clearly and methodically arranged as to have earned for it the name of the code of Atheism" (Buckle, *l. c.*). An extract from Voltaire's answer to it, in which he states his persuasion that the error "proceeds from no badness of heart," is translated in the *Annual Register* for 1771, p. 183, *Characters*. In 1774, Priestley reported that all the philosophical persons to whom he was introduced in Paris were unbelievers in Christianity and even professed Atheists (*Memoirs*, i. p. 74). In 1775, the Archbishop of Toulouse, in a formal address to the king on behalf of the clergy, declared that "le monstreux athéisme est devenu l'opinion dominante" (Soulavie, *Règne de Louis XVI.*, vol. iii. p. 16, *ap.* Buckle, *l. c.*). This, like all similar assertions, must have been an exaggeration; but that there was a large amount of truth in it is known, says Buckle, to whoever has studied the mental habits of the generation immediately preceding the Revolution. Besides a host of inferior writers, among the higher intellects, Condorcet, D'Alembert, Diderot, Helvetius, Lalande, Laplace, and Mirabeau, openly advocated Atheism.

Jacobi, *Briefe üb. Spinoza* (p. 307), 1789. Platner, *Philosophische Aphorismen* (i. p. 543, follg.), 1793. Heidenreich, *Lettres sur l'Athéisme*, Leips. 1796. Malham, *A Word for the Bible, being a serious reply to the speculative Deists and practical Atheists*, London, 1796.

(*f*) *The Nineteenth Century.*—Sylvain Maréchal, *Dictionnaire des Athées*, Paris, 8vo, 1800, reprinted by Didot, 1855. This—"the most extraordinary of Maréchal's books"—appeared just as French society was settling down after the Revolution, "les mœurs dissolues du Directoire s'étaient épurées peu à peu," and religion was reviving under the influence of Napoleon. Silence was imposed upon all journals which desired to criticize or draw attention to the book, embargo was laid upon its circulation, and its author passed over with contempt, and deprived of the *éclat* of a persecution. The original edition is now only to be found in a few private libraries. Alea, *Antidote de l'Athéisme, ou Examen critique du Dict. des Athées*, 1800. Feuerbach, *Das Wesen der Religion*, a set of lectures delivered at Heidelberg in the winter of 1848–9. Iconoclast, *God, Man, and the Bible, three nights' discussion with the Principal of St. Aidan's College*, London, 1860; also, *A Plea for Atheism*, and *Is there a God?* Holyoake, *The Limits of Atheism*, London, 1861. John Watts, *The Logic and Philosophy of Atheism*, London, 1865. Arnold Ruge, *Reden üb. Religion* (founded upon Schwartz, *Ueber den Ursprung der Mythologie*, and Dupuis, *L'Origine de tous les Cultes*), Berlin, 1869. Radenhausen, *Isis*, vol. ii. p. 409, follg.

The modern books, on general or special points of natural science, which popularize Atheistic views in the present day are too numerous to mention in detail; but their general character has been sketched above.

ON DOUBT.

Doubt is an intellectual tendency to deny a proposition resting upon a limited quantity of evidence, on the ground that the evidence is no greater; and it is always accompanied by an opposite intellectual tendency to affirm the same on the ground that the evidence is no less. Doubt is thus the complement of belief.[1] If a thing is known or certain, the evidence or reason for it must be complete, and it is impossible to doubt it. If, on the contrary, there is no evidence for it, or none known to us, we know that it is false, or are ignorant that it is true, and it is impossible to believe it. If, thirdly, there is a limited amount of evidence—much or little—short of that required for certainty, we believe the proposition, because there is evidence for it, but doubt it, because the amount of evidence forthcoming is insufficient to satisfy the demand made by the mind as a condition of its arriving at certainty. This demand varies indefinitely in different individuals, and in different sets of individuals under different circumstances. Thus, the preaching of an angel from heaven would be, to the majority of mankind, conclusive evidence of the truth of a doctrine; but for Christians, St. Paul says, this is not sufficient evidence, unless the doctrine be identical with that already received (Gal. i. 8). Or, again, what is sufficient evidence to produce certainty in an uninstructed, may be insufficient to assure an instructed, person. But apart from this variety in the demand actually made for evidence, there is a certain amount of evidence in every case which is ideally suffi-

---

[1] Belief is co-extensive with knowledge in the opinion of Prof. Flint. "Theism" (Blackwood, 1877), pp. 85-86.

cient, and which is always taken for granted as a standard of certainty, however opinions may vary as to *what* or how much it is. Doubt, then, like belief, presupposes (*a*) that a proposition is no longer received in childlike simplicity without question. "Absit," says St. Augustine, "ut ideo credamus ne rationem accipiamus sive quaeramus." (*b*) "Doubting necessarily implies some degree of evidence for that of which we doubt" (Butler, *Anal.*, ii. 5); and as Archbishop Leighton has it, "when there is a great deal of smoke and no clear flame, it argues much moisture in the matter; yet it witnesseth certainly that there is fire within. And therefore dubious questioning is much better evidence than that senseless dulness which most take for believing. Men that know nothing in sciences have no doubts. He never truly believed who was not first made sensible and convinced of unbelief." Conversely, belief, as the acceptance of a proposition upon evidence less than the amount required for certainty, postulates a margin of doubt (cf. "Lord, I believe, help thou mine unbelief"), which exactly corresponds to the difference between the amount of evidence on which I believe a thing, and the amount of evidence on which I should be certain of it.

In common parlance, when the evidence for the truth of a proposition preponderates over that against it, when the area, so to speak, of our belief in it is more extensive than the area of our doubt about it, we say we believe it, and omit to make record of our doubts about it. Similarly, when our doubts about it preponderate over our belief in it, we say in common speech, that we doubt it, and take no account of our belief in it. And this is all the more the case when, as in most instances, either doubt or belief predominates out of all proportion to its respective opposite. But if we would describe the whole state of the mind in the consideration of incomplete evidence, we must regard it as a double (*du*-bito, $\delta\iota$-$\sigma\tau\alpha\zeta\epsilon\iota\nu$, *zwei*-feln), and not a single state; we must say that we both believe and doubt a proposition which, upon the evidence, is at once probable and improbable.

Doubt does not necessarily imply a state of indifference or suspension of judgment. On the contrary, this is only the case in those very few instances in which the evidence for and against a proposition is exactly equal, and our belief in and doubt about its truth are equal also.

Neither does doubt involve disbelief, except in the same sense as it involves belief; for disbelief is itself a kind of belief, the belief, namely, that a particular proposition is not true.

Belief, then, whether affirming or denying, is a positive, but a limited and imperfect, state of mind, as compared with faith and knowledge. And the limit or imperfection of belief, whether large or small, is doubt.

Apparent States of Belief which exclude Doubt.—When the evidence for the truth of a proposition is complete, we are not said to believe it any longer, but to know it. And this is equally the case whether the evidence consist of an enumeration of the reasons, or rest upon the authority of an absolutely veracious person. The distinction, in truth, between believing in a fact, and believing in a person, will not bear close examination. When I believe in a fact, I assent to a proposition importing that the fact is real and is of a particular kind—as true, on the strength of what appear to me to be adequate reasons; when I believe in a person, I assent to the proposition, importing that the person in question is trustworthy—as true, on the strength of evidence, as in the former case. His trustworthiness, thus ascertained, then becomes itself the evidence for the proposition for which he vouches.

But there are several other cases in which the words "implicit" and "steadfast" are applied to belief to signify the exclusion of doubt: (*a*) A belief is implicit or implied when it is not explicit or explained, *i.e.* when there is no reason or explanation "*why* I believe" to be given, but "*that* I believe" is taken for

granted both by myself and others. This, just like implicit obedience, is the normal condition of the child, and the actual condition of the vast majority of the human race, in whom the mind is in a state of mere passive receptivity in relation to truth, and who are therefore *not yet* able to ask themselves " why they believe."
(*b*) Belief is "steadfast" when the exclusion of doubt is not so much the result of natural condition as of voluntary effort. "Steadfast" means, first, "permanent," or "unwavering," and, secondly, that this permanence is the work of the will, bringing the mind consciously under the sway of habit. "Steadfast belief," then, supposes the emergence of doubt, and its intentional and habitual suppression; not only the state of mind which says, " I believe," but that which, perhaps after experience of the double condition of belief and doubt, says, " I will believe," " I mean to believe," and consciously forms the permanent habit or state of believing. (*c*) The result of this process is again a state of implicit belief, which resembles the first in excluding any explanation or reason for believing, but differs from it in being acquired instead of natural. The child is *not yet*—the "steadfast" believer *no longer*—able to ask "why he believes;" because the attention of the child is not yet—that of the habitual believer no longer—attracted to the fact that he does believe.

To sum up: doubt can only be excluded from belief, either when the evidence for the truth of a proposition is complete, in which case belief itself vanishes in knowledge; or, as in the three cases last mentioned, by the interposition of some determinant external to the mental process of believing, as such, and due either (*a*) to natural condition, or (*b*) to voluntary effort, or (*c*) to the force of habit. In the first case, the completeness of the evidence, while it excludes doubt excludes belief also; in the last three, the intervention of alien causes excludes, along with doubt, the conscious repose of belief upon evidence at all. From this it follows that belief, if it rests upon any evidence whatever, must rest upon evidence that is not entirely complete; and as it is itself (apart from the operation upon it of external causes) essentially an imperfect assent, it postulates the co-existence of doubt, as its limit.

Supposed States of Doubt which exclude Belief.—The attempt to make doubt absolute and thorough-going is still more illogical than the exclusion of doubt from the condition of belief. If doubt be the inherent imperfection of belief, it postulates the existence of that of which it is the imperfection; if it be the consciousness of the incompleteness of evidence, it supposes the existence of evidence which is thus incomplete. It is the recognition of this limit to doubt which distinguishes rational doubt from scepticism. "We doubt," says Descartes, "in order to obtain a ground of absolute certitude." In other words, we traverse the region of doubt in order to arrive at the belief which is its limit. The ancient followers of Pyrrho, however, in setting up doubt as an ultimate and final principle in thought, asserted that there was nothing on which the instructed intellect should allow itself to frame a definite judgment. Such a principle, were it possible to carry it out to its legitimate conclusions, puts an end to all action, as to all thought, and is as subversive of society as it is of religion and philosophy. The consistent Pyrrhonist has no right to eat or drink; if his house is on fire, there is no reason that he should attempt to escape. Why? Because such an action presupposes a series of previous judgments, "I am in danger," "It is well to escape," "To escape, I must flee," &c., none of which he has any rational ground for framing. Fortunately, human instinct is better than philosophy in this case, and comes in to correct the extravagance of theory. But, also, the theory itself, if thought out, annihilates itself. When the Pyrrhonist has doubted the reality of the world and of thought, he at length arrives at a point at which he has the choice of either doubting whether or not he doubts, in which case doubt itself vanishes, or of being sure that he doubts, in which case he has found a limit to his doubt in a definite belief. It was at some such impassable limit, too, that Descartes arrived, and from which the whole of modern philosophy has been evolved. (See Descartes, *Œuvres*, tom. iii. pp. 63–68, ed. Cousin; and the French *Encyclopédie* of 1751, s. v. *Doute*.)

Doubt, then, and belief are the negative and positive poles of the same mental condition, a condition characteristic of the imperfection of human knowledge. They spring out of the same root—viz., the awakening of the mind to the necessity of basing assent on evidence.

Doubt originates, like belief on evidence, in the individual mind. Men never doubt in crowds, nor do communities ever believe on evidence. If we examine the early history of every nation, we find it generating unconsciously an organized system of common ideas, which, like its language or its polity, correspond to its collective character, and from which all marks of individual workmanship are absent. Religion and worship in primitive peoples are always of this gregarious kind, and (to take a familiar instance) it was through the medium of this collective consciousness that the Hebrews came into contact with the Divine revelation. God speaks through His Prophets, but He speaks to Israel at large; and conversely, it is not as a series of individuals, but as a people, that the Hebrews accept the Divine message, and are conscious of being collectively the subjects of the Divine favour (2 Chron. xxx. 12; Jer. xxxii. 39, &c.). So in the primitive Christian Church, the "multitude of them that believed were of one heart and of one soul," and this absence of all individual and private feeling finds its natural expression in community of goods. In all these cases doubt is impossible, because there is no detachment of the individual from the general life of the community. Similarly, the "belief" of this early time is not what is here called belief, *i.e.*, intellectual assent upon evidence, but an immediate apprehension of Christ, as a person, by the "heart," *i.e.*, the whole being of the "believer." So too our Lord Himself discouraged the seeking for signs, and commonly declined to constrain intellectual belief by the evidence of miracles. To St. Thomas alone, who had detached himself for the moment from the common consciousness of the first disciples, and therefore was in the real position of an intellectual doubter, is vouchsafed the evidence requisite for producing individual and intellectual belief. Accordingly, doubt seems to have arisen more generally in the Church, when the original "unity of heart" was broken up by divisions and heresies, when Christianity had become matter of discussion, when "apologies" had begun to be written to produce belief on evidence, and when the saints, no longer finding rest in society, retired into the desert and the cloister. Doubt is thus to the organized authority of common opinion what the monastic impulse is to the organized authority of society—viz., a revolt of the individual from the intellectual and moral world in which he lives. This characteristic is noticeable in the more prominent instances of doubt which are on record. The late Mr. Robertson speaks of the "utter loneliness of spirit," the dreariness and cheerlessness of his life while in doubt. The same is true of Abélard, who, perhaps more than any other, forms a solitary figure in the Middle Ages.

The causes which lead the individual so to detach himself from the ordinary mental life around him, and to demand evidence for the truth of received ideas, lie partly in the educational effect of those ideas themselves, and partly in the fact that they have worked themselves out, and are giving place to a higher development. Plato has described this process under the image of a foster-child, who, after being carefully trained by his reputed parents, at length attains sufficient intelligence to discover that those whom he has hitherto regarded as his parents are not really so; and is led by the discovery to question everything that he has been taught, to break away from all the influences of his youth, and to regard all moral distinctions as merely conventional. In this state of uncertainty he falls into the hands of flatterers and sophists, and becomes a lawless and disputatious person (*de Republicâ*, p. 538). Meanwhile, however, the foster-parents are given up for the real parents. The impulse to demand the reason for traditionary ideas, the formation and emancipation of the individual mind, the capacity of doubt and belief, are the last results of the operation upon man of those common ideas and institutions of which he is the half unconscious author. Their very pressure calls forth the resistance which is the germ of self-consciousness. Man becomes aware of himself as the source of ideas and of institutions, and of his indefeasible right, as a free being, against all that is established. The very reasonableness of tradition and custom have developed in him the faculty of seeking the reasons for them in himself. And the more reason he sees for the traditional and the customary, the less authority have they over him, for he perceives that he is himself, in the last resort, the author of both. The emergence in society of the self-conscious individual is, if we regard it from one side alone, a principle of anarchy; but regarded from the other side, the free activity which is thus called into being is itself a principle of reconstruction. The demand for reason and evidence, while it reveals the insufficiency of what has been hitherto unquestioned, discloses also the quantum of reasonableness without which it could never have been accepted at all. In referring all things to himself, the individual thus refers them not only to a solvent but to an active principle. What he has made before he can again make. The insufficiency of that which he criticizes he discovers to be the result of the insufficiency in himself, its author. And conversely, the sufficiency of himself as the standard of ideas and institutions is the result of the action upon him of that which he criticizes. While he doubts, therefore, he also believes. As the "measure of all things" he creates a new order of thoughts and customs by which he will himself be judged.

The detachment of the doubter from the common consciousness in which all men live is thus the natural way in which ideas and societies correct themselves. If they were wholly adequate at any given time, they could not be criticized; if they were wholly inadequate, they could not have educated their critic. Doubt, therefore, as the characteristic of the individual mind, is at once destructive and constructive, and, as the mean term between an old and a new order, essentially transitional. As transitional it partakes both of the old and the new, and finds its true complement in belief.

The History of the Principal Periods of Doubt further confirms this view. They have all ushered in new developments in religion and philosophy. The period of the Sophists in ancient Greece represents the break-down of the old Polytheism, and introduces the spiritual Monotheism of Anaxagoras and Plato. The sceptical Epicurism of the Sadducees in Israel represents the break-down of that "tradition" by which the "Word of God" had been made "of none effect." What the natural reconstruction might have been, we are left in great measure to conjecture, inasmuch as it was guided, dominated, and ultimately absorbed by the new supernatural principle of Christianity. After the beginning of the second Christian century, the rise of patristic or argumentative, as distinguished from simply or mainly religious, Christianity, points to a period of questioning which called forth the *Apology* of Justin Martyr, and the *Stromata* of Clement of Alexandria. It is characteristic of this period that Clement places the intellectual understanding of revelation (ἐπιστήμη) as the mean term between πίστις in which doubt has not yet arisen, and γνῶσις in which it has vanished in conscious certainty. A little later, the speculations of Origen and the growth of the Arian heresy indicate the continued prevalence of doubt, and the demand for reasons and evidence. In the twelfth century, again, the *Sic et Non* of Abélard indicates the transition from the patristic to the scholastic or metaphysical period of Christian thought. This work, the text of which was discovered and published for the first time by the late M. Cousin, is a discussion of the difficulties arising from Scripture and the writings of the Fathers, and a juxtaposition of the reasons for and against all the main truths of religion. The general point of view is thus stated: "Haec quippe prima sapientiae clavis definitur, assidua scilicet seu frequens interrogatio. Dubitando enim ad inquisitionem venimus; inquirendo veritatem percipimus" (Cousin's *Fragm. de Philosophie*, vol. ii. p. 220–234). This book introduces the method of Enstasis and Solution characteristic of scholastic divinity, which is seen in its perfection in the *Summa* of St. Thomas Aquinas. The doubt, again, of the seventeenth century, as represented by Lord Bacon, Descartes, and Spinoza, is consciously entertained as a solvent of the scholastic modes of thought, and as, what it has proved to be, the germ of the whole modern intellectual movement (Bacon, *N. O. passim.*; Descartes, *l.c.*; Spinoza, *Princ. Phil. Cartes*, Op. ed. Bruder, vol. i. 22–28). Protestantism, once more, the contemporary religious development, as the assertion of the right of private judgment, is essentially a principle of doubt; and, while undermining the dogmas of the later Middle Ages, has in our times shown unmistakable signs of a tendency to destroy itself. For the mere private judgment of one person has no interest for any other; and its maintenance, as such, is subversive both of truth and society; whilst, on the other hand, by becoming illuminated and instructed, judgment ceases to be private, and becomes common.

The last and most thoroughgoing instance of philosophical scepticism which the world has seen, that of Hume and Kant, illustrates the same law. Whilst annihilating the English sensational school of Locke and Berkeley, on the one hand, it is the foundation, on the other, of the vast structure of modern German thought. Doubt is thus, like revolution, an anarchical principle; and its justification, like that of revolution, is its success—*i.e.*, its capability of reconstructing the traditional and customary on a securer basis, "ex fumo dare lucem."

The Consciousness of Doubt in particular cases may arise from a variety of causes. In the majority of minds which have arrived at the stage of demanding evidence for belief, although in reality they both believe and doubt, yet the attention is almost exclusively concentrated upon the fact that they believe. Belief is sustained by the influence of the unquestioning certainty of the world at large, by being more comfortable than doubt, and by the habit of continually asserting or assuming belief in ordinary life. Belief is thus artificially extended, and doubt narrowed almost to a vanishing point. It is most natural to forget that our belief is imperfect, as it is most natural to forget that our actions are imperfect. Belief being not only preponderant, but active, doubt becomes obscured. But if anything occurs to awaken examination of the grounds of belief, this residuum of doubt is brought to light; and doubt is likely to become active for a time, without being in reality different in amount, or in proportion to belief, from what it was before. These are cases in which belief is said to be "shaken," and the occasion seeming, and indeed often being, inadequate to alter the relation of the mind to the evidence, moral perversion is taken for granted, or the inspiration of the Evil One, to account for the emergence of doubt. Whereas the fact is, that a latent condition of consciousness has been excited into activity, and while the excitement lasts—which is not unfrequently prolonged and aggravated by the surprise of the doubter at the existence of doubt in his mind, by the protestation of friends, the social ostracism which he has to undergo, the embarrassment of active duty, the misunderstandings and misstatements of enemies, or, again, by the encouragements of disbelievers, and the clamour on all sides for the supposed doubter to commit himself to definite statements—the discovery of doubt loosens the moorings of all beliefs, or throws an atmosphere of uncertainty over them. Doubt propagates itself, just as belief had done before, and belief diminishes, for the time, to a vanishing point. It is in cases like this that the advice is good to change the sphere of life and engage in active occupation, in order to allow the mind to settle down again before taking any step.

But, again, the mind may become conscious of doubt—*i.e.*, of the imperfection of belief—by an accession of evidence on the negative side of the scale, or by the discovery that a portion of the evidence on the positive side breaks down. Here again the area of doubt may be artificially extended by the novelty of the discovery and consequent exaggeration of its importance, by the self-congratulation of the doubter at his own acuteness in making it, &c., so as to encroach further upon the area of belief than is actually warranted by the new evidence. On this kind of doubt, St. Augustine writes to Adeodatus: " Dubitationem tuam non invitus accipio ; significat enim animum minimè temerarium, quae custodia tranquillitatis est maxima. Nam difficillimum est omninò non perturbari, cum ea quae pronâ et proclivâ approbatione tenebamus contrariis disputationibus labefactantur, et quasi extorquentur e manibus. Quare ut aequum est bene consideratis perspectisque rationibus cedere, ita incognita pro cognitis habere periculosum. Metus enim est ne cum saepe subruuntur quae firmissimè statura et mansura praesumimus, in tantum odium vel timorem rationis incidamus, et ne ipsi quidem perspicuae veritati fides habenda videatur." (*De Magistro*, 31 A B, Bened. ed. vol. i. p. 558.) "The best way never to be a sceptic," says Meric Casaubon, speaking of the same state of mind, "is not to be too quick of belief, and to doubt of many things" (*Credulity and Incredulity*, p. 155). The opposite and more insidious temptation is for the doubter to tamper with his mind, to endeavour to forget the new evidence, to disregard the law of intellectual honesty, and habituate himself to the profession of beliefs for the sake of their comfortableness or utility, until at length he forms a new habit of believing a thing to be true, even in the teeth of a known preponderance of evidence to the contrary. The best remedy against either temptation, and against the continuance of this kind of doubt, is careful, impartial, and methodized inquiry. It is by method that a man arises out of the individual isolation of doubt, and comes into contact with the common thought of all time.

Lastly, doubt may emerge into consciousness owing to the natural inclination of particular temperaments. Just as many are inclined to believe simply because they shrink from the trouble of investigating evidence, others take refuge in alleged uncertainty of evidence because they are afraid of pursuing a subject to unwelcome conclusions (see *Eclipse of Faith*). The remedies for doubt of this order will be the same as those for indolence in the one case, and for timidity in the other.

Relation of Doubt to Action.—Doubt is too often the paralysis of action; and commonly the necessity of action may induce a forcible suppression of doubt which leaves, for ever, a scar upon the character. Of this difficulty Bishop Jeremy Taylor gives the following solution:—In the case of the unlearned, whose assurance may be destroyed by arguments which they cannot answer, he advises that "they stick to their conclusions, in despite of all objections, by a certainty of adhesion." But if the learned "be made to doubt in the understanding by the opposition of an adversary, they are not instantly to change their practice, but inquire further. . . . . In these cases the practice is made sure by a

Y

collateral light, and the 'doubter' is defended from change by reputation and custom, by fear of scandal and the tie of laws, and by many other indirect instruments of determination; which, although they cannot outwit the contrary arguments, yet they ought to outweigh the doubt, and guide the will, and rule the conscience in such cases. There is nothing but a weak man may doubt of, but if he be well, he must not change his foot till it be made certain to him that he is deceived; let him consider what he please, and determine at leisure; let him be swift to hear, but slow to speak, and slower yet in declaring by his action and changed course that his doubt hath prevailed on him. . . . . If the speculative doubting conscience should always prevail in practice, the ignorant might be abused and miserable in all things, and the learned in most" (*Ductor Dubitantium*, p. 184, sqq.). In the analogous forensic case of possession under a title discovered to be uncertain, Taylor quotes the authority of all the principal jurists for his solution, that "whatsoever hath the first advantage of just and reasonable is always to be so presumed till the contrary be proved; a doubt, therefore, may make a man unquiet and tie him to inquire, but cannot interrupt possession . . . . because possession is stronger than doubt, though it cannot prevail against demonstration" (*Ib. l.c.*; see the question discussed at the end of Strauss's *Life of Jesus*, Eng. tr., and in Browning's *Bishop Blougram's Apology*). Robertson writes that he "never allowed his bewilderment to tell upon his conduct" (see his *Life and Letters*, by Stopford Brooke, vol. i. pp. 111–113), although he not only at one time doubted everything except that "it must be right to do right," but even speaks of the misery of a suspicion that even moral goodness and beauty might be a dream. His temptations and doubts he sought to solve by working amongst the poor, by putting his aspirations in practice, and by keen sympathy with the suffering of the masses. He adds (p. 203) that all questioning and doubt left him as he drew near the close of his career.

The Relation of Doubt to Faith is a particular case of the relation of the individual to that spiritual community of which he forms a part. And this may be described as a relation, first, of opposition; secondly, of expansion; finally, of reunion; corresponding in the moral sphere to selfishness, rational self-love, and self-sacrifice, respectively. Faith is, as is knowledge, always of the True Object. But *to us*, who are in process of development, the true object may wear the appearance of the false. Still the true object is there as the condition of the existence of Faith at all: we throw our own shadow upon it by doubt which is the imperfection of belief. If there were no light and no object, we could not throw our shadow (cf. 2 Tim. ii. 13). We see the truth "enigmatically and in a glass," as we see the sun through the medium of the window and the atmosphere; and this truth is our union, in Christ, with God. This is the true object, and, at the same time, itself the reality and substance of faith. But in describing it, we obscure that which we would explain, because the oppositions of speech involve distinctions which in the spiritual sphere are distinctly negative of that which they are meant to express. Faith is a relation, and in thinking of it we cannot but regard it from our side of the relation: we are compelled to think of ourselves as first; whereas in reality God is first, and we in Him. It is this inability of faith to take a true view of itself, which brings it down into the sphere of opinion, and into contact with the divided regions of belief and doubt, which are incidents of the individual life in its state of limitation and growth. And, conversely, it is only by a kind of mental self-denial that we can rise above the region of opinions, misgivings and prejudices, of the contradictions of thought and feeling, and of the opposition of moral and intellectual, which is the province of doubt, and from which we can only describe the truth amiss, and in terms which, so soon as used, require correction. On the distinction of "common faith," *i.e.* belief on evidence, and "true faith," *i.e.*, a supernatural state of the soul, see Perkin's *Exposition of the Creed*, Works, vol. i. p. 126, fol. 1608.

FRAGMENTS.

FRAGMENTS.

We have thought that the following extracts from Dr. Appleton's common-place books would be interesting to many, as giving an insight into the working of his mind upon some important social, political, philosophical and religious subjects. These Notes and Fragments are printed almost exactly as written: for they will, doubtless, be read with more pleasure in their present form than if any attempt had been made to remould some rapidly written and perhaps obscure sentences. They must, however, be taken for what they are—not finished compositions, not matured conclusions, but in great measure as passing thoughts arrested for future use, often tentative rather than expressing formed opinions, and, of course, never intended to meet the public eye.

The extracts range from 1867 to the end of Dr. Appleton's life, but only in a very few cases has it been possible to affix a date.—J. H. A.

Does not every miracle involve two miracles, if not an infinite series? Thus let x, a miracle, be supposed to interrupt the continuity of the series of phenomena A B C D x E F G, &c., at the point between D and E. Then it follows that D as a cause has no effect unless it be x, and E, as an effect, has no cause except it be x. Here, then, we have on the one hand a natural cause, D, producing either no effect (which is miraculous), or else having x for an effect, in which case the cause would be equally miraculous; and further we have C producing such a semi-miraculous cause, B producing C, &c.; *i.e.*, we are landed in a miraculous regress to infinity. In each of the terms of the regress there *is* a miraculous element, although a diminishing one, to infinity. This diminution does not prevent the first term of the series from being *as truly* miraculous as the term D, because all miracles *as such* are equal; *i.e.*, they imply the direct action of the Infinite out of the course of nature. If then this direct action occurs at every point in the series, *i.e.*, in *every* phenomenon previous to a miracle, the distinction between x, as a direct action, and the previous terms of the series vanishes: either they are all miraculous, or else x is natural.

So with the infinite series of terms succeeding x. The series starts with E, which is either the effect of no cause at all, which it can hardly be unless it is the Infinite Being Himself; or it is the effect of D, in which case the continuity of the series has not been disturbed; or, lastly, it is the effect of x, a miraculous cause, and carries on the miraculous element communicated by x *ad infinitum* in a progressive series. This remaining series will thus be miraculous exactly in the same sense that the order of Nature, according to the common conception, is miraculous; *i.e.*, the first term of the series is the effect of the immediate action of the Supreme Being.

The notion of substance arises from breaking the strict relativity between the thinker and the thing; it is identical with the notion of independent "*being*," *i.e.*, of relativity which is relative to nothing, *i.e.*, which is relative to itself alone. Substance is therefore the counterpart of mysticism: as the first is "being" divorced from its relation to the thinker, so is mysticism thought divorced from its relation to things. It would therefore be improper to say that "substance *is*," because it means that that which stands out of all relation to anything but itself, stands in relation (this is the only meaning of "*is*") to the mind; which is self-contradictory.

The only way in which this contradiction can be avoided is by restricting our notion of substance to that which is considered the highest, and indeed which is properly the only case of substantive being, i.e., the self-conscious mind. The mind, as an object to itself, *is ; i.e.*, is relative to a thinker; but, in the case supposed, this thinker, to which the mind is relative, is itself. Its being, or relativity, is thus relativity to self, and is consequently independent of all else. The mind, thinking about itself, is thus the only substance which is not self-contradictory.

Here, however, we appear to be landed in the counterpart of substance, viz., the mind divorced from things, out of relation to things or objects of thought, and in relation to itself alone. Substance is either a self-contradictory notion, or it is indistinguishable from its diametrical opposite and complementary ineptitude, mysticism. In other words, if we arbitrarily sever the relation between the mind and the thing, and try to isolate each member, we cease to be able to distinguish the one from the other.

It is between these two ineptitudes that the mediæval mind, so far as it was not merely commentatory on the past, is continually fluctuating. It is this false opposition which constitutes its fundamental characteristic.

It is only in the sense in which the relativity of mind to itself includes the relativity of the mind to everything, and, conversely, in which the *being* of the mind *for itself* includes the relativity of everything to the mind, that substance ceases to be an impossible idea. The question is, Is such a comprehension possible, and is it necessary? Unless it be, the idea of substance falls to the ground altogether. But if it be, it proves, along with the reality of substance, the fact that there is only one substance, and that that is *spiritual, i.e., neither mind per se, nor things per se, but both together;* and this, not by way of addition to one another, but by way of interpenetration and indiscerptibility.

Does, then, the relativity of mind to itself involve that of everything to the mind? and, conversely, does that of everything to the mind involve the relativity of the mind to itself? (January 10, 1868.)

The substantial character of the Platonic ideas is an instance of the power which the mere act of contemplation has of giving an apparently external character to its object. Thought hypostasizes its idea, as the imagination personifies its image, by merely holding it out at arm's length and looking at it.

The difficulty attending the assumption of initial repose prior to the creative act is exactly equal to that of assuming an eternal movement. That difficulty consists in finding an adequate cause for either. For supposing the creative effort to begin at a determinate time, its quiescence or obstruction up to that time requires to be accounted for. The difference between the two assumptions—one of which must be true, by the law of contradiction—is that the assumption of eternal movement will explain the world, whereas the other will not. But further: physical science reveals no cessation of motion, and philosophy is conscious of nothing but movement or effort in thought. If we penetrate down to the very roots of the mind, we find there not a fixed point of outset, but an initial process.

Whence, then, and what is Repose? It is a merely relative fact, *i.e.*, it is retarded process, as compared with greater velocity. This retardation, if it occur in external nature, *seems*, owing to the want of precision and patience in our observation, to be rest. Or again, if it occur in the world of mind, the consciousness of the process is too sluggish to make any impression on the memory; it may even be so slow as to pass out of consciousness altogether. This experience *and* the frequent sensation of weariness, *i.e.*, desire of repose, leads the imagination to figure what is really only a relative retardation of the cosmic or spiritual effort as an absolute stoppage. There is no such thing as Rest. (January, 17, 1868.)

Infinity, as envisaged in the Imagination.—The constituents of the infinite of the imagination are generally the combined images of air and water. In the difference between the two we get just that minimum of determination which makes the image possible. The image of mere air or of mere water would be no realizable image at all, because there would be no distinction. We find this infinite of the imagination among non-European nations in the form of a state of vacuum immediately preceding creation. Thus in Genesis i. 2 : " The earth was without form and void, and darkness was upon the face of the *abyss*, and the Spirit of God moved upon the face of the *waters.*" In the Hindoo account the creative Spirit is represented as rowing about in a boat upon the ocean. A beautifully pure expression of the imagined infinite is found in the "Popol Vuh," the sacred book of the aborigines of Guatemala :— " There was a time when all that exists in heaven and earth was made. All was then *in suspense,* all was calm and silent; all was immovable, all peaceful, and the vast space of the heavens was *empty.* There was no man, no animal, no shore, no trees ; *heaven alone existed.* The face of the earth was not to be seen; there was *only the still expanse* of the sea and the heaven above. Divine Beings were on the waters like a growing light. Their voice was heard as they meditated and consulted; and when the dawn rose, man appeared." (Max Müller, "Chips," &c., i. p. 333.) In this case the constituents of the image are empty heaven, or space, and—which is introduced as if not at all contradictory to the statement that " heaven alone existed "—the still expanse of the sea. The image of space and water differs here from the Hebrew conception in being dimly lighted as with gleams preceding the dawn: whereas in Genesis all is dark until light is created.

We have substantially the same image of the infinite lying, so to speak, at the back of the Greek mind. But there are two differences. First, the Greek mind dismembers the image;—Thales's symbol is water exclusively; Anaximander's, the void "*in suspense;*" Anaximenes's, the air; Xenophanes's, the ὅλος οὐρανὸς and the sphere. The second difference is, that amongst the Greeks the infinite is not conceived as *preceding* the emergence of finite things, but as *underlying* the process of nature, as it is known to sensible perception.

The tendency of most men is to take part in projecting immaturely a moral order which is ill-considered, in building too quickly a home for the spirit, which, when the winds begin to blow, turns out to be a log-hut full of chinks and crevices. The movement from within outwards is too quick and rash; and these external forms, so prematurely assumed, breed discontent in the finer spirits, and set in motion the process from without inwards.

In the history of Rome the two counter-movements, —the systole and diastole of her great heart—are in the perfect adjustment of health. Stoicism, the centripetal element in the Roman character, is part of the great expansive power that subdues the world and gives its laws to mankind. Curtius leaps into the abyss for the sake of Rome. Marcus Aurelius is a Stoic in his camp on the Danube.

The Roman moral order was never felt as a limitation even for Christianity, which destroyed it. But what a cage for humanity has Feudalism been, and the Catholic Church, and the Treaty of Vienna!

The Greeks, like boys, were wont to build rapidly what might give way at a push. Their profoundly objective temper is seen in their philosophy. Their city-states represent the first moment in the political life of the world. But the Greek notion of freedom is immature. Like Plato's Republic, their political structures are conceived, carried out, and demolished in a day. Cynics and Cyrenaics equally felt the air slipping.

It is a thing not yet generally acknowledged, that the Infinite may be approached, nay, without equivocation, attained not only in Feeling and in Thought (Religious Philosophy), but more than all in Action (Politics). Conscious action is the most complex of spiritual facts: it unites the whole influence of the environment of a man —and each man's environment is no less than the universe of Nature and Spirit in its entirety—with the reciprocal or corresponding influence of the man upon his environment. It raises this unit of interchange into the element of pure or complete Actuality, and projects the whole as a new factor into the world of Being. Every man's deed is in germ the Infinite Actuosity, *actus purus*.

Thought at its highest elevation—at white heat, so to speak—is Action. "Let there be Light, and there was Light." But now go on from the act of an individual to that of a community, of the family, of society, to the highest potency of social activity, the deliberate enactment of a sovereign state; nay, transport yourself in thought to that supreme moment when, just as individuals and families have risen out of the natural relation to one another into the political, so states shall have arisen out of international antagonism into the concrete unity of the world—and we then may conceive Action, Actuosity, at its highest power as the Deed of the Eternal Will, which (just as each man is truly said to be the author of his own moral being), as the Author of all being, creates itself, makes itself to be.

Potential and Actual.—Potentiality will not bear thinking out; it vanishes when we approach it in the actual.

When is a thing possible?—When all the things requisite for its production are present. But when they are all present the thing takes place; it is actual.

Again, we call a thing, in common language, possible, when the *majority* of the conditions being present, one or more requisite to its production are absent. But their absence makes it not possible, but impossible.

The assumption of imaginary entities as the vehicle (*Träger*) of phenomena, although commonly charged by physical science upon metaphysic, is quite as common in physics, apparently quite as necessary, and has lasted quite as long as in the region of philosophy proper—such as fluids, ethers, molecular motion, phlogiston, matter, force, &c.

Bacon was the first to bring in the idea of the *usefulness* of knowledge as a means to material ends, instead of the old idea of knowledge as a liberal pursuit having its end in itself.

The natural *milieu* for ethical theory to grow up in is a sound and healthful politic; when the state is undeveloped or in decay ethics assume the following forms:—

(1.) Commentaries upon ethical systems produced in the political atmosphere.
(2.) Asceticism and the mystical ideal of life.
(3.) The moralization of existing fables, &c., as of the Romance of the Rose, The Game of Chess, the *Gesta Romanorum*, &c.
(4.) The introduction of Oriental "moralities."
(5.) The creation of a moralized fable-literature.

The predilection for the "animal epic" in the Middle Ages is a sign of the absence of political environment normal to ethical thought; men saw a likeness between their own qualities and those of the animals.

Study the anarchical society of Reineke Fuchs.

What was the precise quality wanting to the society of the Middle Ages which rendered it unpolitical and un-ethical?

Scheme of a Book.

1. Religion the first phase of Civility.
2. Nature of Religious Sentiments.
3. Nature of Social Sentiments.
4. Parallel growth of each.
5. Dependence and connection.
6. Different forms of relation between the two:—
    Idea of Israel.
    Idea of Rome.
7. The Natural and Spiritual:—
    a. In Religions.
    b. In Societies.

(The peculiar relation which the higher bears to the lower will in Asceticism.)

8. The two factors constituting Spirituality:—
    The Social Consciousness
    The Individual Consciousness.
    Their analogues in Religion:—
    The idea of God; and of sin.
9. Relations between the two:—
    a. In Authoritative and Sacerdotal Religion. } External.
       In Paternal Government.
    b. In Christianity. } Reciprocal.
       In Democracy.
    c. In Religious Dissolution. } Individual.
       In Tyranny and Anarchy.
10. Transition to Conscience.
    Nature and origin of Conscience.
    Relation to Religion and to Sociality.
11. Transmutation of Emotions:—
    a. Physiologically.
    b. In Consciousness.

12. The idea of God.
    a. Nature.
    b. Society. } Are *a*, *b*, and *c* identical in their laws?
    c. Conscience.
13. Personality.
14. Idea of God not necessarily a religious idea.
15. Subordinate religious ideas and their social analogies.
    a. Idea of Heaven.
        Idea of a Golden Age.
    b. Crime; Immorality; Sin.
16. Conclusion. Persistence of religion as a form of sociality. Variety of these forms. Culture.

Appendix.
    A. Identity of the monastic impulse and the social.
    B. Freedom and Liberty.
    C. The imagination, not the reason, is the true guide of life.
    D. Value of a religion not dependent on the truth of its theology.

                    (December 25, 1875.)

Question for Study.—What are the natural facts of which we are certain, which are represented in the teachings and dogmas of religion? (January 29, 1876.)

The assumption of metaphysic is the Ego or collective consciousness: that of Reason is its own infallibility:

    If she be false, oh then heaven mocks itself.

Personality.—The universal reason or Gemeinbewusstsein is impersonal, like the intelligence which we seem to see active in Nature, and is perhaps simply that intelligence under the form of consciousness. The private reason, or series of the desires, is also impersonal, for they and it exist in the lower animals, to which we do not attribute personality.

Personality consists in the relation between these two impersonal factors.

Against this it may be said that two impersonals can no more make a personality, than two aces can make a deuce: yet it is also true that two ones can make two.

Individuality is produced by the struggle for existence, by the interlacing of circumstances, and is counteracted by the growth of political life. At present the counteracting force is weak; and individuality is becoming selfishness.

Liberty.—When we say we are free, we mean not that human action is unconditioned, but (*a*) that the laws determining it are not material, and (*b*) that the relation of the action to the will, in which if restrained we are conscious of it, is to be distinguished from the relation of the will to the motive, in which if restrained we are unconscious of it. Liberty is thus a necessity of which we are unconscious; or, it is liberty to do that which we are necessitated to will.

Freedom is the expansion, it may be the necessitated expansion, of the finite will, which is necessitated by nature, to the stature of the infinite will, which is prior to necessity, being the operation of that general reason which expresses itself in our surrounding conditions.

Customs grow up amongst a people like flowers out of the ground, and their character is determined by that of the soil from which they spring. The men who make them can give no more account of them than the bee of the honeycomb. They have grown up unconsciously as the fitting framework of particular relations and sets of recurring circumstances, of what Tucker calls "the reason of the thing," until at length they become fixed by habituation.

The origin of each custom, the form in which alone

moral principles are first known, is the single act of one man, an act which, so soon as it is done by him, every body else does, because every body else is like the doer.

The repetition of acts brings with it a quasi-physical necessity of its own, and it is this fixity so attained which really constitutes its sanction as a mode of conduct, and leads men to regard it as a revealed law. Revealed it is: but in this way,—first, a prominent individual, then imitation, then habit and custom. The British Constitution, which has sprung up within the memory of history out of the character and circumstances of the people, is a monster instance of the growth of custom in comparatively late times. Our reverence for it is as superstitious as that of a primitive people's might be.

Three views of the State.—As conceived by Plato and Aristotle, it is a vast lyceum of public instruction: this seems to be an exaggeration of the Pythagorean notion of education.

Rome to the Roman is the infinite reality, of which he is but a mode, and against which he has no rights.

To the Asiatic the king "liveth for ever," and the subject is not even a mode; he has no existence save at the king's pleasure.

The apparent continuity in the structural character of two metaphysical ideas does not necessarily prove that one has been derived from the other; but may be an evidence that both owe their origin to a common parentage and have become differentiated.

Scheme for a Book on Politics.

INTRODUCTION.—The two factors which make up the moral nature of man are the universal and the particular; the objective command and the subject which obeys.

The universal element in thought betrays its cosmical origin.

CHAP. 1.—The first psychological development in the history of the mind is the mere distinction of the lower factor from the higher, preserved in the traditions of the so-called fall of man.

CHAP. 2.—The higher factor then assumes an exclusively external or objective form : and is realized in the personification of the powers of Nature.

CHAP. 3.—Amongst the Oriental races it took form and organization as the Theocratic state : the higher factor being *really, though not consciously* identified with the collective life of the community.

CHAP. 4.—Amongst the Greeks the personification of natural powers passes gradually over into the imagination of a series of ideal human forms, from which the cosmical elements gradually disappear.

CHAP. 5.—In Rome the reverence for the state as such, as the entity to which the individual should be unreservedly sacrificed, ultimately reveals its fundamentally theocratic character in the cultus of the Emperors.

CHAP. 6.—In Christianity, in Buddhism and Brahmanism and in the worship of Osiris the second great psychological stage is reached by the recognition of the hitherto external [and mysterious] *supreme* as a *factor within the mind*, in the same area as that occupied by the subject which obeys. "The kingdom of God is within you."

Cf. the philosophical development in Greece, as expressed in the psychological hierarchy of Plato—the governing and governed.

Cf. also his connection of it with politics.

CHAP. 7.—After Christianity, the consciousness of the two moral factors becomes complicated, owing to the partial identification of the higher of them with the historical Christ (who was, of course, an example, not of one factor, but of both factors), and the consequent subjection to the authority of religion not only of the lower factor in man, but also of the higher moral imperative along with it. (Peculiar relation of higher and lower in Asceticism.)

CHAP. 8.—The growth of knowledge in modern times has replaced reason as a supreme factor in the human mind, and has thus brought it into unavoidable conflict with the authority of historical religion as constituting the higher. This conflict must needs continue so long as the historical element in religion is maintained as indispensable. The effect of the gradual undermining of it by criticism will ultimately be to replace Christianity in its true position as identical with the higher native factor.

But in the meantime the conflict of the two forms assumed by the higher—the native or internal, and the external and historical—leaves the lower and purely selfish factor free partly to indulgence and partly to the gradual origination of a new supreme factor in the shape of prudential morality.

CHAP. 9.—But when the elimination of the historical obstructions of religion shall render possible the solidarity of the moral higher and the religious higher,—then the next step will be to labour to give it a new and permanent outward expression in the laws and institutions of society, and to recognise the reciprocal relations which, through the community, the higher has with the lower ; in other words, to recognize that the *higher in man governs the lower not immediately*, but through the medium of institutions.

CHAP. 10.—What place, then, will religion hold ? It is the primitive and imaginative appreciation of the distinctness and authority of the higher factor, which is its only possible position so long as the lower is *merely* distinguished from it *as lower*, and so long as the higher is therefore regarded as mysterious and external to man.

N.B.—Side by side with the *imaginary religious* projection of the higher factor, there is the *imaginary political* projection of it as the Jove-born and blameless king and the divinely guided legislator. Both these projections are transitory preliminaries to the true and final projection of it, the *practical* projection of it as the self-consciousness of the community.

CHAP. II.—Have we then absorbed the idea of God into that of the state? Not necessarily. The idea of God will then bear the same relation to the polity as it does now to the individual conscience. Only it will be seen that conscience is not an immediate *datum*, as it is commonly supposed to be, but the result, in miniature and in an individualized expression, of the institutions and social relations amongst which it is developed.

APPENDIX.—The Esquimaux, as having the religious sense but no object of worship, seem to have reached the stage just anterior to that crisis which we call the fall of man.

The Ego.—Each mind projects itself. That which is a world to me I cannot know to be a world to you, but as a series of impressions in you, who are merely a function of me. Your power of projection is thus only a function of me: but you say that mine is only a function of you. We are thus reciprocally functions of one another, thus forming a single organism of thought, indefinitely complicated, each part interpenetrating every other. What is the unity which is the *radix* of this organism? The Ego or synthesis, this pure power of self projection.

The world, which is the *datum* we begin with, includes the personal or self-conscious life of man, as that essential part to which all other parts lead up. But, on the other hand, we find that the world of which the Ego is the climax is itself the creation of the Ego: from which it follows that the Ego originates itself; and the world of which, when we assumed the world as a *datum*, the Ego was a part, becomes a self-contradiction when abstracted from the Ego and taken by itself.

Why can we not make out the converse of this reasoning? Thus: the world seems to be the creation of the Ego, if we assume the Ego as a *datum*: but, on the other hand, we see the Ego gradually being arrived at by the world. Therefore the world originates that which when taken as a *datum* originated it, *i.e.*, it originates itself.

These two reasonings are exactly parallel:—the world is self-originated through the medium of the Ego; and the Ego is self-originated through the medium of the world.

To decide which of these is true, we must ask, which of the two can stand in relation to itself without the intervention of the other. The Ego can do so in abstract self-consciousness, which is given in a concrete form in the feeling of freedom, and is given to analysis in every act of thought. Whereas the world can never thus stand in abstract relation to itself, without the Ego as its middle term; because the world apart from the Ego cannot think. That is to say, the Ego originates that which the Ego says originates itself: whereas the world originates the Ego, which it (the world) has no power, apart from the Ego, to say originates itself.

In the last resort, therefore, the question resolves itself into the capacity of self-assertion.

The question of the "cosmological argument," Can we think of a world which did not begin? should be more correctly stated, Can we think of a beginning of thought? And the answer is, Thought itself must always precede any such beginning. But, if we expect to find the same contradiction when we try to think of a beginning of matter,— as thus, matter itself must always precede any beginning of matter;—the answer is, No; matter must not precede such a beginning, but thought must; for matter can be proved to be a function of thought.

The Individual and the Community.—A nation looks back upon the laws which it finds it has made for itself, and believes them to be the work of wise men who have become gods. But the wise man comes later in history; he is the end to produce which the laws exist. The history of man is the history of his emancipation from the animal condition. In the childhood of the race he is emancipated from the brutishness of nature and the " weight of chance desires " by heroes and demigods, by the legislator and the " blameless " king. These are the fathers of polity and its schoolmasters. Freedom first appears in the form of one overpowering personality in a generation, who is a law to himself and to the community. He is ἀφρήτωρ, ἀθέμιστος, ἀνέστιος, but only as containing all these—the family, the clan, the law—in himself. Like the primeval animals, there are but a few of them, but these are giants. While the many are hunting and fishing, scalping and eating each other, he goes up and down in the land and the savage becomes tame in his presence. His personality is a centre and fountain of influence, because he is the embodiment of all the Will and Reason there is in the world, and man is framed inwardly to stand in need of these. He sees relations and utilities which are hidden from others. From him first men learn to " ride on horseback and to shoot with the bow and to speak the truth." As he sits before his door all men come to him for judgment. Wild anarchy finds its complement in Rhadamanthus and Draco. This is the kind of king that Aristotle means when he says, "The first states were monarchical, because those who came together into them had been accustomed to a king."

At length he dies, and all men are the better for his having been : none is fit to succeed him : but all men have become, in some degree, citizens. So they institute sacrifices in his honour and put his kingship into commission. And yet, who can write his character ? Look at the statues of Rameses or the pictures of Charlemagne: they are exact repetitions of each other, and seem to say, " I am Rameses, thou art Rameses, he is Rameses: ye all are what I am; ye are nothing, but as embodiments of me." They have no individual traits, these statues or pictures. They represent the impersonality of the religion and manners, of the laws and inventions; and this is nearly all we know of them. Their character is seen in the history of the nation, whose eponymous heroes they are. The question, Whence came they? is answered by all nations in the same strain—They came from heaven. Whether they dropt out of the clouds, or whether they be an offspring, by a "natural selection," of forces which had been waiting for ages to meet together in order to originate a new type, certain it is that through these gifted persons θείᾳ φύσει δυσχεραίνοντας τὸ ἀδικεῖν a ray of light is shed upon the world and the germs of a new order planted in it. Like the higher breeds of animals which gradually extinguish the lower, our strong and great men are destined to exterminate us who are little and weak. But they exterminate us by gradually and in process of generations raising us to their own level. It is by the complete sacrifice of himself to an external order that man does homage to heroes and rises a step towards their level. Because this external order, which we call the State, is the propagation both in time and quantity of the heroic life.

The hero leaves behind him two legacies, the moral order which he has originated and the memory of himself. By the first he liberates, by the second he continues to oppress mankind; just as when he was alive, his deeds were the emancipation, his caprices (cf. Plat. Rep. IV.) were the terror and the shame of his generation. The moral order which he originated is the true means of emancipation from the influence of his example. To make an image of him and to fall down and worship the idol is just and fitting as well as inevitable for those who cannot fill themselves with his spirit. If they cannot become citizens, let them at least burn incense. When the community is really carrying on his work, it is most likely to forget its hero, as he, in the elevation of heroic endeavour, forgat himself.

These two traits, the worship of heroes—many of them as we should now say of "very questionable character"— and the complete immersion of the consciousness of the individual in the total life of the community, may be said to exhaust the moral characteristics of the ancient world. It is this complete immersion which makes change in early times seem so simple : it is not merely simple from the *naïveté* or imperfection of the record, but was really simple; because the community acted *en masse*, and the variety of individual opposition did not exist. Such changes were the work of great men, and the community moved with the great man.

The hero in the early times is the only *person, i.e.*, he only has attained intellectual and moral manhood. He is scarcely an *individual, i.e.*, a character, though he has certain individual characteristics; and no doubt some only of the heroes of early history were real. A nation creates its own heroes; they embody its total life. The nation itself is the hero; and in looking back, during a subsequent period of reflection, on what it has itself accomplished, it worships the imaginary fathers of letters and agriculture and music as gods.

We may ask, How is the prominence of individuals to be accounted for ? It is an instance of the same law by which all men have poetical elements in their nature, but few are poets, or which in nature has massed earth and water in continents and seas. Why again are peoples, such as the Ionian and the Dorian, different from one another ? and why are they *more* different in religion, language, and outward appearance than in laws and morals ?

The family, in the same way, is, at first, and more conspicuously than the state, one person ; *i.e.*, the moral power embodied in it is not yet capable of distribution among its members. This unity of the family had its projection, its cultus in the Penates: as concentrated in the *paterfamilias*, it was expressed in his autocratic rights. This made the family as arbitrary as the hero. One of the weak points of Roman law was the shifts of the jurists to adapt and modify the *patria potestas*. Its disintegration brought about the dissolution of the family itself. Thus we find Cicero proposing to divorce his wife in order to pay his debts with the dowry of another. But the individual colouring of the collective consciousness is not so strong in the family as in the hero. He was a "natural" individual:[1] his moral force was of an arbitrary and non-moral operation. The real individual, as we know him, is not the gift of Nature, but the long result of time and civilization. The Pythagorean idea of education was, Make a child the citizen of a good state.

In ancient states the play of individuality, wherever it emerged, was regarded as a sign of decay (Plato). There was no idea of rationalizing or educating it: only the idea of excluding it and whatever led to it. The Sophists, Cynics, Epicureans, Roman law and Christianity, asserted the infinite value of the individual *as a possibility:* it has been the work of subsequent history to work out that possibility into a fact. (Cf. Monachism, Protestantism, the abolition of slavery, of feudal violence and highway robbery; change of sentiment about suicide and capital punishment; value of human life in Europe as compared with Asia.)

The relation of the individual to the state has given a peculiar feature to modern education.

What are the elements in civilization which have promoted the growth of individuality? Colonization firstly, and secondly the tendency to form small states during the Middle Ages, due to the successful revolts of the greater

---

[1] Virtues are *natural* when they are not yet the transformation of the desires, but their quantitative definition, *e.g.*, the μέσον.

nobles, and the difficulty of holding large countries together without means of communication. External control, though often severe and vexatious, thus became really weaker and more intermittent. Also the smallness of states rendered escape possible, which in the Roman Empire would have been less so. Then, too, one part of a country subject to one set of circumstances—say a flat soil or a cold climate—gave rise to a different physical type from that produced in a mountainous country, or with a warm climate. The mixture, again, of different types, when migration and communication begin to take place between nations, produces individuality. The Romans and Greeks were *individualist*, as compared with Asiatic nations : the German barbarians, as compared with the Greeks and Romans.

The march of History has been *from the Hero to the State*, and, in the second place, *to develop the individual*, as we now know him. Animals of the same species are much more alike than men : barbarians or Asiatics—*e.g.*, the Jews or Chinese—than civilized Europeans. (Likeness to one another of Assyrian and Egyptian faces, and of Byzantine figures, as compared with the Madonnas and Christs of modern painting). Foreign trade, again, has tended to produce individuality : change of scene, absorbing employments, risk, eagerness, &c. All great nations have pressed towards the sea. India and Egypt suffered greatly from want of a foreign trade.

Corresponding to the two extremes of this process of individualization, we have the absolutism of the ancient European and of the modern Asiatic State, and the mechanical atomism of the modern French and American commonwealths. Both extremes exclude the real relation of the individual to the State, viz., the organic,—the individual acted upon by the State and reacting in his turn upon the community.

The British Constitution is an elaborate system of checks and balances by which the physical individual is surrounded with as much moral vacuum as possible. Demosthenes laments the individualism of Athens. There was a peculiar conservatism in ancient states growing out of their abhorrence of individuality: νόμαια κινεῖν πάτρια is put by Herodotus along with βιάσθαι γυναῖκας, &c., as the deeds of the usurper. (Cf. the rule of the Epizephyrian Locrians which made a man who proposed strange laws appear before the people with a rope round his neck. Cf. also the laws of the Medes and Persians: permanence of Caste in India: Plato's idea of the τύπος and that change is always for the worse: also the Spartan Epitaph at Thermopylæ). The Roman regards the State as an English sailor regards his ship; he will not be saved, if the ship is to perish. (Cf. Brutus and his children: and Quintus Curtius, the "most precious thing in Rome.") The Law of Majesty at Rome, and the practice of Ostracism at Athens are, in like manner, artificial checks to prevent the slightest outburst of individuality.

THE END.

PRINTED BY BALLANTYNE AND HANSON
LONDON AND EDINBURGH

www.ingramcontent.com/pod-product-compliance
Lightning Source LLC
Chambersburg PA
CBHW031430230426
43668CB00007B/484